THE
PERFECT
TUBA

BY THE SAME AUTHOR

*The Least of Us: True Tales of America and Hope in the
Time of Fentanyl and Meth*

Dreamland: The True Tale of America's Opiate Epidemic

*Dreamland: The True Tale of America's Opiate Epidemic
(A Young Adult Adaptation)*

*Antonio's Gun and Delfino's Dream:
True Tales of Mexican Migration*

*True Tales from Another Mexico: The Lynch Mob,
the Popsicle Kings, Chalino, and the Bronx*

THE PERFECT TUBA

Forging Fulfillment from
the Bass Horn, Band,
and Hard Work

SAM QUINONES

BLOOMSBURY PUBLISHING
NEW YORK · LONDON · OXFORD · NEW DELHI · SYDNEY

BLOOMSBURY PUBLISHING
Bloomsbury Publishing Inc.
1359 Broadway, New York, NY 10018, USA
50 Bedford Square, London, WC1B 3DP, UK
Bloomsbury Publishing Ireland Limited, 29 Earlsfort Terrace,
Dublin 2, D02 AY28, Ireland

BLOOMSBURY, BLOOMSBURY PUBLISHING, and the Diana logo are
trademarks of Bloomsbury Publishing Plc

First published in the United States 2025

Copyright © Sam Quinones, 2025

All rights reserved. No part of this publication may be: i) reproduced or transmitted in any form, electronic or mechanical, including photocopying, recording, or by means of any information storage or retrieval system without prior permission in writing from the publishers; or ii) used or reproduced in any way for the training, development, or operation of artificial intelligence (AI) technologies, including generative AI technologies. The rights holders expressly reserve this publication from the text and data mining exception as per Article 4(3) of the Digital Single Market Directive (EU) 2019/790.

Bloomsbury Publishing Plc does not have any control over, or responsibility for, any third-party websites referred to or in this book. All internet addresses given in this book were correct at the time of going to press. The author and publisher regret any inconvenience caused if addresses have changed or sites have ceased to exist, but can accept no responsibility for any such changes.

ISBN: HB: 978-1-63973-548-8; eBook: 978-1-63973-549-5

LIBRARY OF CONGRESS CATALOGING-IN-PUBLICATION DATA IS AVAILABLE

Library of Congress Control Number: 2025943248

2 4 6 8 10 9 7 5 3 1

Typeset by Westchester Publishing Services
Printed in the United States at Lakeside Book Company

To find out more about our authors and books visit
www.bloomsbury.com and sign up for our newsletters.

Bloomsbury books may be purchased for business or promotional use. For information on bulk purchases please contact Macmillan Corporate and Premium Sales Department at specialmarkets@macmillan.com.

For product safety–related questions contact
productsafety@bloomsbury.com.

*To Caroline, my little bird, in hopes she finds
her own perfect tuba.*

CONTENTS

A Word on Tubas xi

OVERTURE

1. Willie Begins 3
2. My Tuba Trek 7
3. The Perfect Tuba 17
4. Bill Bell 30
5. H. E. Nutt I 40
6. Rio Grande Valley: Cortinas in Crystal City 46
7. H. E. Nutt II 51
8. Tuba Woodstock 57

FIRST MOVEMENT

9. The Man Who Tried to Corner the Tuba Market 69
10. Arnold Jacobs I 79
11. The Perfect Tuba: Carpenter 86
12. The Perfect Tuba: Treece 94
13. Rio Grande Valley: Roma 104
14. Rio Grande Valley: Cortinas Takes Over 115
15. Willie and Eugene 124
16. Willie and Weber 127
17. H. E. Nutt III 138

viii CONTENTS

SECOND MOVEMENT

18. The Man Who Made the Tuba Dangerous 145
19. Arnold Jacobs II 154
20. The Perfect Tuba: Sine Waves 163
21. The Perfect Tuba: Zig 170
22. Rio Grande Valley: Neckties 179
23. Rio Grande Valley: All-State 187
24. Rio Grande Valley: J.R. 192
25. Orlando I: Willie and the Mouse 202
26. Orlando II: Willie and Sam Rivers 210

THIRD MOVEMENT

27. The Man Who Built a Tuba Hall on His House 219
28. The Perfect Tuba: Zig's Bell 226
29. Rio Grande Valley: Juan and Frank 232
30. Rio Grande Valley: Roma Gets Ready 240
31. Rio Grande Valley: Lopez High 244
32. Weber's Kids: Roosevelt 250
33. Tuba Fats in New Orleans: In Love 255
34. Tuba Fats in New Orleans: At Rest 273

FINALE

35. The Tuba Player Who Had to Quit 285
36. Arnold Jacobs III: Brian 293
37. The Perfect Tuba: Zig's Last Horn 301
38. Rio Grande Valley: Roma Ascends 312
39. Rio Grande Valley: Treviño at Lopez High 322
40. Rio Grande Valley: *Symphony No. 6* 328

41. Willie Retires 342
42. Rio Grande Valley: Tuba Christmas 349

ENCORE 359
CODA 363

Acknowledgments 365

A WORD ON TUBAS

There are three common kinds of tubas:
A **concert**, or **orchestral**, tuba is held on the lap, with the bell pointing skyward.

A **sousaphone** encircles the player, the bell pointing forward. Invented by John Philip Sousa, these are commonly used in marching bands, and seen often in parades and at football games.

A **euphonium**—aka a tenor tuba—is roughly in the shape of the concert tuba but is smaller and lighter and plays in a slightly higher register.

OVERTURE

Chapter 1

Willie Begins

When Willie Clark was in sixth grade in the town of Harvey, Illinois, a southern suburb of Chicago, he got his hands on his school's tuba.

He had started in the Whittier Elementary School band in fourth grade on the trumpet. In sixth grade, a chance opened up. He had loved the tuba from afar. That year, the eighth grader who played it moved on to high school. This shiny golden Conn tuba was now available. Willie was tiny and couldn't actually hold the instrument, which was attached to a chair. Yet he climbed into it, and it was his.

He was making sounds before he knew it. It was as if the instrument had chosen him, knowing he would feel comfortable with it. This was 1980. He was listening to Earth, Wind & Fire and other funk bands for whom the bass line was the thing. He felt that sound deep in his body, and with the tuba, it was now his alone to make in the band.

The first tunes were a struggle. He couldn't quite make it happen, but he knew the sound would come if he kept at it, so he did. He could be the band's foundation and support. Getting there took over his free time, and he let it, excited by the possibility. He took home a school practice horn. Before long, his mother, Nancy, was telling his friends who dropped by that Willie was busy practicing the tuba and couldn't come out.

I met Willie Clark in Washington, D.C., when he was fifty-five and retiring as tuba player from the U.S. Air Force Ceremonial Brass. We met first over Zoom, then in person a few times. I said I was writing a book about tuba players and band directors. Why, he asked. I said I'd written for years about drug addiction, and now I wanted to write about people who were cultivating their talents, not stunting them, people devoted to finding fulfillment in what they created for themselves and with others, not from a product they bought.

We spoke about a lot of things. His upbringing in Harvey. How the tuba had taken him far from the town. He had worked at Walt Disney World for a decade, when it was one of the planet's great tuba employers. From there, he won the Air Force band job. He had played for presidents, and at Arlington National Cemetery funerals.

He told me of the influence of his elementary school and junior high band director, a man named John Weber. Weber had boxes full of CDs and cassettes of chamber music, jazz, and brass band that he let kids rummage around in and listen to as they wished. Weber one day took Willie and others to see the Philip Jones Brass

Ensemble, with a renowned tuba player named John Fletcher. Fletcher that day let loose with a version of the manic "Flight of the Bumblebee" that so dazzled Willie Clark that he left there thinking, though he was only thirteen, that he might one day play that piece.

His family basement became his tuba refuge. It was a large space with small windows and psychedelic murals left by previous occupants. There he could listen to tapes of John Fletcher and the chamber music from Weber's music boxes. He once brought together some neighborhood kids who could barely play anything and conducted them through the theme to the movie *Rocky*. On his school's big old Yamaha 321, he learned to play a concerto for a higher-register tuba. "If you're trying to play high-register stuff on a large horn," he told me, "it's twice as much work, but I didn't know that."

After we'd gotten to know each other, Willie told me about something that happened at a band competition his sixth grade year.

John Weber cued the band to play the theme to *Star Trek*. The piece called for a sonorous low B-flat note that was Willie's to make. As the band formed before him that day, tiny Willie Clark sitting at the back let loose with a full-bore blow, and the note he achieved seemed deeper and more thrilling than anything he'd ever created.

That note wove finely with those of the others, and as this scrawny little kid blew into that horn for all he was worth, his note took the rest of the band with him, driving them, propelling them all, lifting them off and tickling his spine.

Willie Clark had never felt this before, certainly never from a creation of his own. He did not know it was even possible until right there in sixth grade. For the briefest of moments his horn was taking him soaring. Far beyond the band and John Weber at the podium. Later, Willie had no idea where it came from—all that sound, him being just a little squirt and all.

But it was a moment he never forgot.

Chapter 2

My Tuba Trek

"You end up playing it."

Heroin and the tuba came into my life as a journalist at about the same time.

In 2011, while at the *Los Angeles Times*, I wrote two stories about the tuba in Mexican L.A. The first reported that tubas were all the rage, particularly for backyard parties, which were frequent. The second reported that tubas were being stolen from high schools in those areas, largely due to the instrument's popularity.

After those stories were published, however, I just kept on, pestering tuba players of all styles for interviews. I knew nothing about the tuba. I had never tried to play it, nor any brass instrument, and I never marched in my high school's band. Yet the more players I spoke with, the more the tuba world seemed filled with people devoted to the discipline of nurturing a skill and a creativity solely for the love of it. That seemed a healthy thing, and worth learning more about. So I kept on talking with tuba players here and there.

I heard the story of the late Bill Bell, and of Anthony "Tuba Fats" Lacen in New Orleans. I interviewed Alfredo Herrejón. All three transformed their respective tuba worlds. I spent a couple days at the International Tuba Euphonium Conference, held that year in Knoxville, where hundreds of tuba players came from all over.

Meanwhile, I left the *Los Angeles Times* to write a book called *Dreamland*, about the nation's opioid epidemic: Vast supplies of narcotic painkillers were pushed by drug companies and prescribed by doctors in the pursuit of the eradication of pain. Many people grew addicted. Growing numbers of them switched to heroin, which was cheaper and a chemical cousin to those painkillers. Part of the book was about a town in Mexico where guys who came to the United States sold black tar heroin retail, delivering it like pizza.

My publisher urged me to write a follow-up. *The Least of Us* told, in part, how Mexican traffickers now were producing equally vast supplies of synthetic drugs—fentanyl and methamphetamine—that replaced those pain pills and heroin.

I found it hard to avoid the conclusion that a root of our epidemic of drug addiction was a shredding of community in America, which left us isolated and alone and vulnerable to addiction.

Through these years, I kept a large folder of notes labeled TUBA in my computer. I thought I'd make use of those notes someday, though I didn't know how.

But the drug books dominated my writing life. In all, I spent a dozen years writing about drug addiction. It was a story of our time, I thought, for in essence it was about the search for "happiness" from something you buy that ends up killing you instead.

After that, I needed a break. I wanted to tell other kinds of stories. So I began poking through that TUBA folder again. I went over the notes, contacted the people I had interviewed before, talked to new players. The idea for this book began to take shape.

People asked me why I would be the one doing this. I asked myself the same question. I'm a crime reporter. I've covered seven mass murders, including the first schoolyard shooting with an assault rifle—in 1989 in Stockton, California, where my crime reporting career began. There I covered more than two hundred murders and wrote about gangs, crack cocaine, and methamphetamine. I lived in Mexico for ten years and wrote about immigration and political change. I moved back to California, and at the *Times* I wrote about drug trafficking and the Mexican Mafia prison gang.

Even so, I've always preferred writing about optimistic people. Living in Mexico from 1994 to 2004, I wrote mostly about Mexican immigrants, who were the focus of my second book, *Antonio's Gun and Delfino's Dream*, for that reason: They're betting their own savvy and hard work that tomorrow will be better than today.

The tuba is an optimistic instrument. It brings the band together; it is the community enhancer. Few players choose it. "You end up playing it," said one. Most were just late for the first day of band class and all the other instruments were taken. Some couldn't afford to rent a horn, and they tried the school-owned tuba because it was free.

Yet no matter how they were pushed into the tuba, all the players I spoke to came to love it through the effort they put in, despite the horn's lowly social status, or maybe because of it. Some found refuge in it from a school's cruel pecking order. Most found confidence through learning to make a sound that dug deep into their bones. The horn showed them their own worth and the world's possibilities.

People who do something they have learned to love always have good stories to tell. The beautifully strange tale of the two magical York tubas now owned by the Chicago Symphony Orchestra was proof of that. So I kept at this weird idea of a book about the tuba and people creating something, pushing on through failure, for the love of the endeavor.

I did that because, even after thirty-eight years as a reporter, I am optimistic about the future. Addictive drugs made me so. Writing about them, I met many people recovering from addiction or working to repair their communities. They were unwilling to let failure or lack of acclaim squelch their energies. Our world is drowning in the accepted wisdom of cynics and nihilists. The people I was meeting were the antidote to that.

So were the tuba players who keep at their craft, usually alone, in spite of the disdain or indifference of others, and the poor odds that they can make a career of it.

The tuba virtuoso Roger Bobo once reportedly asked, "Are we tuba players because of the way we are, or are we the way we are because we are tuba players?" In fact, the tuba seems to attract, or forge, loners with quirky artistic visions. Rock guitar players are garbed in rebel chic; unnoticed tuba players, however, are closer to the purity of American risk-taking and solitary toil in pursuit of one's art. They express a bold independent streak quietly, and can look as square as Mister Rogers while doing it.

The tuba, invented in 1835, is the youngest brass instrument. Its youth and lack of entrenched hierarchies help in creating a no-borders attitude that I found refreshing. "If you really want to play the tuba," said one player, "you have to be very tenacious and come up with something that someone's not doing." I don't want to spend hours listening to, say, a large tuba ensemble, but I like the daring it reflects, the flat-nosed pugnacity.

The tuba is very punk rock in that way. Punk rock thrilled me in my youth. It was about just going out and doing something yourself, often when no one else was doing it, whether or not you were good at it at first, and even if you failed. "Just do it" was punk rock ethos long before Nike adopted the slogan. Dare to put in the work to achieve your ideas, no matter how offbeat, instead of thinking you'll get to it someday.

Chalino Sanchez—the slain narcoballadeer who made the tuba dangerous, and about whom I wrote in my first book, *True Tales from Another Mexico*—was like that. Everyone told him he couldn't sing, yet he kept on producing cassette tapes of his own songs of drug shootouts and sold them at car washes and bakeries in the southeast suburbs of Los Angeles. His legend was mightily enhanced by his murder after a show in his native state of Sinaloa in 1992.

Harvey Phillips, the tuba professor at Indiana University for many years, spent his life thinking up strange, big ways to both promote the horn and push it beyond the limitations others imposed on it. One was the event I call Tuba Woodstock. Another is the now nationwide Tuba Christmas.

Phillips was aiming for the liberation of a horn, allowing once stunted players to realize their capacities and shatter expectations. A lot of what I found grew from that liberation—from the tuba's new rambunctious spirit.

Playing "Flight of the Bumblebee" on the tuba was now routine. Jim Self, retired USC tuba professor, built a music room onto his house that is long enough to contain a tuba sound wave. Winston Morris transformed an engineering school in the Tennessee countryside into one of the great tuba centers of the world—molding his "hillbilly" kids into the world's first tuba ensemble and leading them to Carnegie Hall.

I met Bob Carpenter and Tom Treece, the two engineers and tuba guys who set out to recreate the sound of those Chicago York tubas. Through them I met Zig Kanstul, one of America's great brass instrument craftsmen, whose last artisanal act was to try to save his company by replicating those hallowed Yorks.

I kept hearing about the player who took the Chicago Yorks to their awesome fame: the late Arnold Jacobs. At the Chicago Symphony for forty-four years, Jacobs was a titan of the twentieth-century tuba and became almost a Zen master of music instruction. Somewhere in there, too, I heard of Fred Marrich, who tried to corner the U.S. tuba market.

Along the way, I discovered the story of the high school marching band from Roma, Texas, at the northern end of the Rio Grande Valley, on the border with Mexico. I met Al Cortinas, seventy-eight, who in the mid-1990s became Roma High School's band director and tuba instructor. Later, I met George Treviño, who took Roma's rival, Lopez High School in Brownsville, on to become the state's Honor Band. Al Cortinas, George Treviño on the border, and John Weber up in Chicago each devised methods for training kids who could not afford lessons and turned their bands into statewide powerhouses.

They also showed me the connection between what kids learn playing the tuba and what they learn in band: focus, patience, perseverance, and sacrifice, all through working with others, yet without so much of the glory, and perhaps without the privilege, accorded to athletes. Maybe that's what made band and the tuba fundamentally healthy pursuits—you did it because you learned that you loved it.

"Band is just the tuba player on a bigger scale," George Treviño told me.

That had not occurred to me. But it struck me that both endeavors taught values that sustain community.

I came to see how marching bands, in fact, create community in this country. They find a place for kids of all kinds to thrive, not based on their size or speed, but instead on their willingness to work hard. Without a band, every school football or basketball game would feel empty, lifeless. Without the tuba, the band wouldn't be much at all.

Understanding this, major Division I college football schools have been involved in a tuba arms race for some time. Just look at their bands in the stands—ringed now by mighty lines of gleaming sousaphones. Like Mexican immigrants, who, as you'll read, hire the horn at parties to show they have succeeded in America, those schools see throngs of tubas as proof to the nation that their football programs are to be respected. ESPN ought to create an entire talk show dedicated to band directors and tuba players—so essential are they to nurturing the network's final product. Yet we ignore them. That seemed unfair, even unwise. I figured I might be in a position to do something about that, writing this book about the tuba. So I expanded my project to include band directors, too.

Brownsville schools in particular had some of Texas' best bands for years, run by band director graduates from a place called VanderCook College of Music in far-off Chicago. Much of their philosophy grew from VanderCook's director, H. E. Nutt, a monk of music education, whose story his students recounted to me.

I had embarked on all this wanting to write about something very different from the topic that consumed my previous dozen years. By the end, though, I realized the tuba was actually not as far from the issue of drug addiction as I had imagined. Or, better put, the tuba is *so* far away that it is the mirror opposite of addiction.

Drug addiction is obedience to a substance, forsaking all else in the lonesome pursuit of immediate gratification from something you buy. It is the final expression of our consumer culture's empty promise: that we can find happiness from a product that is for sale. An opioid overdose shuts down the respiratory system, stifling breath, and life itself.

The tuba requires nurturing that precious breath. It is about finding purpose from the wonder of sound you learn to create yourself, and from which you forge a sense of fulfillment, but which cannot be purchased other than by hard work, preparation and persistence, collaborating with others—and the love of it all.

Call it the tuba approach to life.

No one ever got rich or famous playing the tuba. No internet adulation, no stadium shows, no posse. Only an unnoticed, middle-class life of nurturing your abilities. But that's why it is a sane thing. It's paring life to what we need, not what we're told to want and insistently demand.

Our epidemic of addiction began with pain pills and our desire to avoid pain, even discomfort, at all cost. The tuba is about enduring discomfort, patiently pushing through it, postponing gratification and gaining sweet moments of well-earned contentment. Again, it's the opposite of drugs.

The tuba approach to life feels especially important today.

We live in a distrusting, lonely, manically distracted world. We look for purpose and can't find it. We swim in a toxic soup of *legal* goods and services that are engineered to prod addictive behavior—from rapid-fire slot machines and gambling apps to ultra-processed "food," hyperpotent pot, social media apps, porn, cable news, and videogames. That's not even mentioning the addictive illegal drugs these things mimic. A simple cup of coffee has mutated into a towering concoction of fat, sugar, and caffeine, sold on every downtown street corner.

We allow corporate marketers to push addictive values. "Warning, contents will cause happiness," read Amazon big rigs, which dock at places the company calls "fulfillment centers."

"Think less is more? No, more is more!" claim the folks at Taco Bell, echoing the motto of every drug dealer and internet influencer out there, as they sell us their "Luxe Cravings Box," an eye-glazing combination of a "Seasoned Beef Chalupa Supreme®, a Beefy 5-Layer Burrito, a Double Stacked Taco, Chips & Nacho Cheese Sauce, and a medium fountain drink." All for $7.

Tuba players and band directors are underground resistance fighters amid all this gunk and muck, and may have something healthy to remind a world like ours. After all that I had written about the effects of drug addiction and community destruction, their stories seemed worth telling, too.

So this book, a celebration of working hard for purpose in life, ended up as a perfect sequel to the two I wrote about drug addiction. Maybe all along I was seeking some antidote to what ails us as a country. But that may be too grand an aim to ascribe to this tuba quest of mine. For all I've ever wanted was to find some good tales no one else has told.

That's always been enough for me. I hope it's enough to intrigue you, and for a book like this.

Chapter 3

The Perfect Tuba

"the most wonderful sound"

It is a historical, though little noticed, peculiarity that as humankind has invented and improved a world of musical instruments, in all that time we have been able to produce only two perfect tubas.

They are owned by the Chicago Symphony Orchestra and were made in the 1930s by the York Band Instrument Co. in Grand Rapids, Michigan.

The Chicago Yorks, as the two horns are known to tuba players everywhere, are considered simply the greatest tubas ever made. The All-American tubas. The Holy Grail of tubas. "To be even in the same room with them is a big deal, let alone touch them or play them," said Mike Roylance, who is the principal tubist for the Boston Symphony and has played the Yorks. "If there was an instrument that could understand what you want to do before you know what you want to do, that's the instrument."

"The York tubas are like the Stradivarius [violins]," said Wayne Tanabe, a master instrument repairman who for years serviced the two horns in his shop in Chicago. "In the violin world, people know what a Strad is. I can't think of another brass instrument that has that kind of pedigree, that kind of story behind it, that magic, that mystery. It's very strange to think it's these two tubas."

The York company was formed by a man named James W. York in the 1880s. He later brought in his sons. In 1917, though, James York had retired to Los Angeles. His sons sold the company to investors led by York's foreman and one of the best brass instrument makers in America at the time, Alfred "Bill" Johnson, also known as Pops.

Bill Johnson had begun his career as a teenage apprentice early in York's history. By the 1920s, he was thoroughly trained in musical instrument production and was running the company.

The 1930s were years when the U.S. instrument industry reached a mastery of craft, just before the post–World War II era when the demand for cheap student horns grew to such a level that it often removed the incentive for excellence. Making horns was factory work and artisanal at the same time. Instrument workshops were often family affairs, made up of employees and their children who spent decades forging brass into horns and talked about it at dinner. "You were immersed in a culture of intended excellence as opposed to a culture of belligerent apathy" that emerged in factories decades later, said John Hagstrom, a Chicago Symphony trumpet player and a brass instrument historian.

During World War II, many brass manufacturers became munitions factories. York was one of those. It never recovered from that wartime transition. In 1946, Johnson retired and spent the rest of his years running a Grand Rapids instrument repair and pawn shop. Many of his craftsmen moved on. York, meanwhile, turned to student horns for a period. As the industry consolidated, the company was sold a few times, and finally, in 1972, York closed for good. Its market share was digested by companies from our erstwhile enemies Japan and Germany.

The Depression years, though, were York's best. The company had a valued brand, supremely experienced workers, and an expert supervisor. Bill Johnson earned a half dozen patents in horn improvements. The company made trumpets, cornets, trombones. But under Johnson, it was for tubas that the company acquired a fame that years later would become almost mystical. The York tubas made during those years had a sound that was warm, bold, and enveloping unlike any others—"an American sound" is the way some players describe it to me.

York's skill apparently reached its peak in 1933, when, under Johnson's supervision, the company built a custom orchestral tuba for the tubist of the Philadelphia Orchestra, Philip Donatelli. The orchestra's director, Leopold Stokowski, the story goes, asked Donatelli if he could find a tuba with a deep, powerful tone, like the bass register of a church organ. Donatelli contacted Bill Johnson.

Johnson built two. These would become the hallowed Yorks, the perfect tubas.

Both horns were C tubas, which were unheard of in America. No one made C tubas. But the thing about the C tuba is that if you straighten out its tube—all those bends, switchbacks, and hairpins—it measures 16 feet. Sixteen feet is also the length of the bass organ pipe. So a 16-foot tuba would presumably give Stokowski the low organ sound he wanted. Johnson sent one of these custom horns to Donatelli. He kept the second horn, which he may have intended as a prototype, for once Donatelli was known to play the instrument, orders would surely pour in, and the company would have a copy from which to mass-produce his horn.

Little is known about how the brass for the tubas was chosen, or how those two instruments were designed or made, or by whom. While probing all this, I happened to read a book about the King James Bible and how it was produced. We know King James and the names of a couple of the Bible project's supervising religious scholars. The rest of the monks who gathered for years to translate the Bible into English are lost to history. Something like that happened at York. Other than Bill Johnson, the identities of those who actually built these tubas are unknown—anonymous workers toiling on instruments whose legacy they may never have guessed.

It's likely they didn't know how good the horns were. From York's perspective, in fact, the tubas were failures. Donatelli, being short and chubby, couldn't play the horn the company sent him. "Donatelli didn't have a lap," said one tuba player I spoke with. Donatelli later sold the horn for $175, on a $5-a-week installment plan, to a teenage student of his at the renowned Curtis Institute of Music, a conservatory in Philadelphia.

This teenager was a wunderkind named Arnold Jacobs. Arnold Jacobs grew to love that horn's sound. It tantalized players who heard it, it filled a hall, it stirred those who listened, it unified any orchestra it supported. That so often it didn't stand out is precisely what made it perfect. You didn't so much hear the York as feel it. What you heard, instead, was the whole orchestra, powerful, resonant, lush, and majestic. The York exemplified the tuba's most essential role: It was a community enhancer.

Jacobs was an unknown, playing for the Curtis Institute's student orchestra. Then came World War II. He held on to that horn and with it over the next fifty years became one of the century's greatest tuba players. He played for a time for the Indianapolis and Pittsburgh orchestras. In 1944, he was hired as the tuba player for the Chicago Symphony.

That's where he and his tuba stayed.

In the early 1950s, Donatelli called Jacobs. He had seen the second custom York; it was owned by the University of Oklahoma. Jacobs traded the school two new tubas for the now twenty-year-old York. It arrived dirty, and littered with insect corpses, yet still possessing that rich, warm sound.

I'LL TELL YOU much more of Jacobs' story later. But in his hands, in an orchestra soon of world renown, those two York tubas became "the Chicago Yorks," recognized for the dazzling creations they were. This happened as U.S. tuba players thirsted for respect. Here now were instruments that might help make that happen. Two perfect tubas. Yet there were only two, and York was in no position to recreate them.

Most every major brass instrument manufacturer since then has tried. By my count, nine companies have attempted to replicate these two tubas. The Swiss Hirsbrunner firm was the first, with a horn everyone now calls the Yorkbrunner. Yamaha made one years later, known affectionately as the YamaYork. The Chicago York tubas themselves have been almost gynecologically examined. Measured millimeter by millimeter. This pursuit of perfection has consumed decades of effort, mountains of money, and the fervid energies of many an obsessed tuba player. York made many excellent tubas, though none like the two in Chicago. Yet mania for the Chicago horns drove players to spend great sums on York bootlegs. These were lesser York tubas cut to approximate the Chicago horns and known, after their operations, as "frankentubas."

Still, the Chicago Yorks remain unparalleled in the classical tuba world, spoken of with an awe that startled me when I first heard about the horns. "It was an obsession, and still is," said Kevin Powers, a longtime brass instrument repairman in Michigan. "A mass hypnosis. A state of mind."

Powers told me of a band director who brought in a prewar York tuba missing some parts. Finding replacement parts, Powers told her, would be impossible. So she took the horn home, buried the tuba bell and filled it with water, and used it as a birdbath; when the water froze, the bell cracked. A year later, though, she found the missing parts and dug up the horn. Being brass, it hadn't rusted. She returned to Powers, who patched the bell and put the horn back together. She was still able to sell the horn, once a birdbath, for $3,000. Demand for old York tubas was like that.

The frenzy, though, was based on something absolutely real. It was the gorgeous, mesmerizing York sound, vibrating with luscious overtones of possibility and reminding legions of American tuba players of what they might create for themselves if given a chance.

Don Little was a student of Arnold Jacobs in the early 1970s when one day the maestro asked if he wanted to play one of the Yorks. Little, who is now a tuba professor at the University of North Texas, played the horn for fifteen minutes he never forgot: "It was the easiest tuba I've ever played in my life with the most wonderful sound. It was amazing."

The original Yorks are 6/4 horns, which means they are big, the only such tubas York is known to have made. They are nearing a century in age.

The man who now plays them is Gene Pokorny, a Southern Californian and the Chicago Symphony's tuba player since Jacobs retired in 1988. Pokorny maintains a studied indifference to the technical aspects of the horns that have so obsessed the American tuba world. "I drive the car. I don't get under the hood." This detached attitude is in contrast to a lifelong fascination with trains and their intimate details that has gripped Pokorny since childhood.

He allows me to view the Yorks one morning at Orchestra Hall in Chicago. Both horns are ornate, with mother-of-pearl buttons and gorgeous tubing—marvelous monuments to human ingenuity. Pokorny lets me hold York I, which Arnold Jacobs purchased as a teenager.

York I is, above all, an enormous thing. On my lap it rises a foot above my head. It takes up the space on my lap that I imagine a linebacker might and is almost as hard to wrap my arms around. The horn is heavier than I imagined. To fill it with a sustained supply of air would seem life-threatening. It's then that I understand tuba players when they shake their heads at musicians who complain that their own instruments are tough to play. Tuba players, you can probably guess, bow to no one on that score. (The only other wind instruments that require as much air, strangely, are flutes, as so much of the air a flautist uses is wasted. Particularly true of beginners—their air just flies right over the flute's opening without creating any sound. "Flutes?" scoffs one tubist when I mention this observation. "You hold them out the window of the car and they play themselves." It is, however, another strange fact I notice that tubists and flautists seem to marry each other a lot.)

The tubing of York I winds in the most graceful curves, and its silver plating adds to its luster. I'm awed at such a gleaming creation that I've heard so much about for so long. I'm overcome with guilt at the injustice of my holding this masterpiece when so many great tuba players would love to be in my chair. I can, however, appreciate its stately beauty, so much of which resembles our intestinal tract.

Pokorny puts a freshly cleaned mouthpiece on York I. In my lame non-player way, I buzz my lips into the mouthpiece. I've never tried to play a tuba. The first tone I ever make on one is on this legend. After a few seconds, the best I can produce sounds something like a growling stomach. I feel the need to apologize, as if I just burped in a cathedral.

As worshiped as the Yorks are, they are not identical. York I, which I'm given to hold, is taller by 2 inches. Someone, it's unclear who, added a fifth valve to that horn. And the horns are showing their age. Each has scratches, chips in the plating, and patches where the original brass wore through from continuous playing. An iron cable around the bell of York I rusted away and had to be replaced years ago. That same horn, in a case, once fell down an elevator shaft.

Arnold Jacobs used York I exclusively for years. With it he found his distinctive lyrical voice at the bottom of the Chicago Symphony that captured the imaginations of so many tuba players.

One day, on his lunch break, Jacobs took the horn to a repair shop to patch what's known as the lead pipe—the thin metal tube that "leads" from the mouthpiece to the horn's intestines. It was wearing thin and leaking air in a couple of places. A repairman thought he was doing Jacobs a favor and replaced the whole pipe. He threw away the damaged pipe and it was never found, despite strenuous effort at the shop when Jacobs came back from lunch and discovered the error. The horn hasn't played the same since. The lead pipe fiasco is counted as one of the great disasters to befall American tubadom.

All this added to the mystery of the horns, as no one I've spoken to can decipher what about the makeup of the lead pipe made it so essential to the sound. Pokorny once had a German master craftsman make several replacement pipes. None sounded as sweet. "Maybe it's the thickness of the metal," Pokorny said, "maybe the content of the metal. I don't know." He has kept York I in a closet for years, waiting for brass repair technologies to improve to the point where the horn might be returned to its former glory.

Gene Pokorny and the Chicago York tubas. "It's just a sweet, organic sound."

York II, which Jacobs purchased from the University of Oklahoma, has been Pokorny's go-to ax ever since. The companies that have copied the horns came so close, he told me. "Yamaha in fact made as much of a perfect copy of this thing as they could, but it wasn't the same. It's so mystical. There's something about the sound that's unique to this one."

Pokorny has test-played an array of York copies at Orchestra Hall for small groups of musicians and designers. He first plays through the copies. "Then, at the end, I'll get this thing out," he said, pointing to York II, "and everybody goes, 'Oh!' It's just a sweet, organic sound."

Wayne Tanabe, the repair tech, told me he was sitting toward the top of the hall during one of those sessions. Tanabe still remembered that moment decades later. "When he finished playing the York," he told me, "the sound hung in the room like you were sitting in a big church. You could feel the room ring—feel the sound in the room just hanging in the air. None of the other [tubas] really had that."

Still, the day may come when the Chicago Yorks won't be playable at all.

It is this possibility that alarmed two tuba obsessives down in Orlando, Florida.

Tom Treece and Bob Carpenter are engineers. Treece, the older of the two, is a retired candy confectioner and baking consultant. On the side, though, he has nursed a lifelong tuba jones. He has played the tuba as an amateur for decades, sold the horns, collected them, traded them on eBay.

Carpenter, meanwhile, once worked for NASA, where he managed a space shuttle, then worked for various military contractors, all while holding the tuba chair at the Orlando Philharmonic Orchestra. Carpenter is from Orlando and spent his postcollege years there as the town became a tuba hotbed. From that tuba scene, a new generation of players emerged to occupy many of the orchestral tuba jobs in America. Bob Carpenter is among them.

What united Carpenter and Treece, apart from a lifelong love for the tuba, was that each had an engineer's curiosity they applied to the horn. They were captivated by that immense York sound, and wondered how it was created and might be replicated.

As an instrument, tubas lent themselves to that. As with any young invention, the horn's kinks were still being worked out. The trumpet and trombone each had a standard size, but tubas, like humans, were short or tall, fat or skinny. (Human intestines are 15 feet long, almost the length of the tube of a C tuba. If our intestines were straight, we'd all have to be close to 20 feet tall. Instead, nature found a way of doubling back our intestines, neatly folding them into a confined space. Tuba makers did more or less the same thing.)

A mutual friend, knowing their similar interests, brought them together in 2007. Carpenter brought his horn to Treece's house. It was a Holton, an old and respected company, which had made its own stab at a York replica years ago.

But Treece had heard Carpenter and his horn at a couple of concerts. The horn's sound seemed to just flop dead on the floor once it left the bell.

Carpenter played it again at Treece's. Treece did, too. It was a tough horn to play.

"Do we know each other well enough that I can tell you something insulting?" Treece said.

Well, they didn't know each other at all, but Carpenter was willing to listen.

"That tuba and its bell aren't doing you any favors," Treece said.

As it happened, Carpenter had heard the same from a couple of tuba players who had heard him in the orchestra. But his big Holton was a York replica. It had once belonged to Arnold Jacobs. How could there be anything wrong with it?

That began a friendship, and a years-long conversation on the topic of how to improve tubas. Both men knew the Chicago Yorks' history. Naturally, as devoted tubists and engineers, they turned to the problems involved in replicating their sound.

Gradually, and without at first meaning to, the pair set off on a trek that would consume years and a lot of money, to see if, without the assistance of a conglomerate, they could do what those companies could not, and recreate those two perfect tubas residing at the symphony up in Chicago.

Chapter 4

Bill Bell

"He looked like a tuba player."

In the year 1957, raw rock 'n' roll was shredding eardrums and shocking parents.

Elvis Presley released "Jailhouse Rock" that year. Little Richard put out his first album, including the song "Rip It Up." Jerry Lee Lewis seemed to understand it all with "Whole Lotta Shakin' Goin' On."

That year, another earthquake of a record appeared to no less stunning effect on those who heard it. The man on the cover looked like a Madison Avenue ad exec. He had black lacquered hair, black horn-rimmed glasses, and a black suit and tie. In his arms he held a magnificent golden orchestral tuba.

Bill Bell and His Tuba, the record was called—the first album with tuba as lead instrument.

The man on the album cover was Bill Bell himself, the tuba player for the New York Philharmonic Orchestra.

Bill Bell and His Tuba begins with him singing "When Yuba Plays the Rumba on the Tuba (Down in Cuba)." But he also recorded a tuba version of Mozart's "Isis and Osiris Guide Them" and variations on Handel's *Judas Maccabaeus*. Those composers died long before the tuba was invented. Yet Bell was fresh from premiering in America the first tuba concerto from a major composer—Ralph Vaughan Williams. He cheekily insisted on staking out new territory for his horn, so he brought it to these great composers. Bell then led the record's B side with "Carnival of Venice." The Niccolò Paganini piece based on an Italian folk song was usually rendered by trumpet players. But here was Bill Bell, double- and triple-tonguing the mighty horn, adding sixteenth notes, and ending with a big finish that was unashamedly, unabashedly, proudly low.

As it circulated into the next decade, *Bill Bell and His Tuba* created among tuba players stirrings of the kind that jazz musicians in the 1940s remember the first time they heard Charlie Parker, or that awed rock guitarists upon hearing Jimi Hendrix. These tuba players were young, alone, hidden at the back of school bands where little was expected of them and less was required. The record opened their eyes and minds. Those I spoke to remember conceiving of their instrument one way before *Bill Bell and His Tuba* and quite another way after.

Bell was a large man, 6 feet 2, 250 pounds—"He looked like a tuba player," said one student—with equally large tastes. He enjoyed eating and drinking with other people, and he drank a lot. His sound on the tuba was described by some players as the most full and beautiful they'd ever heard the instrument produce. He loved to sing, too, and his voice matched the baritone depths of his horn.

Bill Bell was born on Christmas Day in 1902 in the town of Creston, Iowa, southwest of Des Moines—the second youngest of five children born to a mother and father who both became school superintendents. Bell took up the tuba at age ten, playing in the kind of brass band that was then spreading across middle America. As a boy, Bell had no formal lessons, but he learned along the way.

The rules for a tuba career were still unwritten. He set an unorthodox "just do it" path that others followed in spirit. He became a classical musician yet spent no time in a conservatory. His training came in the marching bands and circuses that were his first musical love.

At fifteen, he studied music at North Dakota University, then in 1918 won the job in an ensemble called Bachman's Million Dollar Band run by a Col. Harold Bachman, an early promoter of U.S. military and marching bands.

Bell's tuba renown was spreading in 1920 when John Philip Sousa offered the teenager a job without ever having heard him play. Sousa was a Portuguese immigrant. In the first decades of the twentieth century, before radio and TV, before even universal electricity, he became one of the most influential musical figures in the country. His military-style marching bands toured middle America. They played live, breaking the monotony of towns where little else happened. Sousa brought the gospel of band to a silent, still rural country. He preached music for commoners, a band in every town, lessons for every kid.

Soon a marching-band craze began across middle America that is depicted in the musical *The Music Man*. In New Orleans, the town's Black residents made that style their own, creating jazz and jazz funerals along the way.

Sousa, meanwhile, designed a wraparound tuba that could be carried—the sousaphone. It became a fixture at football games and is today the image most people have of the horn.

Bell played tuba for Sousa on three national tours between 1921 and 1924, then landed a job at the Cincinnati Symphony. In 1937, he moved to New York as the tuba player for the NBC Orchestra under Arturo Toscanini. Toscanini found Bell's playing so beautiful that one day he asked him to play the same section of a symphony over and over. "Please play it once more," Toscanini said, "just for me."

Bell was hired by the New York Philharmonic in 1943, and there he spent the rest of his playing days.

New York is where he became *the* Bill Bell. He embodied the old and the emerging tuba worlds and had a hand in shaping both.

He gave the American debut of Ralph Vaughan Williams' "Concerto for Bass Tuba and Orchestra," and wrote perhaps the first tuba textbook, *Foundation to Tuba and Sousaphone Playing*. He taught at the Juilliard School and in studios around New York. He was generous with his time. His lessons occasionally drifted into hours, sometimes surrounded by tuba pals kibitzing on the student's playing, or sharing tips on breathing.

His recommendation was all a student needed to find an orchestral tuba job. His New York City students went on to populate the emerging symphonies around the country—Kansas, Minneapolis, Houston, Oklahoma City. Bell taught the first woman to play tuba in a symphony, the late Connie Weldon, who won the job at the Boston Pops orchestra in 1954.

For our story, though, perhaps Bell's more important role was presiding over the country's first authentic tuba "scene." Broadway shows all had orchestras needing tubas. So did a lot of clubs. The city teemed with tubists, as much as a city can.

Bell was New York's reigning tuba monarch for twenty-five years. He established a tradition of heavy drinking that tuba players of the time adopted—just as bebop jazz players of the 1940s and 1950s turned to heroin because their hero Charlie Parker was an addict. He spent notorious hours at McSorley's Ale House in the Bowery, a bar known for "Good Beer, Raw Onions, and No Women." Word would somehow spread when he would show up at McSorley's, and a dozen tuba players would arrive for an all-night drinking binge.

Bell also liked nothing better than to play in a circus or a parade. He was said to have kept a sousaphone in a locker in Grand Central Terminal in case a parade was planned near the city. Then he was gone. He and his circus buddies from years gone by would carouse whenever they came to New York. He loved, too, playing in the municipal bands in which he'd first learned his instrument. He would occasionally take a powder from the New York Phil and head to Asbury Park, New Jersey, where the municipal band was renowned and one of his favorites.

In New York in 1956 or thereabouts, he met a man named Clark Galehouse. Galehouse was from Bell's hometown of Creston, Iowa. He had just started a record label, Golden Crest records, out on Long Island. Galehouse was balding and in a business suit. He looked like the plastics businessman he had been. But he harbored a fondness for offbeat musical visions that the major labels ignored. He was his own musical scout and recording engineer. Galehouse remains one of the unheralded renegades of American recorded music. He produced records of jazz, doo-wop, college choirs, garage rock, and classical piano. Paul and the Four-Mosts and the New York Brass Quintet were Golden Crest labelmates. The Wailers were the label's best-known act, with their 1959 instrumental hit "Tall Cool One."

Galehouse died in 1983 and his label soon closed. In 1957, though, he was just getting started. With one of his first records, he brought Bell and a piano player in to record ten pieces.

For *Bill Bell and His Tuba*, Galehouse spared no hyperbole. "It's difficult to find suitable words to describe a triumph of this kind," read the record's liner notes, which went on to claim that "professionals who know and understand [the tuba's] difficulties shake their heads in wonder and amazement" at Bell's mastery. His achievement was comparable, Galehouse insisted, to a runner breaking the four-minute mile, a track-and-field landmark set three years before.

Bill Bell and His Tuba is out of print and sold today on novelty music websites. (I scored my copy on bizarrerecords.com, which proclaimed him King of the Tuba.) But every tuba player I spoke to from those years could tell me when and where he first heard the record.

In Chicago in 1961, a high schooler named John Weber, early in his tuba education, heard of the record from a friend during summer band. Weber went downtown to Rose Records and bought a copy, brought it home, and listened to it all summer.

Me and Bill Bell and his Tuba. *"I was just hooked by his sound."* Photo by Sheila Tully.

Paul Krzywicki was in the band room at St. Joseph's prep school in Philadelphia. He had only recently taken up the instrument at the urging of his teacher but loved the deep resonance he produced. "That's when the Bill Bell record was given to me, in the band room at St. Joseph's," said Krzywicki, who went on to become principal tuba player for the Philadelphia Orchestra. "It was the only tuba record there was at the time. I was just hooked by his sound. It's the basis of what I've always tried to produce: that deep rich sound."

In Barnwell, South Carolina, a junior high student named Winston Morris, the son of a doctor, remembers that his band teacher gave him the record. It bent his mind. Young Morris was the lone tuba player in his school. He now realized he had gravely overestimated his own skills and saw how little had been expected of him. "I would have been a doctor and I'd be retired, and I'd be living in Santa Barbara, right up on a hill somewhere, but this recording came out and I literally said, 'That's what I got to do, man!' "

In 1962, five years after Golden Crest Records released *Bill Bell and His Tuba*, Bell left New York for a teaching job at Indiana University. His playing days were ending. He was a poor money manager, especially after his wife, Aggie, died in 1960. He was likely approaching poverty. Within a few years, a revitalized union movement took hold among U.S. orchestras. Musicians' unions won fifty-two-week contracts, real health insurance, and protection from arbitrary firings and hirings. But none of that safety net yet existed in 1962. Bell had to keep working, though his skills were declining.

His arrival at IU was a revelation to young tuba players around America whose lives his record had changed. Suddenly, he was available to them at a Midwestern public university. They flocked there. Bell knew every major composer of the midtwentieth century. He had performed their music at the New York Philharmonic. He could tell his students of the time he played with Aaron Copland or Richard Strauss.

Yet he could be tyrannical. His daily warm-up exercises wore out students. He had them play Paganini's dizzying piece for violin, "Moto Perpetuo" ("Perpetual Motion"). "I don't think he believed there was a place in music for everybody who wanted one," said one student. Some fled the program, which was likely Bell's point. Two may have entered mental institutions.

But Bell had a lighter side that revealed itself to those who stayed. His students replaced his New York bar cronies. His house that he shared with some students, back when that kind of thing was done, became the tuba's social center at IU. Under Bell, drinking became part of tuba life at Indiana, almost a test of tuba manhood. Some of his students were from small Midwestern towns and found this disturbing. "He did not drink by himself," said Paul Krzywicki, one of the students who rented a room from Bell. "He loved people too much. It was a social thing, 'C'mon, let's have a drink.'" Krzywicki, who loved to cook, would prepare mountains of potatoes, sauerkraut, and steak, and music students would descend on the house. "He could consume a shitload of food," Krzywicki told me.

Bill Bell spent ten years at Indiana University. Without his wife, though, he grew depressed. He barely managed to pay the electric bill. His body was crumbling from years of neglect and the physical punishment a tuba exacts. He couldn't play as he had before, and that likely hastened his decline.

Bill Bell retired in 1971 and moved to his sister's home in Perry, Iowa, then to a nursing home, where he died on August 7. He was sixty-nine. His students were by then at major universities or orchestras around the country. A *Bill Bell and His Tuba* album cover remained tacked above the bar at McSorley's in New York City long after.

At a memorial service, a minister eulogized Bell as *not* an "organization man"—no conformist despite his relentlessly square attire. Bell instead embodied the tuba approach to life. He played a solitary instrument yet was inspired by an equally powerful gregarious impulse. He was a man of great cheer, the minister said, who loved "publican and sinner" and lived with purpose, a taste for hard work, a love for the sound he could create, and a generosity that helped others "laugh, cry, and sing."

For many years there was a William Bell Memorial Tuba Day in Iowa on the first Saturday of November. Tuba and euphonium players gathered in Perry, Iowa, for a concert, then adjourned to Bell's grave, where they played two of his favorite pieces, Bach's "Come Sweet Death" and Ralph Vaughan Williams' "Dona Nobis Pacem"—Latin for "Grant Us Peace."

Bill Bell and His Tuba inspired young players to bridle at how little others expected of them, and how little they expected of themselves. Bill Bell's rendition of "Carnival of Venice," in particular, might as well have been a cavalry charge to his lonely tuba troops across middle America. They had languished at the back of every school band while trumpeters played soaring crescendos, and they, the tuba players, huffed away, hidden behind a mountain of metal, supporting the enterprise with plodding whole notes because, well, what else was the tuba and its player capable of?

Then *Bill Bell and His Tuba* showed them a path out of the back of the band and into the instrument's future.

Chapter 5

H. E. Nutt I

"He was so focused on . . . the roots of the paper bag."

In 1921, a college student in Chicago was seeking a cornet teacher.

The student's name was Hubert Estel Nutt, but everybody called him H.E. He was studying biology, though music is what he loved. He had long played in marching bands, but somehow never found a good teacher. His skills stagnated.

Then H.E. contacted a fellow named H. A. VanderCook. VanderCook already had a long career in circus bands behind him. He was a strange-looking man, gaunt with a mop of hair perched atop an elongated head, round glasses, and a stern manner. He was a frugal, practical "Holland Dutchman" with a knack for analyzing student weaknesses. What's more, he burned with the faith that he was remaking music instruction by focusing on real classroom problems facing band teachers.

His practicality spoke to H. E. Nutt, who was of Dutch extraction himself, raised on an Indiana farm, and impatient with theoretical constructions. Suddenly Nutt's cornet playing improved.

H. E. Nutt was not a man given to half measures. If he had planned for a life outside music, it ended after he met H. A. VanderCook. Like a monk giving up earthly pursuits to follow a spiritual master, H.E. ditched biology to spend his life promulgating the methods of his music teacher.

In 1928 the pair founded what is today called VanderCook College of Music, famously writing out its band director curriculum on a paper bag (preserved at the school). H. E. Nutt was in its first graduating class in 1931. VanderCook, married and childless, would come to refer to Nutt as the son he never had. In 1941, VanderCook moved to Michigan to care for his ailing wife. He died there in 1949.

H. E. Nutt never left the college. He was its dynamo, its force. H.E. was a short man, thin and wiry. Life's luxuries that others dreamed of were to him frivolous distractions. He instead found an ascetic devotion to the teaching of band conducting in the way of his departed mentor.

It had taken H.E. three wives to find one who could live with him. H.E. and Thelma, a violinist, lived at the school in a small apartment. They received no salary, taking only enough from the school he cofounded to pay for food, clothing, and gas.

Many nights, H.E. cleaned the school. Some students at first mistook him for the janitor. He repaired instruments. Band directors do what needs doing, that was H.E.'s motto—or one of them; he was a man of many mottoes. His devotion and energy kept the school going when other music colleges failed. "This became his life's mission," said Ruth Rhodes, a Nutt student, later a teacher at the school.

H.E. believed in the cleansing power of music. He didn't curse, smoke, or drink, and avoided parties where any of that was going on. He went only by H.E., not Mr. Nutt. His frugality was legendary. He always dressed the same way: gray pants and a light-blue long-sleeved nylon shirt, with suspenders underneath. He once wore the same green nylon-Dacron shirt every day for a year, washing it nightly to test the material's new "drip-dry" properties. He ate cereal without milk, believing it was important to activate his salivary glands in the morning, and he did eye calisthenics, believing they would postpone the need for glasses.

He was personally conservative, dreaded depending on anyone, despised Franklin D. Roosevelt and the New Deal, and refused Medicare and Social Security. Nor did his school accept federal scholarships, because H.E. hated the idea of the government telling him what to do. Yet he was professionally democratic and fought for underdogs—rural kids, poor kids.

He created a system of teaching based on his master's methods. He became the system's "messianic evangelizer," and "more like VanderCook than VanderCook himself," wrote George Borich, an alum and Nutt disciple, in a 1984 dissertation on the teacher's life.

He sometimes walked the halls in his pajamas at night. Students with questions had only to knock on his door, even late at night, and they'd get a lesson. Some students avoided him because he often stopped to quiz them on this or that scale or baton motion.

H.E. rarely played an instrument. Conducting was his thing, and what he taught was unbending. Every student took his conducting classes and repeated the motions exactly as H.E. insisted. How to hold the baton, how to prepare kids to begin to play—to these and other questions H. E. Nutt committed his life. He made all his students sing what they conducted in solfège—using "do," "re," "mi," and so on.

Conducting also relied on body language. It required not just the arms, but the entire face and body to convey nuance to a band. H.E. admired the French mime Marcel Marceau, and he made a study of semiotics, the science of communicating without the voice, through gestures, facial expression, and body movement.

He believed in drilling until a skill became second nature. His life's magnum opus was the two-page *Directing Etude #1*, an exercise he wrote to take students through the conducting motions and time signatures they would encounter in school band music. He required every student to sing the etude and conduct it exactly the way he instructed. No variations. You don't know enough yet to be creative, he told them. "That etude was part of his soul," said Ruth Rhodes. "We had to mimic him. He would not stand for anything less."

Only with a solid base of conducting fundamentals could they create their own style as directors. This he believed, and in time his students understood. Three VanderCook alums, decades out of school, could still sing *Directing Etude #1* to me over the phone.

Meanwhile, H.E. co-organized a small clinic in 1946 for local bandmasters returning from the war. The Midwest Clinic today is one of the world's largest music education conferences, attended by more than twenty thousand people, still run in part by VanderCook students and administrators.

Through it all, H.E. remained largely oblivious to anything going on beyond the school. "He was so focused," one student remembered, "on being true to VanderCook, the school, and the roots of the paper bag."

His writing was as frugal as the man. The sum total of H. E. Nutt's more than forty years of musical life was contained in two hundred pages, now conserved online, each page concisely packed with his accumulated wisdom regarding band and choral directing, or fingering tests for saxophone and clarinet, or "101 discussion topics for band clinics" (including "Getting along with school officials" or "Most bands have too many woodwinds").

Above all, H.E. believed directors must focus on "beginning the beginners better." Kids with good instrument foundation were on a path to improvement, and to a lifelong belief in their own abilities.

To this end, Buddhist in his brevity, he wrote the "8 Teaching Points," his guiding principles for teaching beginner music ensembles. His first was focus on "Tone Production and Intonation," and, connected to that, "Start, Sustain, Release." Teach students to start the note perfectly, sustain it perfectly, release it perfectly.

Through the decades under H. E. Nutt, the college became a reflection of the man, a place of joyful yet intense devotion. Band "was all we talked about, all we cared about," said Willie Owens, a saxophonist from Gary, Indiana, who arrived shortly after H.E.

died in 1981, to study band directing. "This was what we wanted to do and I absolutely loved it. This was the crowd I was meant to be with."

VanderCook graduates spread across the United States. Among the places they landed was the town of Brownsville, Texas, which borders Mexico where the Rio Grande flows into the Gulf.

The town was growing fast. More VanderCook graduates followed and found their first jobs as band directors in Brownsville schools. As time went on, so many arrived that they created what you might call a colony of devotees to the teaching methods of H. E. Nutt.

Chapter 6

Rio Grande Valley

Cortinas in Crystal City

"Let's go show them what we can do!"

In 1972, a young man from south Texas named Al Cortinas, just out of college with a degree in band directing, was looking for work.

At about that time, the small Texas town of Crystal City, southwest of San Antonio, was in the middle of a racial reckoning. The town was three-fourths Latino, but the White population dominated local politics. In 1969, cresting on the Chicano power movement, Latino kids walked out of the Crystal City schools. The next year, Latinos won all the city and school district elected posts through a local alliance, Raza Unida (United Race). White families moved away or put their children in private schools.

The high school marching band lost about half its members, including its most proficient musicians. Most of those who remained were children of migrant farmworkers.

In 1972, the district brought in a man named Roberto Botello to direct its high school band. Botello was a short, thin man of bounding positivity when it came to teaching band. His energy cut through the political tension. He'd stop students in the halls with "You want to be in the band?" He called the group La Banda del Animo—*animo* being Spanish for a combination of energetic spirit and pride.

He hired three student teachers. Al Cortinas, then twenty-five, was one. Cortinas had deep-brown skin and jet-black hair. He wore glasses and possessed a manner that was both amiable and unsure, betraying his youth and lack of teaching experience.

He came from the south Texas town of Taft, where Whites lived on one side of the tracks, Latinos on the other. He played saxophone as a kid, hiring out to some of the Tex-Mex bands in the area. He played for a time for Freddy Martinez, whose Freddy Records became Texas' first Mexican American–owned record label.

When Cortinas graduated from high school, a vice principal refused to send his transcripts anyplace other than a vocational school, believing Latinos weren't capable of much else. It was only because a band director, another White man, intervened and threatened the vice principal that Al Cortinas attended Del Mar College in Corpus Christi, studied band directing, and got the chance to change his life.

He arrived at Crystal City to find that Roberto Botello dressed in a suit and tie, no matter the heat, and insisted his assistants do the same. Cortinas bought the first tie he ever owned. Botello addressed his assistants as "Mister," and insisted they do the same.

Band had been largely the domain of White students. But Botello and his assistants recruited seventy kids, all Latinos. Many could play no instrument; those who could play couldn't march.

So Botello and his team taught them. Al Cortinas would remember that year as one long essay in relentlessly hard work. The kids who could play couldn't sight-read, so the teachers helped them memorize the pieces they would perform, note by note. Nighttime rehearsals, weekend rehearsals. On the field, Botello had his assistants pound in 6-inch stakes, then had them tie cords between the stakes—mini-hurdles for the kids to practice high-stepping.

As months passed, the kids found themselves in Botello's enthusiasm and rigor. Their confidence began to build.

Well into that year, Botello took them to a regional band competition. The marching band on the field was Fredericksburg High School, a band twice the size of Crystal City's, and mostly comprising German American students. Each band was judged on its marching and musicianship, then given numbers from 1 to 5—1 being best.

Crystal City's band timidly walked around the field that day, suddenly feeling exposed, vulnerable. Botello would have none of that. We're the children of farmworkers and manual laborers, he told them. Nobody expects anything from us. The kids stared at him intently. They think we're nothing, he declared. Their jaws jutted as he spoke. Their teeth clenched. Some of them nodded.

"Well, they can think what they want. But you know what?" he yelled. "Let's go show them what we can do!"

The kids roared onto the field as Botello took the microphone. "Damas y caballeros, ladies and gentlemen: La Banda del Animo!"

"He had a deep voice that moved mountains," Cortinas remembered. "You'd think he was the good Lord when he spoke on the microphone."

All that work, the racial tensions, going it alone without the White students, it all came to that moment of marching and playing on the field. When it was over, they stood at attention alongside the other bands. The judges gave Crystal City the highest qualification. Kids broke down crying. Botello stood there, nodding, a grimace of vindication on his face, as if to say, See! See!

This moment made no news anywhere. Most of the kids' parents weren't even at the event. It lives only in the memories of those in the band that day. One of them was Al Cortinas, who, exhausted from that season of work, remembers it as the most deliriously happy moment of his life up to then.

Over the years, that small achievement rippled through Crystal City. Band became a prized activity. Parents pushed their kids into it. Older kids trained the younger ones in attitude and practice habits. By 1977, Crystal City's band was marching in the state finals at the University of Texas. Band kids began to go to college and to professional careers. Seeing this, other small south Texas towns, mostly poor and Hispanic, began investing in their school bands too.

Roberto Botello left Crystal City to spend decades directing in Texas and New Mexico. He died in 2016, a legend in the south Texas marching band world.

In 1973, Al Cortinas took a job as band director in small Rio Grande City, over on the border with Mexico. But for the rest of his life, he remembered Crystal City as a master class. That whole year, he said, "was about teaching those kids they can be whatever they want—we did it through band."

Chapter 7

H. E. Nutt II

"You learned from the masters and the masters were learning from each other."

The first VanderCook grad to arrive in Brownsville, Texas, was a man named James Murphy, in 1946.

Murphy had played in a military band during the war. He was a demanding, stubborn, blunt, and profane guy, yet a disciple of H. E. Nutt and devoted to music. "Proficient in his comprehension of the [music], and attuned to its emotions, he became one with it," read one obituary after Murphy passed in 1982.

He was just as devoted to merit, his students remembered. In Texas in the 1940s, Hispanics were second-class citizens. But in Brownsville under Murphy, White and Brown kids played side by side, winning or losing their instrument chairs based on how they played. A youth boxer of some skill, he once boxed and beat a gym teacher who mocked his band kids when Murphy prohibited them from boxing, as it might damage their lips.

Murphy hired other VanderCook graduates, starting with Bob Vezzetti, and Arcadio Guajardo, who grew up in the nearby town of Pharr, Texas, but hitchhiked to Chicago to attend VanderCook. Then a half dozen others. They forged a culture of high school band excellence based on H. E. Nutt's teachings. Brownsville bands soon were winning top honors consistently throughout Texas.

As Brownsville's band fame grew, more VanderCook graduates found their way down from Chicago for band directing jobs in which they would teach some of America's poorest kids, many of whose lives resembled their own.

These men—almost all were men—were poor and working-class Midwesterners. They were the first in their families to graduate from college. Band directing was their path to the middle class, away from farm and factory. The job brought something that many hadn't associated with work, which was fulfillment, a feeling that one's labor could actually mean something to oneself and to others. They saw this in the eyes of their students.

Most of these VanderCook grads came to Brownsville intending to stay just long enough to hone their craft. They spoke no Spanish and were foreign to the insular world of the U.S.-Mexico borderlands. But as years passed, they found they couldn't bring themselves to leave. Many married, had children, and stayed.

Up in Chicago, H. E. Nutt came to view Brownsville as a band-directing city on a hill. Toward the end of his life and no longer school president, H.E. may have felt unwanted. Those around him, he felt, were too removed from the demands of the working school conductor and thus had lost "the 'true' VanderCook credo," wrote George Borich, an alum, in a 1984 dissertation.

The VanderCook teachers in Brownsville invited H.E. down in 1976. He and Thelma came for a week, were feted and thanked and shown what his ideas had created in practice. H.E. ran clinics for junior high kids. He was seventy-nine, with a shrinking role at VanderCook. To him, Brownsville remained a bastion where his acolytes preserved the purity of his methods by subjecting them to the real world.

By 1981, the year H.E. died, Brownsville schools had twenty-two band directors, eighteen of whom were VanderCook graduates. They met often at the home of the district's head director, Bob Vezzetti, to eat barbecue and brisket and talk band. Band directors can have sizable competitive egos. Here, though, they were all in this together and creating what the rest of Texas thought unlikely coming from the impoverished southernmost outpost of the state: excellence in band achieved by Mexican and Mexican American kids.

"Over a martini, the older guys taught me how to teach a beginner class: ways of expressing an idea to the kids, ways of demonstrating it," said Paul Flinchbaugh, an Ohioan who arrived in 1981 from VanderCook and spent his career teaching band in Brownsville. "I used it the rest of my career. You learned from the masters and the masters were learning from each other. We were all obsessive compulsive, and all focused on band."

Willie Owens graduated from VanderCook in 1985 at age twenty-two, then went to Brownsville intending to visit for three days. "These guys were making great strides, making a difference in people's lives, and had phenomenal ensembles. That's what I dreamed of doing all my life." So Owens stayed, entering the Brownsville band director crucible in which he was shaped in the daily fire he came to love. A group of directors, he said, "would show up at six A.M. at the Dunkin' Donuts on Boca Chica Boulevard. Then we'd go to our band halls, knock off about eight or nine P.M., then get together for dinner after that. Get home about ten, then get up next morning and do it again. We ran that way for years. None of us were married at the time. We did our Thanksgivings together, spent all day together. You learned stuff you could never, ever learn in school. It was a life."

Brownsville directors put enormous effort into teaching kids the proper embouchure—the shape and position of the mouth as it meets the mouthpiece of a brass or woodwind instrument. In doing so, they created not only some of the best high school bands Texas had ever seen, but what became known as the Brownsville Sound.

To do so, teachers spent the first semester of sixth grade band having kids play literally one note—B-flat—every day. They'd make tapes of their bands playing that note and would play the tapes at conferences, to the befuddlement of directors elsewhere.

In 1981, a young teacher named Rolando Zapata took a job in Brownsville after finishing his master's degree at VanderCook. He visited a Brownsville band class playing one note over and over. He expected an atmosphere of tedium and rebellion. Instead, he was struck by "the intensity of these teachers and the eyes of the kids, sitting on the edge of their chairs, ready to play. The kids were like, 'Yes sir! Yes sir!' They'd take a breath, play the note, then stop."

This was the second of H. E. Nutt's "8 Teaching Points." "Start the note with a beautiful beginning, sustain it with the same quality, and release it with the same quality," Zapata said. "One note, every day, for weeks. You see the kids. They're mesmerized. Focused. 'We're going to do it.' And when they got a compliment, it was like, 'Yes!!!' "

An entire basic music curriculum, Zapata realized, was being taught through one note. "How do you get kids focused that long on just one note? It was just the intensity teachers put into everything they did—the way they breathed, articulated the note, the tone as they were sustaining it. They were teaching all the fundamentals: balance, volume, tone quality. By the time they got through, the kids knew what a note's supposed to sound like."

From there, students went on to high school trained to listen and expecting to work hard. This was the basis, Zapata came to understand, of the "Brownsville Sound." Orchestral and confident yet not brash. "It was warm, clean, clear. Strong . . . but never loud," said Zapata, who stayed at the district until retiring in 2013.

Early on, Brownsville bands won competitions across Texas. Up through the Rio Grande Valley their sound spread, and many in the south Texas band world aimed to replicate it.

Among them, and of particular interest to our story, was young Al Cortinas.

Cortinas was then in the early years of directing the band at Rio Grande City High School, a hundred miles upriver. The sound those Brownsville bands produced simply enthralled him. When H. E. Nutt visited the Valley in 1976, Cortinas met him at a reception, "then I saw him the rest of my life through what he taught other people."

Cortinas set out to study how Brownsville bands worked. As he did, one thing struck him more than anything else, and it was this: The sound those bands produced came from kids not one of whom could afford a private music lesson.

Chapter 8

Tuba Woodstock

"We were pushing the envelope, man!"

In March 1973, legions of tuba players began quietly descending on the tiny town of Bloomington, Indiana.

They streamed in from all over the country. Flying in from the coasts, they came. From throughout the Midwest. Some hitchhiked in, tubas on their backs. Others grabbed rides with friends and threw their horns in the trunk. Bloomington is home to Indiana University. In the end, close to three hundred tuba players came to the school in the Indiana hinterlands for a four-day gathering—the first of its kind in America, maybe the world.

It marked the beginning of a collective tuba consciousness, an awakening of the tuba tribe to the fact that they were everywhere and greater in number than any of them had thought. The event at the university was officially called the First International Tuba Symposium-Workshop. But the gathering was so momentous, the numbers so unexpected, that some who attended would later call it Tuba Woodstock.

"It changed our world," said Bob Tucci, who went on to a long tuba career in Germany.

Young people everywhere were questioning the established order of things. Tuba Woodstock was the first collective indication that tuba players were doing the same. They were fed up with the low expectations, the jokes, the fat elephants and tuba-playing clowns, the plodding whole notes. A radical tuba underground, fragmented across America, had been imagining a new day for the horn. Tuba Woodstock showed them they were not alone. That nothing less than a tuba civil rights movement was in order.

"We were tired of sitting in the back of the damn band," said Winston Morris, a young tuba professor at the time.

"Most of us had never seen so many tubists," Robert Ryker, then a thirty-four-year-old tuba player with the Montreal Symphony, told me. "It was just thrilling to be with so many."

At the event, the Young Turks also formally established the first tuba association in America. The idea for an association had been jokingly proposed by Bill Bell during a drinking bout at McSorley's in New York City. The Loyal Order of Shit Pots, he called it.

Ryker, a Bell student and acolyte, took the idea somewhat more seriously. A half dozen years before Tuba Woodstock, Ryker was conducting a brass ensemble at McGill University. He and others were discussing the need for a tuba association. Players were isolated across the country. They needed to know that there was a tuba nation out there, of which they were a part. Ryker had coincidentally accumulated hundreds of their addresses. So, one night, he volunteered for action.

He and a friend sneaked into the McGill University Press and printed a letter announcing the new organization. Only they had no name for it. That night, Ryker said, they coined a more concise synonym for "tuba player": "tubist," which conveyed their lofty intentions for the instrument. If "violinist" and "cellist," why not "tubist"? The word stuck and today is commonly used.

From that they crafted the name: the Tubists Universal Brotherhood Association—the T.U.B.A. "We couldn't think of a better name," Ryker said, "so that's what we called it." The four hundred letters they sent out informed recipients that they were now "tubists" and founding members of the T.U.B.A. Tuba players paid $1 and received a certificate of membership.

Ryker's energy for the project faded, however, in the face of other commitments. For several years, the new association faltered. Winston Morris wrote a quarterly T.U.B.A. newsletter. But tuba players were loners, not joiners. They brought a powerful streak of American individualism to the horn. No band had more than one tuba player. So they rarely hung out together. In fact, nothing was more terrifying to one tuba player than another tuba player hungry for work.

The T.U.B.A. tried to corral these stubborn souls. Morris would head to H. E. Nutt's annual Midwest Clinic in Chicago. Tuba players would peel off from the convention and go meet at Miller's Pub nearby. But many of them wouldn't join the T.U.B.A. because—why? They had work. Their careers were testaments to their own self-reliance. " 'I don't need this organization telling me what to do.' I heard that a lot," Morris said.

Then entered the man who would change it all. The P. T. Barnum of the horn. The man who harnessed the tuba to his passion for grandiose marketing and the kind of cornball that has characterized, perhaps afflicted, the horn for years. A man who came to be known, in fact, as *Mr. Tuba*, a title he would use for his autobiography.

Harvey Phillips was a tuba virtuoso, a Bill Bell protégé and as large as his mentor. He held the tuba chair at Indiana University now that the great man was gone. He named his farm outside Bloomington the TubaRanch, home to his family, cows, and a duck named Confucius that sat and listened to Phillips practice. TubaRanch became a tuba mecca. To it over the years came students, horn makers, and the leading lights of brass. One student lived in a teepee on TubaRanch. Phillips met them all with kingly generosity and ample "libations" (his word), the ranch being intended as a tuba wonderland and Harvey being a drinker in the Bill Bell tradition.

Born in 1929, Phillips grew up in rural Missouri, and like Bell, another Midwesterner, he never got over his love of the circus. Rural Missourians were inclined to view circuses as roving sinkholes of sin. But Phillips loved them. He deferred college at eighteen and left home to play in not one, but three. This eventually included the band with the Ringling Bros. and Barnum & Bailey Circus under conductor Merle Evans.

Phillips was a circus "windjammer"—jamming wind into his horn at the manic tempo the circus required for three hours a pop. On the road, Phillips met a one-legged cornetist, a dapper drooling drummer, and European acrobats. He learned to play craps. He practiced his horn in town cemeteries, and the tuba took him across America together with clowns, lion tamers, cooks, and roughnecks.

It was about as cool a time playing the tuba as a kid could imagine in those days, this being just after World War II.

Phillips' high school teacher once told him, "Remember, you play the horn, it doesn't play you." This was a liberating concept for any young musician. It intrigued Phillips. It meant that the shape, register, and tone of the metal beast did not constrict its options the way many assumed. Rather, these qualities endowed the horn with a bounty that only the player's dedication and talent could unlock.

This insight gave Phillips his path in life. He became a tuba philosopher, even ideologue. He bridled at the instrument's limitations that other musicians, and even some tubists, accepted. "If you told a [tuba] joke around him, he'd give you hell," said one.

Phillips studied at Juilliard, where he met a professor and composer named Vincent Persichetti. So little music was written for the tuba, Phillips complained. Persichetti was sympathetic, but, he asked, who would make the change? Violinists? Conductors? "If you want better music to play on the tuba, you better do something about it," Persichetti is said to have told Phillips. With Persichetti's DIY exhortation ringing in his ears, Phillips commissioned tuba music until he died—more than a hundred pieces, including two from Persichetti himself.

Composers, Phillips believed, needed to see that there was tuba talent out there eager to play their new work. Players, alone in the world, might falter and quit without hearing new voices. It was only together that each player could find individual tuba freedom. A reinvigorated T.U.B.A. was necessary, Phillips believed. When tubists saw they were part of something big, their enthusiasm for a tuba association would surely grow. To achieve that end, he conceived that 1973 Tuba Woodstock symposium.

The Indiana University music school dean supported the idea. Phillips slated the event for March 22–26, 1973, and convinced a slew of composers to come, among them the jazz and classical pianist Gunther Schuller, who taught at the New England Conservatory. And as the event approached, legions of shaggy-haired, born-to-be-wild tuba players began trucking into Bloomington from out of state.

Don Little was a tuba student in Chicago when he grabbed his sleeping bag, tuba, and some food and piled into a friend's Datsun station wagon. They arrived at Tuba Woodstock without money for the registration fee and slept on a friend's dorm floor. There were composers, and tubas he could try out. Little, who went on to teach tuba at the University of North Texas for forty-nine years, left amazed to have met so many aspiring tubists like himself in one place.

Participants held recitals. Younger players auditioned for judges. Breakout sessions dealt with "The Tuba in Jazz" and "New Directions and Techniques."

The whole group—hundreds of tuba players—posed for a photo that is now tuba-world famous.

In a major coup, Phillips persuaded Merle Evans to attend. Evans was by now retired from the Ringling Bros. and Barnum & Bailey Circus band. Yet no one was more renowned in tuba and circus circles than he, "the Toscanini of the Big Top." Evans appeared on a panel about the evolution of the tuba's image from 1900 to 1940. "For people who knew what he was about, and what he'd done, it was like seeing Elvis," said Ed Firth.

Firth was in the U.S. Army's West Point band. In crew cuts, he and a few bandmates drove out in a Volkswagen van and were starstruck at the tuba galaxy before them. "It would be easier to name the great tuba players that weren't there," he marveled.

In from Southern California flew Gene Pokorny to play a piece composed especially for him, "Three Essays for Solo Tuba." Later he would describe the conference as a kind of gravitational pull that attracted tuba players, then flung them out into the world with greater energy "inspired to [move] beyond whatever their reality was in the tuba world. People felt that they were all kind of in a cause."

Brian Frederiksen, a freshman tuba student at Illinois State that year, hitched a ride with a friend and found an empty dorm room. He talked with players and composers he had actually heard of, and it amazed him that he was speaking to them on a first-name basis. "It was a tuba renaissance," Frederiksen said years later.

Conference participants wrote a T.U.B.A. constitution. Dozens of composers and horn makers mingled with students and players; they performed until late at night, then everyone hung out and drank and talked. Using a technique called circular breathing, a former Bill Bell student named Don Harry, just starting a career at the Buffalo Symphony, played a Bach cello concerto on the tuba with no breathing breaks, for Bach was writing for the cello and intended none. Harvey Phillips, meanwhile, was hospitalized from overwork and missed most of the event.

Finding one another, tubists perhaps saw the reason to form the community they had avoided. "It was one of the most important things that ever happened in the history of the tuba," said Winston Morris. "We were pushing the envelope, man!"

The T.U.B.A. from then on would give formal voice to the spirit of Tuba Woodstock. Membership grew. It founded a quarterly

Tuba Woodstock, Indiana University, 1973. "It changed our world."
Courtesy of Ed Firth.

publication—the *T.U.B.A. Journal*—and held annual tuba conferences. In 2000, the name was changed to include women and euphoniums, the tenor tuba: International Tuba Euphonium Association (ITEA).

Morris himself showed up at the 1973 gathering with a bizarre new concoction: a mighty tuba ensemble, ten tubas, eight euphoniums, all students at the school where he was now the tuba professor—Tennessee Tech University, in the rural town of Cookeville. Nothing quite reflected the collaborative yet barrier-breaking intentions of these tuba rebels better than a massive ensemble of bass horns.

Tuba Woodstock convinced Phillips that tuba players needed to bridge their isolation, to come together and play. To honor his mentor, Bill Bell, Phillips organized tubists to play Christmas carols at the Rockefeller Center ice rink in New York City in

December 1974. More than three hundred showed up, and Tuba Christmas was born.

In 1976, Phillips went on to sponsor Carnegie Hall's first solo tuba concert series. He reserved one day for Winston Morris' ensemble that had premiered at Tuba Woodstock three years earlier.

Morris trained the ensemble like a football team. In late night rehearsals, he challenged their commitment. "I was a drill sergeant. No bullshit," he told me. "It's business."

His students were country, self-described hillbillies, who grew up in the 1960s in rural Tennessee far from the decade's tumult, and of whom, like the tuba, little was expected. Many were the first in their families to go to college. Tim Lawhern had plowed land behind a mule named Big John on the family farm on the Cumberland Plateau. The father of Joseph Northcut, a euphonium player in the Morris ensemble, was a pastor and a handyman in Waverly, Tennessee (pop. 3,800); Northcut's mother was a teacher.

Morris was from the South too, and knew his students' origins. That's all they needed, he told them: work and focus. Talent was overrated. "He was the only one who said those words to me," said Lawhern. "We knew he meant it because he came from rural South Carolina, with that accent, and ended up studying with Bill Bell, the world's greatest tuba player." So, from across small-town Tennessee, as years passed, countrified tuba players flocked into Cookeville—not for the school, but for the man.

Morris insisted they burst the world's view of Tennessee hillbillies and the tuba simultaneously. After the 1973 symposium, word of the daring ensemble spread. "In our own little world, we were sort of celebrities," said Nancy Holland, a euphonium player in that ensemble. "Once I got outside of that, I realized people did not have positive views of tuba players."

They sold doughnuts to pay for the trip to Carnegie Hall and spent two days on the bus, their faces pushed up against the windows. In New York, they ate at Jewish delis, heard raging car horn symphonies, saw jaw-dropping skyscrapers, subway drunks, and streets with no trees. They swung by Golden Crest Records and recorded an album.

The concert was held on March 2, 1976, in the smaller Carnegie recital hall. It was half full. Many in the crowd were family of the musicians onstage. A *New York Times* reviewer wrote something like "Tuba music for people who like tuba music."

Perhaps, but the reviewer missed the point, which was in the daring. As the tuba world groped for new ways to play, the ensemble suggested a path and, maybe more important, an attitude. They returned to Cookeville as stars, heroes. "Nobody thought a tuba ensemble could ever do anything like that," said Joseph Northcut.

Winston Morris continued his ensembles until his retirement in 2022. They played Carnegie Hall seven more times, and JazzFest and the Mardi Gras parade in New Orleans an equal number.

But it was that first ensemble of Tennessee hillbillies, nourished in the soil of Tuba Woodstock and the early days of the T.U.B.A., that set out in New York City a fresh stance—proud, unashamed, even pugnacious—that the young rebels were bringing to their lowly horn.

FIRST MOVEMENT

Chapter 9

The Man Who Tried to Corner the Tuba Market

"He'd get so excited doing the deal."

One sunny day in 1999, a man named Kevin Powers boarded a train in Beijing, China, and headed north into the province called Hebei. Powers was from a suburb of Detroit and carried with him only a couple of small suitcases. For five years he had been visiting China as it was becoming the industrial giant it is today.

Parts of Hebei province hug Beijing. But the state also reaches to the north, where it borders Mongolia. Its terrain gradually becomes a windswept desert. It was to this part of Hebei province that Powers, forty-two at the time, took that train, then a bus, and finally spent three hours in a Chinese jeep with a board for a back seat and doors that didn't quite close. They took him into a barren outback, past an occasional lonely village with a few stray dogs and kids in gunnysacks, until finally he arrived at a fenced collection of buildings, without another structure for miles. All in search of a cheaper tuba.

Hebei province was the center of Chinese instrument making. Those buildings housed a trumpet manufacturer run by a certain Mr. Shi, who, Powers had been told, might be willing to try his hand at tubas.

Powers was on assignment from his employer, a man named Fred Marrich, and was used to this kind of trip.

Fred Marrich was by then a tuba legend, and as bare-knuckle a businessman as the horn had ever known. He had established his Tuba World brand out of his Custom Music shop near Detroit.

A short, thin man with large glasses, and a famously bad driver of a boatlike tan Cadillac, Fred Marrich had the instincts and manner of a fast-talking used-car salesman—by turns abrasive, unctuous, fun-loving, ornery, generous, and loud. He loved tubas and tuba players, though he never played a note. Just as often, he argued with customers, nickel-and-dimed buyers, aggravated and fought with employees. Those who knew him said he at times hung out near the hazy line between shrewd and unethical. From his shop, Fred Marrich also drove improvements in the tuba worldwide, just as its players were demanding respect and better instruments.

Marrich traveled the world, urging manufacturers to improve their tubas, financing those improvements, and sealing exclusive U.S. distribution deals. Tuba World became America's premier tuba spot. Loads of players, especially younger ones and especially in the Midwest, traveled to Tuba World to buy their horns.

"He wanted to corner the tuba market," said Paul Kryzwicki, retired tubist with the Philadelphia Orchestra. "He was intense."

Fred Marrich saw China as the tuba's future. In the mid-1990s he sent Kevin Powers to find it.

China had a conflicted relationship with the horn. In the 1960s, the Communist dictator Mao Zedong decreed that China was elitist, too effete, too separate from the workers. He ignited the so-called Cultural Revolution. Foreign influences were rooted out, the party re-revolutionized. Intellectuals and others were seen as class enemies and sent to work camps in the countryside.

The Cultural Revolution lasted until Mao's death in 1976. It stripped the country of its most educated, talented people in the arts and sciences. It devastated China's economy. Massacres killed more than a million people.

One Cultural Revolution moment is important to our story. Mao placed his wife, Jiang Qing, an actress, in charge of remaking the country's arts with revolutionary fervor. Madame Mao, as she was known, was an impulsive ideological inquisitor. When it came to music, said legendary orchestra conductor Li Delun, "she couldn't understand a fart."

At one orchestra performance, the story goes, she objected to the trombone as too loud, insisting it be banned. As Li told the authors Sheila Melvin and Jindong Cai, as reported in their book *Rhapsody in Red: How Western Classical Music Became Chinese*, he could not imagine his group without a trombone section, and he suggested it might be the tuba she didn't like.

With that, Madame Mao banned the tuba. (Though, undeterred, she later did ban the trombone. The bassoon, too.)

In 1980, Stan Freese, a tuba player with the University of Minnesota, was touring China. A Chinese tuba player in the orchestra whom Madame Mao had objected to introduced himself. He had been sentenced to five years in a rural labor camp, Freese wrote later, but had his tuba smuggled to him in a hay cart so he could practice.

After Mao's death, Madame Mao was tried, sentenced to prison, then released years later for medical reasons, after which she killed herself. Meanwhile, the violinist Isaac Stern had visited China in 1979. His playing mesmerized the country, reigniting its fascination with Western classical music, which was now officially allowed once more.

The tuba was again taught in schools and included in the state orchestra.

By the 1990s, China was learning to make the horn. The quality was abysmal. Still, Marrich sent Kevin Powers to comb the country. Be on the lookout, Marrich told him, for companies we might tutor and coax into making horns just good enough to export, then rework and sell at Tuba World.

The first person to ever tell me about Fred Marrich was Tom Treece, the Orlando engineer and tubist. "All the tuba players met Fred at one time or another. We all bought our first tubas from Fred Marrich." Marrich's empire in suburban Detroit, Tom told me, qualified in fact as "the center of the tuba universe in the U.S."

That there was a U.S. tuba universe, and that it actually had a store you could call its center, were startling ideas to me at the time. I began to poke into the story of Fred Marrich.

Right off the bat, I learned that his Tuba World became a badge of tuba cool. When talking to other players, you were hip if you could say something like, "Dude, yeah, got this horn at Tuba World," and let that hang in the air for a bit as others, envious, quickly changed the subject. How Marrich did that—how he turned a cornball name like Tuba World into something edgy—well, Kevin Powers never could figure that out.

Part of it, though, had to be what was known as the Tuba House. For years, Marrich had a two-story wood-frame house a block or so off the main drag from his official store, Custom Music, in the town of Royal Oak, north of Detroit. This house was packed top to bottom with tubas. Even the attic burst with them. The kitchen was for trombones; tubas were everywhere else. Dozens of them, some still in shipping boxes. From beginner horns on up to professionals, stacked on plywood shelves in the dining room, the living room, the bedrooms—a million-dollar inventory. The largest congregation of tubas in North America. A magical tuba wonderland.

Marrich kept smaller instruments on display in his store on Main Street. He branded them as well. Bassoon World. Flute World. He sold a lot of marimbas. These instruments were bought by customers usually oblivious to Marrich's other, more hidden life as king of the tuba dealers.

No matter what was on display in Custom Music, "the tuba community knew the good stash was in the Tuba House," Powers said. "Everybody in the whole country who played the tuba knew about the Tuba House. Players would come, stay for two, three days, sit on folding chairs, and play their way through all those tubas. To buy one, though, you had to get past Fred. His style of [price] negotiation could burn you out in no time."

Many tuba customers remember him fondly nevertheless. "He gave them something they couldn't get their whole career, which is a great tuba," said Powers. But Powers worked for Marrich part time for twenty-seven years and, wearied by the experience, never considered him more than a "business associate."

Marrich's store had grown from an instrument pawn shop his father owned. Marrich took over the shop, saw legions of competitors for violins, guitars, and drums, and decided instead to specialize in harder-to-find instruments. The tuba above all. He didn't always say so in so many words, but Marrich gradually realized that if he could arrange exclusive distribution deals with manufacturers, he could corner the North American tuba market.

American horn makers, however, balked at investing in tuba research. They already had the student market. Orchestral tubas cost too much. Why make these costly finer horns? They could sell four or five trumpets for every tuba they sold. So Marrich crossed the Atlantic, extending financing to struggling European brands. Meinl in Germany was one. Nirschl another. In return, they gave him exclusive distribution rights in the United States.

The Swiss Hirsbrunner family had been making instruments in the small town of Sumiswald since the late 1700s. The family started out making woodwinds, but during the Napoleonic occupation in the early 1800s they saw French soldiers playing brass instruments and began making them as well.

Like Napoleon, Fred Marrich had a hand in transforming the Hirsbrunner enterprise. He pushed the family to produce tubas and financed the expansion. U.S. players were mesmerized by the Chicago Yorks that Arnold Jacobs played and were frustrated by their lack of options in fine horns. With Marrich's backing, the Hirsbrunners turned out the first copy of the mythical Yorks—dubbed the Yorkbrunner. In exchange, Marrich got the U.S. rights to sell their horns.

Through these years, Fred Marrich connected players and technicians and manufacturers. His most important collaboration was with two young Americans named Bob Tucci and Dan Perantoni. Tucci played for a German orchestra. Perantoni taught at the University of Illinois. Tuba Woodstock had just taken place, the T.U.B.A. was a functioning organization. Tucci and Perantoni were charter members: Tuba radicals they were, unwilling to accept the musical segregation of either their instrument or themselves.

"When I was in college, there was only one [kind of orchestral tuba] available that you could buy," Perantoni told one interviewer. "It was pretty good, but that was it. We wanted something that played better. Trumpets had all these mouthpieces. We had one."

Fred Marrich asked their advice on how to improve the horn. The two musicians set off in search of their own perfect tuba. The collaboration produced the PT-6 (PeranTucci-6), a towering marvel and beautifully curving horn that soon became the choice of many orchestral tubists.

By 1990, Marrich had locked up deals with some of Europe's best-known tuba makers. York was long dead. German horns, along with Yamahas, were ascending. In the United States, you could buy a horn from someone other than Fred Marrich, but no one had his exclusive selection of the best tubas, and of course no one had the Tuba House.

His world-beating dreams at fever pitch, Fred Marrich now looked to China to complete his full-service tuba empire. He had a fine Hirsbrunner for which he charged $10,000. He needed a usable Chinese horn for a quarter the price to grab kids early in their tuba lives. No American dealers were buying China's cheapo horns. But Marrich believed their quality would improve and wanted an early foothold in the Chinese market.

Powers figures he made at least fifteen trips to China for Marrich. He rarely saw another foreigner outside the major cities. He traveled in creaky buses on bumpy roads, ate suspect food. Along the roads, he occasionally spotted dead bodies, left after being hit by vehicles. Dozens of brass instrument factories all used poor-quality metal, shoddy tooling, cheap finishings, soldering that fractured. Using an interpreter and his own halting Mandarin, Powers lived in a vortex of misunderstanding and cultural misinterpretation, making handshake deals over cigarettes and green tea. He developed a serious smoking habit—all for a cheaper tuba.

Sometimes Marrich came too. Groping through the cultural and linguistic fog put Marrich in a foul mood. He was often irritating and irritated during negotiations with factory bosses over the tubas they could make and at what cost. "The quality wasn't there," Powers said, "and Fred would be yelling at them, 'I can't sell that shit!' We'd all take a break, drink beer, eat, then go back at it."

Mr. Shi, who ran the company in that compound in Hebei province that Powers visited, was indeed interested in making tubas. Until he calculated the cost. Then his enthusiasm waned.

Powers and Marrich eventually struck an arrangement with Dalian Hue Mie, a brass instrument company in the international free trade town of Dalian, on the peninsula near North Korea. Their horns were of poor quality, Powers remembered, and he had to modify them when they got to Michigan. He spent a lot of time shuttling between Michigan and Dalian.

"There'd be times where I'd be taking three prototype tubas to China, with notes on improvements needing to be made on the company's horns, and a change of clothes. It dawned on me that I was really influencing tuba manufacturing in China."

Over the years, Fred Marrich midwifed not a perfect tuba, but a better one. His financing funded collaborations that led to better tube and valve design, improvements in plating, lathing, soldering, and more.

Marrich ran Tuba World until 2008, when at the age of ninety-two he died. The *International Tuba Euphonium Association Journal* published an eight-page spread on his life and contributions to the horn.

"He was proud of the instruments he helped develop, but the [distribution] deal was what he was after. The conquest," said Dan Perantoni. "Fred Marrich wanted to control the tuba market. He'd get so excited doing the deal. He was a pawnbroker in his heart. I understand it now. I didn't at the time. We had a lot of fights along the way. But we always kissed and made up. I also remember some hard times in my life. Who was the first guy to call me? Fred Marrich. I admired him greatly."

Kevin Powers tried to buy Custom Music and Tuba World. Instead, the Marrich family sold them to another. Custom Music still exists, but it isn't the same as when Fred Marrich ran it as the mothership of world tuba domination.

Chinese tuba makers, meanwhile, have spent the last two decades investing in top-quality machinery and brass, finer finishes, soldering that actually holds an instrument together—"all the things I was trying to get them to do years ago," Powers said.

Now even the Chinese can take a stab at replicating the perfect American tuba.

Chapter 10

Arnold Jacobs I

"everyone else just went for the ride"

When Arnold Jacobs bought that first York tuba from his teacher, Philip Donatelli, he likely had little idea of what had fallen literally into his lap.

He was a teenager at the Curtis Institute, several years younger than the other students and perhaps a bit timid.

One day, the story goes, he brought the horn to a Curtis student orchestra rehearsal of Bach's *Toccata and Fugue in D Minor*. You've heard the *Toccata* whether you know it or not. It's a piece almost synonymous with old-time vampire movies. Bach wrote it for organ, with a bone-shaking bass line. His piece has since been adapted for the orchestra, and there it requires a tuba up to the task.

During that first rehearsal with the York, from the back of the band, Jacobs suddenly produced a sound so deep, so perfectly ominous, that his conductor, an exacting old-school maestro named Fritz Reiner, is said to have bolted upright at his podium. Throughout the rehearsal, Reiner stared at Jacobs, marveling at the sound this teenager was now producing.

Reiner insisted that Jacobs bring the horn to rehearsals from then on. For a time, Jacobs lugged the horn onto Philadelphia buses. But when a woman tripped and fell on the tuba, bending its bell, Reiner sent his chauffeur to pick up Jacobs and the York for every rehearsal—three days a week for the next three years.

That was the beginning of one of the most illustrious careers in American tubadom.

Arnold Jacobs was born in 1915 and grew up in the community of Willowbrook near Los Angeles. His father was a shipyard accountant, his mother a silent-movie pianist.

He fell in love early with the trombone, and with it he won a scholarship to the famed Curtis Institute of Music in Philadelphia. The entire family moved to Philadelphia so he could enter the school. But on a family trip through Texas his trombone, tied to the car's running board, fell off, thus changing the tuba world forever.

Curtis had no extra trombones. Without enthusiasm, Jacobs switched horns. But he had prodigious musical talents. He learned the upright bass, playing in nightclubs. He was such a talented singer that Curtis offered him a vocal scholarship. By then, however, Jacobs had learned to love his adopted tuba.

He went to work for the Chicago Symphony in 1944. About that time, as it happened, Bill "Pops" Johnson retired from York Instrument Co., and its decline began. Johnson founded and ran something called the Musical Instrument Exchange in Grand Rapids. Near as I can tell, the place was akin to a pawn shop, where Johnson appraised and repaired used instruments. And in that endeavor, the man who had overseen the creation of the two greatest tubas ever made spent the rest of his working life. He died in 1972 at the age of ninety-one about the time York closed its doors for good.

Over those decades, meanwhile, the brass section of the Chicago Symphony grew world famous, due in no small part to that custom York tuba that Johnson and his crew crafted. That brass section was a monster, a leviathan of bold, ringing sound, reflecting perhaps some larger American confidence in the world during those postwar decades. The section's players were, in the words of one writer, "a collection of superheroes," each one a virtuoso, though none a star outside the orchestral world. Together the CSO's brass section forged what became known as the "Chicago Sound."

That sound was powered by Arnold Jacobs—Jake, as he was known to his colleagues. Together, Jake and his York provided a vocal, lively bottom that seemed to jump from the horn. "A new kind of orchestral tuba sound evolved," wrote the tubist Bob Tucci for the *ITEA Journal*. "Broad, possessing great power and volume on the one hand, yet having a beautiful singing core on the other." Some concertgoers would come early just to hear Jacobs go through pre-performance cadenzas. Jake's sound on the York began to inspire a devotion among young tuba players that would last the rest of his life.

Bob Rusk was a freshman tuba student of Bill Bell's at Indiana University in the 1960s when he heard a Chicago Symphony recording of Igor Stravinsky's *Song of the Nightingale*. Over and over Rusk listened, entranced especially by an F note Jacobs played at the top of a crescendo. Rusk learned that the symphony was soon to play the piece, and he wanted to hear whether Jacobs played that F note as powerfully in person as he had on record.

He borrowed two cars to get there, switching cars in South Bend, Indiana. That night Bob Rusk sat in the audience in Chicago, waiting for that one note, that F at the top of the crescendo. The symphony played and when it came time, Jacobs' F soared above the band, and Bob Rusk decided that it was, yes, as powerful and as moving in person as on the recording. Then he drove back to Bloomington, changing those cars again in South Bend. Rusk, later the tuba player for the Milwaukee Symphony, "drove almost 600 miles to hear one note," read his obituary decades later, "one excellent note."

The Chicago Symphony's first trumpet was Adolph "Bud" Herseth, the son of a school superintendent in rural Minnesota. Herseth was the greatest orchestral trumpet player of his era. "With Jake and his York at the bottom and Bud at the top," a symphony observer said, "everyone else just went for the ride."

Dale Clevenger joined the section in 1966 as its French horn player, fitting in between the two legends. He had listened to their symphony recordings every lunchtime in his high school band hall. Now seated in that same symphony, achieving the greatest brass sound ever recorded, Clevenger was awestruck. He recalled a German phrase sung in a symphony by the composer Gustav Mahler, which Clevenger translated as "That which is indescribable, here we are doing it."

Jacobs, meanwhile, would come to call the Yorks "the tubist's version of a Stradivarius," and he spoke often of how lucky he was to have encountered that first horn so young. But, said one veteran tuba player, "Arnold Jacobs made every horn sound like that. He'd put any mouthpiece on my horn and he'd sound like a York. Nobody sounds like that. Nobody still sounds like that."

Within this story, though, are the desperate lives that many orchestral musicians lived, represented by unions that had become corrupted. For the first half of Jacobs' career, players had only twenty-eight-week contracts and paltry health insurance. Management and conductors might replace them without warning. End-of-life poverty was a real possibility. To make off-season ends meet, one Chicago symphony player sold rugs; another sold garage door openers.

Jacobs taught. For more than two decades while he was employed at the symphony, his teaching revenue sustained him and his young family for half of each year. His manner with his students was gentle. He was naturally that way. He was sincere in urging them to imagine their potential, even if the chance of finding work was scant. This was intoxicating stuff for any music student, but especially for tuba players, who rarely heard such encouragement. "Often, he was the only person who told you, you had a chance. You did sound better. Whether you were better enough to get a job was another thing. But he gave you hope," said John Hagstrom, the Chicago Symphony trumpeter and brass historian. "Showing he was the best choice for students—managing his brand—that was right thing to do." For Jacobs, it was also a matter of survival.

In those years, especially, tuba players longed for heroes. Jacobs became one. His sound was bold and solo-like on the Chicago Symphony records, which benefited from advancing stereo technology in the 1950s. In lessons, master classes, and interviews, Jacobs spoke often of the York tubas he played—the only two of their kind, unique and irreplaceable, almost mystical. Students clutched to what he said, "believing in it," Hagstrom said, "as much as you believed in your own potential because of his teaching." The Yorks were every bit the tuba's counterparts to Stradivarius violins. This intoxicated young tubists who had never heard this kind of talk before. But why not? Why should the tuba world not have such precious instruments?

"Nobody would know those two tubas existed were it not for Arnold Jacobs," said Joseph Agnew, who wrote a history of the two horns for the *ITEA Journal*. "So this story is about the tubas, it's about the guy who's playing the tubas, and it's about the guy who's playing the tubas' *opinion* of those tubas."

But it's about even more than that. Jacobs would become one of the most important music teachers of the era largely because he transcended the technical aspects of the tuba to become almost a philosopher of breath and brain. By the 1970s, he was intrigued by neuroscience, then still in its infancy. Apparently long before the view was widely held or documented, he believed that the brain was plastic—that it could adapt to new circumstances, new demands—and that this quality was in fact healthy and necessary. "Strangeness is your friend, sameness your enemy" was a Jacobs aphorism.

His fame as a teacher spread. Flocking to him then were not just tubists, but singers and wind musicians of all kinds, who would travel sometimes days for a lesson at his home on Normal Avenue on Chicago's South Side, or, later, his fourth-floor studio in the Fine Arts Building on Michigan Avenue downtown.

That a tuba player followed this branching path was natural. The horn required great physical capacity, so what a player learned might be of use to others. More than that, its relegated place in American music tended to make tuba players—some that I met, anyway—intellectual omnivores. Their instrument had grown from the circus and brass bands, after all, not conservatories. This made them, I came to believe, comfortable exploring new influences and possibilities and resistant to narrowing tradition.

Were they that way because they played the tuba, or were they tuba players because they were that way? I don't know.

But Arnold Jacobs was all that, and thus he moved from metal to the mind.

Chapter 11

The Perfect Tuba

Carpenter

> *"I can literally feel the vibrations, and the frequencies of those vibrations I'm making."*

In 2007, Bob Carpenter, an electrical engineer and tuba player for the Orlando Philharmonic Orchestra, went on eBay.com to buy a horn.

The online site had emerged as a forum for a lively tuba trade. Tubas that had been taking up space in attics around America for decades, reminders to their owners that they, too, had once harbored dreams of a tuba career, were now coming out to be sold and to find new lives.

On his first foray, Carpenter spotted an old tuba for sale. It was in the key of B-flat, built in 1906 by—and this is what keyed his interest—the York Instrument Co. of Grand Rapids, Michigan. Carpenter knew the York name. While in college at Northwestern, he had studied with Arnold Jacobs and knew the sound and renown of the two great Chicago Yorks. So he took a chance.

He contacted the seller in Virginia. The guy said he had bought the horn more than twenty years before, disassembled in pieces in a case, at a small-town store in New Hampshire. It had lain there for decades by then. Tubas can be taken apart and put back together fairly easily, if you know what you're doing. This guy did. So he fitted it back together and it played well, and he said he'd used it occasionally in the years since purchasing it. He was just about to sell the instrument to a family without much money whose daughter had multiple sclerosis; tuba playing was her main form of exercise, he said. The tuba was probably too heavy for the girl, but at least she'd have something to play.

Carpenter struck a deal with the vendor. He'd buy the horn the guy was selling for $1,000, then give the girl one of his tubas, even smaller and lighter, more fitting for a child than the York. It was a Martin, made in America, and unpummeled by the years.

That's how Bob Carpenter came into possession of his first York tuba.

As a kid growing up in Orlando, Florida, Carpenter didn't know what a tuba was. Nor did he know band or orchestra music, which wasn't played much around his house. His mother was a social worker, his father an attorney. Upon entering seventh grade, he was somehow assigned Home Economics as an elective. A few days into the semester, Carpenter knew this wasn't for him, and he mentioned this to the school's band director, who, as a friend of the family, gave him a ride to school.

Seeing the chance to recruit a band student, the director asked, "Would you play the tuba?"

Sure, Carpenter said, eager to get out of Home Ec. What's a tuba?

The teacher led him to the band room and to a monstrous sousaphone of white fiberglass. It was on a stand connected to a chair, and Carpenter, a tiny kid, had to climb up underneath and into the thing. It dwarfed him in its embrace.

To his surprise, he made a sound that first day. Soon he was playing scales. Within two weeks on the tuba, he told me, "it was just this visceral 'I have to do this.' " Within two months, he was in advanced band. "I was instantly into the timing, the intonation."

Later that first year, Carpenter's band director led the youngsters through an adaptation for band of Austrian composer Franz Schubert's *Unfinished Symphony*. The sound was more of a chaotic wail than music. Nevertheless, seventh grader Bob Carpenter was transfixed. He was able to play only basic notes on the tuba. But he was a scientific kid, enthralled with rockets and electronics and with understanding how the world worked. Through these tuba sounds he felt connected to all that, which was something he had not expected. "Science is a description of the world and how it works," he told me one day, in one of the many chats we would have over the years. "You use math as a language to describe the physical things going on around you—liquids, solids, air. I was fascinated that in space there is no sound because there is no air. Now, here on the ground, playing an instrument, the vibrations are floating through the air and they're interacting with other things . . . I'm playing a note and can feel the other instruments coming back in through the bell. I can feel it in me, and I can hear where things are in tune or out of tune with what I'm doing. I can literally feel the vibrations, and the frequencies of those vibrations I'm making. These concepts can exist when you're young. I'm thinking about all of that stuff."

Despite the mess they made of the *Unfinished Symphony*, Bob Carpenter felt the sound he produced, and from that he felt an inkling of the possibilities of life. He couldn't believe it was of his doing, on an instrument he couldn't even identify months before. The band fell apart around him. Still, he could make out the melody, the chord structure. Through the din he perceived how he was part of something grand, and how he actually seemed to steer it all forward, and at that moment he thought to himself, like a rider on a bucking bull, "Whoa, man! This is great!"

ON THE COVER of the 1973 Pink Floyd album *Dark Side of the Moon*, a beam of light is fed through a prism, separating into a rainbow of colors. Scientists know that this is proof that the light we can see is made up of many kinds of light that we cannot. Fans of the album have interpreted the beam on the cover to refer to a life, and the rainbow of colors as the many paths one may follow.

Years after the *Unfinished Symphony*, Bob Carpenter came to realize that a musical note was formed in a similar way and offered similar paths to follow. This was the mid-1980s. He was studying engineering and the tuba at Northwestern University. He took engineering classes in radio frequencies, and tuba lessons with Arnold Jacobs.

Under Jacobs, Carpenter became fascinated with overtones. Overtones are the notes hidden within a note. It turns out that one note can be, in a sense, mined for each note of its major scale that lies within it: the second note, the third, fourth, fifth, and sixth, and finally a seventh note, but that is flatted and thus not part of the major scale. All those tones lie within the fundamental note. On a wind instrument—from a tuba up to a flute—these tones can be isolated by varying the lips and air flow, while retaining the fingering for the original note. Each is called an overtone, and musicians call these tones together the "overtone series."

What the overtone series means, among other things, is that, like light or life, a musical note is made up of a lot of possibilities that we may only gradually come to perceive. That inkling he had on the tuba as a kid during Schubert's *Unfinished Symphony* wasn't far off, Carpenter realized.

His lessons with Jacobs in his sophomore year at Northwestern were focusing on how to create a sound full of overtones. Arnold Jacobs was obsessed with them. Overtones were in fact the foundation of the American tuba sound he pioneered with those mythical Yorks. A sound with a full range of overtones was not only big and rich, it also blended with the other instruments while standing out, too, but in a good way. With Jacobs, the York horns produced rich overtones that aligned the orchestra, and Carpenter came to see this as the key to their majesty.

At Jacobs' urging, producing overtones became Carpenter's obsession. He went into a building known to students as the Beehive near the university's music school. It was winter and the building had little heat, so Carpenter was often alone in the cold with his tuba and its tones. Endlessly, for most of a year, he blew long notes, sustaining them until he'd emptied his lungs, then starting again, searching for that sound Jacobs urged him to find as his horn echoed through the building's empty corridors. Then only gradually did he concoct the combination of lip position and air required to create it. That sound had what tuba players call "grit"—which is not necessarily pretty to hear up close, but from a distance, in a hall, say, it fills the room.

At the time, Carpenter was taking an engineering class in radio frequencies. The radio textbook laid out a graphic, a map, of frequencies and the harmonics—the overtones—embedded within them.

In that practice room at Northwestern, struggling to produce overtones, Carpenter found a unity to all he was then studying; sound and light and radio frequencies were all systems made up of other elements that had to be culled to understand the whole and its potential.

Sound depended on vibrations. To physicists, vibrations are the basic waves of the universe. They are energy that disturbs, fueling both creation and destruction. In engineering, vibrations can be damaging. They lead to the decoupling of things that technicians have devised to snugly fit together—a NASA space shuttle, for example.

In contrast, vibrations of air are what creates music. Nothing is more dramatic proof of this than the tuba. Its sound begins with a damp and unpleasant buzzing as lips vibrate air through a metal mouthpiece. Those vibrations are transformed milliseconds later through the widening tube and out the great metal bell as a note that can fill a concert hall and shake your bones. Stacked atop each note are overtones in hiding. Some horns produce them powerfully, enhancing the sound of others.

That beat-up York horn he bought on eBay, when Carpenter got it home, was one of these. It was only 33 inches tall. Yet when he played it during orchestra rehearsal, it stood out far beyond his main horn, a mighty Holton tuba, which sat like a bear on his lap. Or, better put, the York blended seamlessly with the other instruments, as if they all had melted together. This synergy magnified their collective sound.

Carpenter puzzled over what could be within each note of the old horn that made it sound this way. Why was its sound so much more unifying than what his bigger tuba produced?

That bruised York contained a lot of Bob Carpenter's professional life up to then—his music, his engineering, and especially his questions about the physics of sound and light, and all that went into creating them.

As an engineer, meanwhile, Carpenter grew interested in systems. Managing groups of people toward a larger goal promised greater rewards than focusing, as a lone scientist, on an isolated question. A good system was greater than the sum of its parts.

He began to think of the tuba in this way as well. It produced a sound only when its parts worked together—a system that included metallurgy, screws, braces, valves, tubes that were curved and tapered, and the gaping mouth of the bell spun just right. At rehearsals, Carpenter felt the York's power. He was startled to hear how the old horn helped the orchestra to fit together until it, too, became more than the sum of its parts.

The York was not one of the mystical tubas that Arnold Jacobs had played in the Chicago Symphony. But its sound had their essence.

York, it seemed to Carpenter, had figured out so much more than any other company of the time about how to make great tubas. As he pondered all this, it occurred to him that perhaps those grand custom-made Chicago horns weren't unique after all. Perhaps they were produced by an impeccably designed factory system that the York company had devised for making tubas—a marvel about which little was known but that had functioned for years.

To Carpenter, that meant that the secrets to a perfect tuba might then be harvested from almost any York from that time.

Chapter 12

The Perfect Tuba

Treece

"just always interested in how things worked"

When Tom Treece was sixteen, he played tuba in a church band in his hometown of Toledo, Ohio. One day at rehearsal he felt a hand on his horn from someone sitting behind him.

He looked back and a boy turned away. A bit later, Treece again felt the hand touching the bell of his horn. The same boy. "Do you want to play the horn?" Treece asked. The boy nodded.

His name was Tom Whitacre, and he was deaf, but he could hear the lowest tones of the instrument; above all, he could feel their vibrations. "Don't mind him; he's deaf and dumb," Whitacre's father, the church band director, told Treece.

Treece hadn't many friends in school; he made candy, he was beginning a lifelong fascination with the world of molecules, and he played the tuba. So he knew an outsider when he saw one. Treece gave Whitacre his tuba. Right away the boy played a note. Over the next three years, Treece undertook to teach the tuba to his new friend.

That idea did not seem strange to Tom Treece. If many young tuba players felt wedged into limiting boxes, Tom Treece was discovering the horn to be a world of unexpected possibilities. It possessed strange tones that no book then described. He learned to play them. He brought home a half dozen school sousaphones, took them apart, cleaned them, understood them. His tuba teacher was also an opera singer and had Treece playing with vibrato—that wavering sound common to romantic singing and rarely used then on the tuba. "I played the tuba as though I played a solo instrument. I was taught it was okay to do that," he told me, "that I should do that. I got the Bill Bell treatment early."

So he and Whitacre sat at the breakfast table in the Treece home after school and played. Whitacre would feel Treece's throat as Treece played overtones on the horn. He watched Treece's embouchure and copied that. A music director told Treece he was cruelly raising the deaf boy's hopes. But Whitacre "could hear enough of the tuba that he could distinguish things," Treece told me. Hearing aids, new on the market, helped.

By his senior year, Tom Whitacre was marching at football game halftimes and playing "The Star-Spangled Banner" before each game. "I saw him march down the street in a parade," Treece told me. "All this stuff he didn't think he could ever do." His father, a stock car driver as well as church conductor, came around. He bought his son a sousaphone. In church, the two Toms doubled on tubas on hymns like "Abide with Me."

Tom Whitacre graduated, found a career in mechanical drafting, married, and had a family, and he and Treece have stayed in touch ever since.

"It all started with the tuba and its vibrations," Treece told me.

I met Tom Treece through Bob Carpenter. I had first called Carpenter years before. I was interviewing tuba players to see what I might learn. Carpenter was nice enough to take my call. He happened to be doing tests of radio software on the runway of a Marine Corps air station—which right there I thought was a strange place to find a professional tuba player. But Carpenter told me he was also an engineer, so that intrigued me as well.

During our conversation, he mentioned that he and Treece had undertaken to replicate two historically great tubas, and had I heard of them?

I had not.

Carpenter was the first to tell me the story: There were these two magical tubas out there, only two of them, and they could create sounds so wondrous that, like the Sirens to Odysseus, they inebriated generations of American tubists, many of whom spent their lives trying to capture them. Major instrument companies had done the same. But he and Treece had done tests, autopsying tubas, measuring their frequencies, and thought they had the data, the metallurgy now to succeed where others had failed.

Many companies had attempted to replicate the York sound. Yet it seemed that few had tried to understand the makeup of the brass the York company used. These companies were looking at the structure of the tubas, the physical beauty of the horns, and tried to replicate that. That was understandable. But Carpenter and Treece thought they also needed to look into the horns' bloodstream, their soul: the brass and what went into it.

Treece told me, "The sound of the two Yorks is the same, though the horns are physically different." How is that possible? The metal itself, Treece believed.

No one could chip away at the Chicago Yorks' metal and analyze it; that would cripple the horns. But Treece and Carpenter came to believe that York tubas from the same era could give them clues as to what made the Chicago horns great. The sound of Carpenter's old York that he bought on eBay hinted that that might be the case.

I would probably have dropped the whole tuba thing years ago had I not heard this beautifully strange story of these perfect tubas and these two guys in Orlando trying to recreate their sound.

"You should talk with Tom," Carpenter told me.

I got to know Tom Treece in phone calls and visits to his modest 1970s ranch-style home near Orlando, Florida. At seventy-nine, he was a soft-spoken, outwardly square fellow. His living room featured a couple of La-Z-Boys, a grandfather clock, an aquarium, and Tiffany-style lampshades. Yet beneath these placid personal waters roiled a rambunctious curiosity that had goaded him since childhood.

Treece was never interested in college. He was self-educated. He tried his best, on general principle, to avoid full-time, salaried employment in corporate America. By the time I met him, he had been a music teacher, candy maker, rosin inventor, lacquer inventor, doughnut maker, caterer, supermarket baking consultant, food factory consultant, paid and unpaid musician, and, with his knowledge of metallurgy, a collector of tubas.

He leaped from one fascination to another because he was, he told me, "just always interested in how things worked." Part of that was understanding the tuba, and how "this little buzz you make in the mouthpiece, when it comes out the bell, is something that'll just about rock the room." That, I agreed, was a magical idea.

His curiosity was almost preordained. His mother played jazz vibes and in the 1950s was one of Ohio's best marimba players. His house was packed with instruments. Chimes, a xylophone, a set of orchestra bells. As a child, he would sit under the family piano and listen as his mom played. "I never knew when I'd hear 'Lady of Spain' on the marimba at four in the morning," he told me.

His mother's people worked as music teachers, organists, interior decorators; one was a blacksmith. His grandfather was a preacher, developed a solution that added grain to wood, and for a while owned a plaster of paris company, making figurines he sold at carnivals and county fairs. Treece spent childhood summers going from city to city, living among carnies. His grandfather urged him to become an expert in things he was good at and liked to do.

At age twelve, researching candy making, Treece bought the 1954 confectioners' bible, *Choice Confection: Manufacturing Methods and Formulas*, by Walter Richmond. Tom Treece never was much for novels, but he stayed up nights with *Choice Confection* until he figured that his own recipes—for saltwater taffy or Mackinac Island fudge—might work better. He tried them in his basement until he got them right.

At about that age, he began to study molecules and how with heat they might be combined and changed, and how this in turn might lead to remarkable things. Soon candy's molecular makeup intrigued him. He could go on at some length about chocolate, for example, and its melting points, how manipulating them allowed for its shine, the snap when chocolate breaks.

He subscribed to *Candy Industry* magazine as a boy. He called people who knew more than he did and drained them of knowledge. As a teenager, he opened a store to sell boxed chocolates, eventually employing nine people. Later, he worked for many years as a baking consultant, opening Albertson's supermarket bakeries across the South.

Treece found a combination of wax and petrolatum that could form a rosin for upright bass bows, which helps create the sound vibrations as the bow is drawn across the strings. He concocted a lacquer for decorative glass.

This work consumed him, and from it he made his living. But the tuba devoured his spare time. He was sixteen when he asked his parents to drive him from Toledo to Detroit, where Fred Marrich's Custom Music and his Tuba World brand were becoming a tuba mecca. Treece voraciously played the horns, felt their vibrations, compared their sounds, and bought his first professional tuba.

He heard the story of the Chicago Yorks while living in that town in the 1970s. They reminded Treece of a tuba he had once borrowed as a teenager that played like no other. It was the summer of 1960. "You played about four notes on it," he said, "and it comes over you. So easy to play, such a sweet sound, and it has this deep richness to it." He later discovered the horn was in fact a 1930s-era York, made for another company that stenciled its name on the bell.

His interest in the York company grew from that. As it did, a York tuba underground revealed itself. Across America, tubists frothed for York horns made before World War II, when "Pops" Johnson ran the company and it was strong. These old Yorks were traded, sold, envied, and sought—fed by the mystique surrounding the two Chicago horns. But, like Carpenter, Treece noticed that even run-of-the-mill York tubas from that era were some of the best around.

The country during those years had the skill, patience, and cost advantage to make great tubas. But York must also have taught horn-making fundamentals to the lowest apprentice, insisting each job be done the right way, Bill Johnson's way, every day. Tom Treece, factory consultant, had thought about this and concluded this had to be true of York. Otherwise, he said, "we wouldn't have the quality of York horns that we have today" from that era.

So, to Treece, the York story was also about what the country had lost. There was something essential to innovation, and to community, about skilled workers and management side by side, not separated by oceans. Elbow to elbow, they found the smallest improvements, solved the smallest problems. Innovation happened in the least perceptible daily ways but accumulated over time.

People who make a living in that kind of environment are good to have in your town. Their kind of realistic optimism doesn't just improve companies. That's how the healthiest social change is made as well: through patient daily effort, working with others toward the tiniest improvements that in time will make larger solutions easier to find. This was in fact a theme of my last book, *The Least of Us*. I just didn't expect to encounter it in a book about the tuba as well.

Some prewar York tubas were mediocre. But the many that survived decades did so because their sound was so sublime. Players loved them, hoarded them, refurbished them. They nabbed them wherever they found them. Pawn shops, yard sales, classified ads. It seemed to Tom Treece that every tubist in the country must have a 1930s-era York hidden in a closet somewhere.

Treece kept working as a consultant to baking factories around the country. Meanwhile, he began to acquire a mighty tuba collection. In 2016, he retired from consulting with time and money to nurture his tuba thing.

I visited him a few years later. From the street, his house stood out in no way whatsoever. Inside, it was a tuba temple. Some 175 horns had passed through his home—bought, sold, traded. "I was out of my mind for a while," he said. Treece studied each one, took them apart, trying to understand why any two of them might look similar yet, to him, sound so different. He had forty-two tubas in the house by the time I visited. Many were stacked in his garage; his family room became the tuba room. A few were up on the walls. He loved their feel, the glow of the

Tom Treece at home. "It all started with the tuba and its vibrations."

brass, their elegant curves and ornate intestines, even the musty smell of their cases.

He was their temporary caretaker, he told me. He kept a folder on the history of each one, as best he could learn it. Serial numbers told him when the horns had left their factories. He researched where each had been since. Had the horn played Radio City Music Hall? In a circus? A symphony orchestra?

In 2007, Tom Treece was semi-retired from consulting and hitting full tuba mode when he met Bob Carpenter. They could speak to each other as engineers and as tuba players. Naturally, they got down to the sound of those Chicago Yorks and how they might be recreated.

That was the big question. It would consume them for years.

But their story really started over something much smaller.

It really started because Bob Carpenter had just bought that York on eBay. With that, he began to realize that his other horn, his big old Holton, which was one of the first Chicago York replicas, which he had been playing for more than twenty years, which he had purchased from his teacher, the great Arnold Jacobs, wasn't sounding all that good anymore.

He just wanted to know why.

Chapter 13

Rio Grande Valley

Roma

"I'm not sure if you're prepared for this."

The state of Texas classifies 251 high schools as 5A, the second largest level of high schools in the state. These schools have enrollments between 1,300 and 2,224 students, and each presumably has a marching band.

In 2023, only twelve of those bands made the 5A finals in the state championship held that November in San Antonio's Alamodome football arena.

A week after those marching band finals concluded, a map of the state of Texas circulated on Facebook. The map showed a red star for each one of those twelve schools.

Six stars were clustered on the wealthy outskirts of the Dallas–Fort Worth metro area. Another four were nestled in the suburbs north of Austin, home to many of the area's high-tech firms and employees. One was on Houston's southern edge.

Then way down at the bottom of the state, a distant outpost off on its own along the Mexican border, so far away from the other stars that you could easily miss it on the map, was a star for the high school of the little town of Roma, Texas.

Roma has a population of eleven thousand and is in Starr County. Starr is among the poorest U.S. counties, known in part for a robust traffic in drugs and people.

The town lies at the northern end of what's known as the Rio Grande Valley, at the southwesternmost edge of Texas. The Valley stretches upriver from the Gulf of Mexico for 135 miles. Along the way, a string of towns hugs U.S. Highway 83, which roughly mimics the Rio Grande's meandering path. Most of these towns are small and well above 90 percent Hispanic.

Roma is the most isolated. It is ninety miles from the nearest northbound interstate, an hour from the closest Best Buy, and four hours from an Apple store. Many of Roma's schoolkids live cross-border lives, with deep family connections to Mexico.

People here are poor or working class. They live in neighborhoods of modest stucco or concrete block homes, driving dusty used trucks on streets without sidewalks. Though the town has grown in the last two decades, most of these neighborhoods still aren't far from the native mesquite, the scrub, and nopal cactus that dominate the Valley's rugged natural topography. People here work in oilfields, on ranches, as nurses or teachers or truck drivers, they run small businesses. In some cases, they're in drug trafficking. By and large, though, Roma is made up of people used to the necessity of unnoticed hard work.

A lot of that goes into the story of how a marching band from this speck of a town grew into a statewide contender among 5A

Texas high schools. It has to do with band directors who, against all odds, did the small but important work: They taught skills, combined them with discipline and with love, and from that prepared fertile terrain for kids' achievement and confidence.

To a significant degree, the story has to do with the tuba.

And this being Texas, it begins with a high school football game.

DURING THE FALL of 1993, Roma's team traveled eleven miles downriver to play its rival Rio Grande City High School. Both towns are small and almost entirely Mexican American and Mexican. Yet they are quite different.

Roma sits on cliffs overlooking the Rio Grande. Across the river is the small town of Miguel Alemán, Mexico, so close that a pedestrian bridge connects the two towns.

Roma's residents are viewed as Mexican in custom and outlook, more rustic and country. Many kids with relatives on both sides cross from Mexico every day to attend Roma High.

The town of Rio Grande City, meanwhile, has always viewed itself as sophisticated, more middle-class American, more Texan. The bridge to Mexico is several hundred yards from Rio Grande City's highway. No one walks it. Family connections to Mexico are thinner.

Between the two towns are "eleven miles of day-and-night difference. One world there, another world here," said a teacher who taught in both towns. A resident put it like this: "At the Whataburger in Rio Grande City, they answer you in English. At the Roma Whataburger, it's in Spanish."

Those differences and the schools' natural rivalry make their residents—particularly Roma's—tender to perceived slights.

In the bleachers at the game that night was Eloy Vera, an engineer born and raised in Roma and just elected to its school board. Vera had played trumpet in the school band when he attended Roma High in the 1960s. His daughter now marched with the Rio Grande City band.

Vera had divided loyalties, but he paid special attention to the halftime show, and was dismayed at what he saw. The Rio Grande City band marched up and down their home field, sharply executing maneuvers to a tune that years later Vera no longer remembered. He did recall how good they looked. Roma's band just sat in the bleachers and played "Amor Eterno," written by Juan Gabriel, Mexico's great romantic balladeer. They didn't sound bad. But Roma's Mighty Gladiators looked mighty weak, Vera told me when I spoke with him. "The least they could do was march, and they couldn't march."

Rio Grande City won that game, but Vera left feeling stung more by the sight of his alma mater's band just sitting there as its rival strutted the field. The town had had enough reason to feel dilapidated and overlooked, particularly compared with Rio Grande City.

Eloy Vera spoke to his district's new superintendent, Walter Watson. We need teachers who can take the band to a higher level, Vera told him. Watson was all for it. He had just moved from the Rio Grande City district. He knew its band director, Al Cortinas.

Cortinas had been with the Rio Grande City school district since leaving Crystal City that summer of 1973. He had done good things with its high school band in those two decades. They'd been to state championships a time or two, though never to the finals. Several of his players were All-Staters on their instruments. One or two of his students had even been to college on music scholarships.

"We need to get Al Cortinas to come to Roma," Vera told Watson. "I don't care how you do it."

THE BEST WAY to describe Al Cortinas twenty years into his career was as a softhearted disciplinarian. The tough lives his kids came from meant they had to meet standards and expectations. Asking anything less would cripple them as they went out into the world, and they already faced enough disadvantage. Yet he was from their world. He felt their circumstances. Above all, he knew the immense power of marching band to change the lives of poor kids, for he had been the beneficiary of it himself.

By now, band was what Al Cortinas thought about most. He had ideas of how, in the impoverished Rio Grande Valley, you might raise the level of musicianship of a school band. This seemed to him an urgent task because during his years at Rio Grande City High School, two things had begun to happen.

First, Mexico's drug cartels had begun to coalesce and expand operations. A major pass-through point was the Rio Grande Valley, and Starr County, in particular.

"A thirteen-year-old with a radio in his pocket, looking out on a riverbank—they could make a couple hundred bucks just on one load coming through," said a long-time federal narcotics agent. "All of a sudden they become their own little gangsters and set up their own little smuggling operations."

As band director, Cortinas was selling hard work, practice, postponed gratification. He saw Rio Grande City kids seduced by the easy money and envied for their new pickups with fancy rims.

Meanwhile, Texas marching band was changing. For many years, bands from middle-class districts and those from poor districts competed on roughly equal footing, during a time when the economic differences between them were not as pronounced. For years, Texas band performances were graded—from 1 to 5, 1 being best. This was music and marching and highly subjective. No one felt the need to have bands compete like sports teams. That changed in the 1980s at state-level competitions. Bands vying for state were now to compete head-to-head. Judges declared a winner and ranked the rest—second, third, fourth, and so on.

This ignited a high school band arms race. With the Reagan era, predominantly White and suburban school districts grew wealthier. Their parents paid band fees of hundreds of dollars a year. Their band budgets and booster clubs expanded. Above all, kids in these districts had private music lessons. In time, it wasn't even enough to get your kid private lessons. The lessons had to be with certain teachers known to place children in a school's top band.

The first powerhouses in the Texas high school band world were from the suburbs of Houston, then from the Dallas–Fort Worth region and, lately, from Austin's tech suburbs.

For families in the Rio Grande Valley, even renting a musical instrument could be an insurmountable expense. By the 1990s,

Texas band competitions reflected the economic separation going on across the state, and the country.

These trends alarmed Al Cortinas. He saw band as an antidote to drugs and drug trafficking. Band kids learned community values that prepared them for life: discipline, punctuality, collaboration, postponing gratification, not to mention the love of music in its many forms. Yet he could see a time when Valley bands, if they didn't change, would be shut out of competitions, crippling their ability to attract and keep kids.

AT RIO GRANDE City High, Cortinas had hired a long-time friend, Roel Elizondo, who came down from the tiny town of Zapata (pop. 4,500), where he was the lone band instructor. They brought in a former Cortinas student named Rudy Barrera, who had returned home after earning a music education degree at Baylor University. Other directors came and went.

The three men formed almost a think tank on new ways of doing band. They were inquisitive types and single, searching for new ideas that might make them better teachers. They went to competitions in San Antonio or Corpus Christi. They brought in teachers from across Texas to hold clinics. Cortinas pestered his administration for a big-screen television on which he showed his kids videos of opera and classical music, which they had no chance of attending in person.

Band directors from across the Valley met each month. Cortinas and his team drove to these meetings and sat quietly next to veteran directors, drinking in their discussions. "We'd be like little pups running around behind them, asking them questions," he said.

Cortinas and his team were especially interested in understanding why the bands in Brownsville, Texas, had a fuller, more powerful sound than any in the Rio Grande Valley.

Brownsville band directors spoke constantly of the VanderCook school in Chicago, and of this man named H. E. Nutt. Nutt's ideas were on display in their band halls and in the gorgeous sound they produced. When H.E. and Thelma Nutt came to town, feted by band directors across the Rio Grande Valley, Cortinas met them. He spent so much time around the VanderCook crowd that he ended up speaking their jargon and being mistaken at times for a graduate of the school.

Gradually, his ideas wove with theirs into something Cortinas thought could work if a school district would commit to it. He could use band directors as teachers of specific instruments during the day, then as marching instructors on the field after school.

For years, the districts hired one or two band directors per school. In districts where kids had private music lessons, that might be sufficient. In the Valley, though, they were spread too thin. Rudy Barrera, for example, taught not only trumpet and cornet, but French horn, all woodwinds, and rifle twirling. Students barely got basic instruction on their instruments. So much young potential went undeveloped.

Cortinas concluded that enough band directors could fill the role that private teachers played in wealthier districts. Cortinas imagined a system in which one instructor could teach tuba, another saxophone, a third trombone, a fourth percussion, and so on. These teachers could more easily focus on teaching their individual instrument and bond with kids through the years. Kids who started on trumpet in sixth grade would, by, say, sophomore or junior year, under the same teacher, reach a higher level.

A sense of excitement would grow as kids saw themselves improve and compete to best their friends. A band with those elements might keep kids, Cortinas thought, even when drug trafficking money beckoned. They might also compete with bands from wealthier schools.

Trick was, of course, finding districts that would pay for it.

Then in the fall of 1993, up the road in tiny Roma, Texas, Superintendent Watson picked up the phone and called Al Cortinas.

CORTINAS' FATHER HAD just died. He was proud of what his team had accomplished at Rio Grande City, but he was looking for a change. So when Walter Watson called, Al Cortinas was interested. He explained his ideas to Watson.

"I'm not sure if you're prepared for this," he told the superintendent.

Write up a proposal, Watson told him. We'll see.

So, one night, he did. He poured into the proposal years of learning, listening, of trying ideas that had filtered down from H. E. Nutt and all those VanderCook grads and their Brownsville band scene. The focus would be on the youngest kids first. Roma had four band instructors—one for the high school and one for each junior high. Cortinas proposed that the district hire six more, each an instrument specialist. He would scour south

Texas for an instructor who could teach marching and clarinet. Marching and French horn. Marching and flute.

No district in the region, probably none in Texas, had so many band directors for so few schools. But Cortinas figured it was better to be clear about what he thought was needed.

The next afternoon, Watson called back. "We just held an emergency board meeting. You're hired."

Before signing on, Cortinas and Barrera visited Roma High's band. There wasn't much to do in Roma, and band was kids' social scene. So almost three hundred were in the band. Girls were busy doing their makeup; boys were horsing around or lounging on chairs. Some seemed comfortable with their instruments, but their sounds were uneven, and they couldn't read music. "They seemed to have a lot of pride and wanted to do well," Cortinas remembered. But when he asked one or two of them to play a C, they stared back.

Their instruments were old, bought by the trailer load from an outfit in north Texas. Also, the band had fifty cornets, fifty sax players, and only three tubas—a sign that the teacher hadn't pushed kids to explore other instruments. When he asked the director to have the band play something, the kids wobbled through a pop tune.

Al Cortinas was alarmed.

Yet within the band's sorry state lay the new job's appeal. It couldn't get much worse and was his to reshape. The job offered him a chance to deploy ideas he'd been mulling over for years and show how band could change poor kids' lives the way it had changed his.

So he took it.

That decision would turn the high school marching band from Roma, Texas, into a state competitor. More than that, the Cortinas system honed the talents of hundreds of young musicians, many of whom were children of migrant workers. More of these kids began to go to college and return as lawyers, as dentists. Others were recruited by universities to study music on scholarship and came back as band directors, as those jobs proliferated across the Valley and offered a ticket to the middle class.

It would further transform the life of Al Cortinas, who, among other things, became the Roma district's tuba instructor when they could find no one else.

Chapter 14

Rio Grande Valley

Cortinas Takes Over

"It'll work if we give it time."

As the fall 1994 high school semester began in Roma, Texas, the three hundred kids enrolled in band crowded into the hall.

Before them, sitting in a row, sat the school's new band directors, the men dressed in shirts and ties and the two women in prim, modest dresses.

Al Cortinas stood and introduced himself as the district's new band director. They would be implementing a new system, he told them, that would start in sixth grade and run through high school.

Students would be getting better instruments. Each instrument would have one instructor. That instructor would teach all the kids in the district who played that instrument. From now on, students would be responsible for learning their parts, for daily practice, and would be graded accordingly. There would be a focus on music fundamentals—scales, exercises, tone improvement—and one nighttime rehearsal per week. Band room would be open all day, beginning at six in the morning.

The next day, a third of the band students dropped the class.

Before that first meeting, one trumpeter then in seventh grade told me, "We were told it was going to be all fun. Then these band people came instilling this new discipline. Structure. A culture of practice. My friends were all leaving. I said, 'I'm staying. I think I like this.' Something with structure got my attention."

Cortinas gave the job of writing the new Roma band curriculum to his assistant and former student, Rudy Barrera. From now on, the lifeline to a stronger Mighty Gladiators band was sixth graders. Get kids early, train them properly, and they would be skilled players as juniors and seniors. Barrera delegated to teachers the responsibility of making sure their kids achieved the year-end goals. Sixth graders would be learning exercises that were then beyond Roma's older students.

One gruff older teacher of many years took a look at the new plan as the school year began. "Hey, boy," he said to Cortinas, "who the hell do you expect to be playing this stuff?" Sixth graders, Cortinas told him. By the end of the year, he maintained, they'd be playing like eighth graders elsewhere.

"Pues, no estas más pendejo porque no estas más viejo," the teacher replied. (Roughly: The older you get, the dumber you get.) "Not even our seniors can do that now."

True, Cortinas said, but we're going to get it done.

Doing so might achieve another goal Al Cortinas had in mind. Those first weeks, he noticed, none of the kids looked teachers in the eye. They looked at the ground while talking. "They need to look up, not down," Cortinas told his team. Real musical achievement, he thought, might change that. "My goal was to get all of these Hispanic kids to be confident about what they were doing."

Mr. B, as Rudy Barrera became known, wrote out goals for each instrument that each student must achieve by the end of sixth grade. The curriculum distilled decades of studying how to teach band in a poor region.

First week, they taught the sixth graders how to sit erect on the rounded edge of their chairs—Feet Flat on the Floor, Rump on the Bump, they called the posture. Opening instrument cases was used to train kids in rhythm and following instructions. Barrera taught kids to listen to the metronome, then open the case latch on the fourth beat. They worked on blowing air through pursed lips. They didn't touch their instruments for three weeks. Then they worked on single notes, on blowing long tones, to build kids' control of their instrument. The trick was to slow it all down, teach them to practice a musical phrase or exercise only at the speed at which they could play it perfectly.

A key to all this was the band's foundation—the tuba. Tuba players had been limited to whole notes and half notes—a kind of musical foot binding that crippled not just the young tuba players, Barrera figured, but the whole band. To play the kind of music he imagined, the tubas had to advance beyond the instrument's traditionally low expectations. He envisioned tubas cleanly playing eighth notes by seventh grade, and fluidly running through high notes by ninth grade.

To get there, they first had to develop the column of air coming from their diaphragm. It would take time and physical maturation. In middle school, they were out of air by the second beat. "They'll start yawning and falling asleep, because it's using up all their air," Barrera said. "You have to be patient with the tuba."

One of three beginning tuba players that year was a skinny, outgoing kid named Lizardo Hinojosa.

Two years before, in fifth grade, Lizardo had had the tuba chosen for him. His parents had already purchased a trumpet for an older brother in band and couldn't afford another instrument. So Lizardo had to choose a school-owned instrument. His older brother nixed the trombone and the euphonium.

"He said, 'Just play the tuba,'" Lizardo told me. "So I signed up for tuba. I didn't know better."

Lizardo's sixth grade year was especially fruitless. His seventh grade year, Al Cortinas and his team took over. On the first day, a teacher showed the students lined paper, with bass and treble clefs. What's this, he asked. Lizardo had no idea. No one else knew, either, except one kid who had played piano in church.

"They were basically reteaching us everything you were supposed to have learned in sixth grade," Hinojosa said. "We were little kids. We didn't know. So we just went with what they were teaching us."

THOSE FIRST WEEKS of fall 1994, in fact, tried everyone's stamina. One teacher, hired to form a flute section, burst into tears her first day upon seeing how little the students knew and the enormity of the work before her. At one point that semester, even Rudy Barrera wanted out. Every kid played like a sixth grader. This is agony, he told Cortinas. Let me go back to Rio Grande City.

"It'll work if we give it time," Cortinas told him. "Stick with it." So he did.

As the teachers figured, shaping sixth graders' skills in their instruments was the easy part. The youngsters had no understanding of how hard all this was. Tell them what to do and they did it without question—like the fundamentals of sitting, blowing air, or just practicing slowly. With those came skills that the older kids hadn't developed.

At the middle school, kids were caught just before they learned bad musical habits. They struggled but moved forward. One eighth grader who stuck it out was Daniel Rentería. The exercises were boring, he told me, but "I saw that it was getting me better. So I'm going to keep on doing whatever they're telling me to do. The people who were fighting it, not buying into it, they weren't improving."

A senior named Carlos Maldonado had some skill on the trumpet. But that first year under the Cortinas system showed him how far he had to go. "I never had purposeful home practice on my instrument before. We were not pushed hard enough," he said. Now his teachers demanded scales, warm-ups, arpeggios, flexibility exercises to improve his fluidity on the horn. Maldonado began practicing at home and won the high school band's first trumpet chair.

Many upperclassmen, though, rebelled. Having spent their formative years without real instruction, they hadn't advanced. They couldn't march and play their instrument at the same time.

For the teachers, meanwhile, the new system was a heavy lift. They met at the high school at six forty-five each morning to drill the kids in marching. From there, they drove together to the middle school to teach their instruments, then to the elementary school for the sixth graders, then back to the high school for more instruction, then drilling the kids in more marching after school, and headed home after dark.

They ate lunch in their car, drank their coffee on the run, and spent more time with one another than they did with their own families. Like brothers and sisters, they didn't always get along, but they felt part of a team and thus came to enjoy the journey together. Many were single, most were youngish.

They dressed formally during the week. Jeans were acceptable only on Fridays. They used Miss and Mister when speaking to each other in front of the kids, who addressed them, in turn, with "Yes, miss" and "Yes, sir."

They relied on exercise books that Cortinas and Barrera had stockpiled. There were the Clarke II studies—exercises to develop lip endurance, written by the cornetist Herbert Clarke in 1912. New York Philharmonic trumpeter Max Schlossberg's flexibility studies, Eastman Music School trombonist Emory Remington's warm-up exercises. These exercises amounted to a massive infusion of accumulated musical wisdom new to the Roma High band.

The new Roma teachers created insular spaces for their designated instruments. Within them, they had freedom to create what they thought was necessary for the kids to progress and had just enough resources to unfurl their own excitement for teaching.

One of these was Daniel Carrera. After college, he found work as one of four Roma High band directors. Those first years, Carrera taught trumpet, trombone, and euphonium to several dozen kids at a time. Then in 1994, Al Cortinas took over. Carrera stayed on, now able to focus only on euphonium students. "I was like, 'Finally,' " he said. Kids could move ahead faster. He got to know them well enough to judge their moods and whether to push or ease off. He worked with them on tone production and technique, then put the books aside and let them have fun at the end of class playing any tune they wanted. "It just felt really good to be able to do that," he said.

Lizardo Hinojosa's tuba playing was rudimentary but getting better. In eighth grade, the district's tuba teacher left and, with no one else available, Al Cortinas took his place. Cortinas' relationship to the tuba was as to a foreign language learned later in life. He could play it, but his vocabulary was limited. He could teach it, just as a teacher of a foreign language who speaks that language haltingly could teach children. But he knew the instrument's importance to what he was creating at Roma.

He invited Richard Morgan, the tuba instructor from Texas A&M University, Kingsville, to visit occasionally to help guide youngsters like Hinojosa. During his eighth grade year, Lizardo Hinojosa won a tuba chair in the Valley's All-Region band.

He wasn't quite clear what All-Region band actually was. But "it helped the way our band directors would sell it to us, that All-Region was a real cool thing for us," he told me. "When you make an All-Region band, there's a two-day rehearsal, then a concert. Our teachers took us to that. No one in Roma had ever experienced this. I was the first tuba player to do it."

Sitting in the dark bus on the way home from the concert that night, Lizardo listened to Claudina Anderson, the clarinet teacher, recount her memories of studying band directing in college, learning all the instruments. She was pregnant one year and still lugged the tuba all over campus. Lizardo sat there mesmerized. And that was it. He never thought of doing anything but becoming a band director.

Roma's new band teachers, meanwhile, believed themselves at the beginning of something exciting, untried yet possible in this part of Texas amid the mesquite and the ranches. "We didn't realize how lucky we were," said Claudina Anderson. "We were able to just teach."

"Give it seven years," Cortinas told Walter Watson, when the superintendent asked him how long before the band would be competitive. Time enough for those first sixth graders to reach twelfth grade.

That fall the Roma High School Mighty Gladiators marched during a football halftime show for the first time. Carlos Maldonado was on the football team, too, and marched with the band in his pads and socks. Eloy Vera watched them all, amazed. "It was a tremendous feeling," he said.

In Texas, the high school band year divides into two seasons. Fall is for marching band, and most every kid who signs up for it is on the field. Spring is for concert band, in which kids at each school are divided into several bands according to their skill. For each season there is a series of competitions: local, to regional, to state. In concert season, they compete on musicianship and then on sight-reading. Kids also compete individually on their instruments.

Roma High School's band had never competed in any of this. The school had no football team for many years, so had no need for a marching band; Roma was known instead for its stellar basketball team. The band did parades and some concerts, and that was all.

Yet that first year, the Mighty Gladiators got a 3 in marching—which in Texas band parlance means "not bad, needs work." At least it wasn't a dismal 5.

At the end of that first school year, Carlos Maldonado got a partial scholarship to study trumpet at Texas State University, south of Austin. No Roma High band student had done that before. He went on to become a band instructor, and now runs the mariachi program at a school district in central Texas.

These were the highlights for the high schoolers that first year. The seventh and eighth grade bands were outplaying the high school band. "From there on, that group of kids just flourished," said Claudina Anderson.

And true to Cortinas' expectations, coming up fast behind the seventh graders, Roma's sixth graders arrived at year's end playing exercises that the seniors had trouble with, and were controlling their tones with the skill of eighth graders.

"I'll be damned. I never thought we were going to get this done," that crusty veteran teacher told Cortinas.

Chapter 15

Willie and Eugene

"Flight of the Bumblebee"

In 1986, two high school students from Harvey, Illinois, walked into the studios of Chicago's NPR affiliate, WBEZ, to play one of the most manic pieces in classical music, "Flight of the Bumblebee," on the tuba and euphonium.

They appeared on the station's weekly program showcasing new Chicagoland musical talent.

Willie Clark was a senior. What had begun with his exhilaration that day in sixth grade playing the *Star Trek* theme had evolved into full-blown dedication to the horn. He was playing it with a maturity beyond his years, and seeing his future there. His duet partner, Willie would say years later, was probably the best euphonium player he would ever encounter in what would become a lifetime of brass playing. The kid's name was Eugene Campbell. Eugene was then a junior.

On the euphonium, if Eugene thought it, Willie told me, "he could play it."

Though they were in high school, they returned often, late in the afternoons, to Brooks Junior High, their former school, where their old band director, John Weber, gave them a practice room, encouragement, a ride home at night, and maybe a trip to McDonald's along the way.

They set up in a room at the back of Weber's band hall. The youngsters coming up in Weber's band didn't dare interrupt them. Willie and Eugene were their heroes who, if the time was right, would give them tips on how to get better. Everyone saw how hard these two practiced. They almost made a life of playing challenging pieces. Nothing set that standard like "Flight of the Bumblebee."

"Flight of the Bumblebee" is a fusillade of sixteenth notes. It's meant for the violin. Playing it on the tuba, the piece becomes a punishing sprint to see whether the player can get through it before stroking out. Woody Allen, who began as a stand-up comedian in the 1960s, satirized the idea in his act: "My father used to play the tuba, tried to play the tuba. Tried to play 'Flight of the Bumblebee.' Blew his liver out through the horn."

However, as the search for the perfect tuba gradually improved the horn, and a tuba liberation raised players' expectations, "Flight of the Bumblebee" became both a novelty and a sign of maximum tuba studliness. Something akin to how much can you bench press—only on the tuba it's more like, how fast can you play "Flight of the Bumblebee"?

The Russian composer Nikolai Rimsky-Korsakov, who wrote the piece as part of an opera, had in mind roughly a minute twenty. Charles Daellenbach, a tubist and the business mastermind behind the ageless Canadian Brass quintet, at one point reportedly played it in thirty-eight seconds, beating the previous (unofficial) record of forty-two seconds. (For that and many other reasons, Daellenbach is viewed by tuba players as both a reason to keep trying and maybe, too, a reason to give up.) In the 1980s, playing "Flight" on the tuba, however, was still perhaps a bizarre notion, not to be tried at home, and best left only to virtuosos.

Yet neither Willie Clark nor Eugene Campbell knew this. In fact, since that eighth grade day when Willie saw the tuba player John Fletcher perform the piece, he thought "Flight of the Bumblebee" was something he would get to sooner or later.

One day John Weber dug out the sheet music to the piece. Learn this, he told the youths, and you'll go places. Willie and Eugene started in practicing it every afternoon in the room Weber provided for them at the back of his band hall in the school they no longer attended.

They were his prized students. They had moved on to high school, but to John Weber they remained his kids, the greatest talents to emerge up to then from a system he had cobbled together through trial and error, with spit and string, to teach music to kids who had no access to music lessons.

Chapter 16

Willie and Weber

"It was the small steps. That you can advance without being perfect."

John Weber had come to Harvey, Illinois, in 1972, a young tuba player just out of college, hired as band instructor for the school district's elementary and junior high students.

He was short, wore tinted glasses, and his brown hair would thin as he aged. He spoke sparely and softly. He was a native of north Chicago and had played the horn since high school. A lot had happened since *Bill Bell and His Tuba* had opened John Weber's mind.

His father was a vacuum cleaner salesman and his mother a secretary. They couldn't afford to send him to college. After high school, Weber found work as an office boy while figuring how he might make a life from the tuba. From the office phone one day, he called Arnold Jacobs to ask for lessons. "First thing he had me do was jog around his basement playing on the mouthpiece," Weber told me when I met him at the duplex where he lived in north Chicago that his parents had bought in 1948. "He punched me in the stomach, too. I was holding my stomach tight." Loosen up, Jacobs told him, and free your lungs. "From weakness there is strength." Weber never again clenched his diaphragm while playing the tuba.

In 1964, Weber's draft number made it likely he'd be called into the Army and shipped to Vietnam. He sent the Army's West Point band an audition tape and on that basis was accepted. He spent 1965 through 1968 in the band, playing the tuba eight hours a day, through the war's bloodiest years.

Leaving West Point, he enrolled in a local university on the GI Bill and graduated with a degree in music education, and that August, at the age of twenty-eight, John Weber arrived at School District 152 in Harvey, Illinois.

"Do you mind having a Black principal?" was among the first questions he was asked. He did not, but he was not expecting this question.

The question reflected much that was then on the town's mind. Harvey had formed in the late 1800s as a Protestant experiment in temperance, a refuge for those who believed that drinking was the root of much of the evil afoot in America. Then Catholics began moving in. Someone opened the first bar in Harvey. The town's temperance experiment ended.

Still, it remained a White town for most of the twentieth century. The 1964 Civil Rights Act opened the way for Blacks to move outside the enclaves to which they'd been confined. In Chicago, many middle- and working-class Black families moved from the Bronzeville district south of downtown to suburbs where they perceived life was better. One place was Harvey, south of Chicago, where, supported by large factories and one of the region's first malls, the schools had a reputation for excellence.

But Harvey went rebelliously into this new era. Race riots erupted at a high school in 1969. Harvey's population, more than 90 percent White in 1960, was 80 percent Black by 1990. Deindustrialization closed several Harvey factories; the mall closed, too. In their place, gangs and cocaine grew potent.

Oblivious to much of this, John Weber arrived to teach band to elementary and junior high students. As a White man teaching Black kids, he came to understand the fault lines of America in deeper ways during his years at the school.

He had never taught before, but he soon realized he loved watching kids find themselves as they honed their abilities. He spent from seven A.M. to nine P.M. in his band hall for thirty-three years and did not begrudge the hours. He never married. As years passed, it seemed natural to him that he simply grew wedded to his job. His students became his kids. He occasionally battled budget-cutting administrators or school district officials who didn't understand how being in band helped his kids academically.

His one personal splurge was to buy himself a big, gorgeous Yamaha B-flat tuba, which accompanied him to gigs for the rest of his life.

Few of his students could afford music lessons. He told them, nevertheless, that they were talents, though at that age they had no evidence that this was true. Instead, he allowed them to discover this for themselves, through a system he called Check Off.

The system divided into tiny segments the skills each kid would need on each instrument—say, a C major scale and a C major chord arpeggio, for a start, then the G major scale and a G major chord arpeggio.

For each skill mastered, the student got to place a check mark on a chart that Weber displayed in class so students could see their own progress, and that of others. This kept his students vying with each other to get better. To fall behind on checks was shameful.

Weber didn't give praise for no reason. But his kids were just starting on instruments that they could find dishearteningly difficult, so his system was set up to make it hard for them to fail. Each week, he'd sit with them, listen to each one play a scale or exercise. Weber was not interested in perfection at each step, but rather in energizing his students to keep moving forward. "A sense of accomplishment," said Willie Clark. "I think that's what he was trying to draw out of you. So you double down on what you're doing. You want to play better, do more." If there was something not quite right, it was not a reason to refuse a check. But to those who clearly needed work, he explained how they could earn that check.

A check, meanwhile, became a badge of honor, and the quest for checks kept his kids moving in small and steady steps. "When we would get to next level, we'd tell everyone. 'I got to E!'" said Frank Parker, who is now a jazz drummer in Warsaw, Poland. "We were all into the Check Off." By the end of the year they (and their parents) could look with pride at the long row of checks by their names.

"I didn't realize it when I was in it, but now I realize he was teaching us how to practice," said Christopher N. Davis, now a professional trumpet player and teacher in Chicago. "It was the small steps. [The idea] that you can advance without being perfect."

Through Check Off, perhaps thousands of Weber kids without private music lessons learned the fundamentals of their instrument. By the end of eighth grade, they had the skills to excel in high school band, and did. Weber, meanwhile, learned most instruments—sax, flute, clarinet—well enough to get each student going. He brought in a drum teacher for a while until he learned percussion basics.

"He showed me paradiddles and flams. I had no idea this was the foundation of drums," said Frank Parker. But "he wasn't afraid to let the kids know who the adult was in the room. You have to earn this. It was showing us we had to work for what we got."

Weber kids often tested his boundaries. When that happened, Weber's face would turn red. He'd slam a music stand. His strongest language was "jerk"—as in "Don't be a jerk"—and "baloney."

"That's a bunch of baloney!" he would yell. Then his kids would realize they had gone too far. Occasionally, when he wasn't around, some of the brasher kids would imitate Mr. Weber, with "That's a bunch of baloney!"

His system amounted to a campaign to push students to their potential while understanding that at that age kids needed a social world as much as they needed discipline. Every year, they went to the Indiana Beach amusement park on Lake Shafer. They held roller-skating parties at a nearby rink. They held candy sales, and all-you-can-eat pancake breakfasts, and spaghetti and fish dinners, to raise money.

Through it all, Weber bands competed across Chicago and the state and emerged as among Illinois' best junior high bands. Weber wanted them to see more of the world than Harvey. Competing created goals and teamwork. They competed against White high schools in a rough time for race relations in Chicago. "It was important to show people that my kids were just like everybody else," Weber told me one day. "Back then, that was something people needed to see."

"What he got out of us was incredible," said one student. "I always think of him as this Pied Piper of band—he was, for me, leading me away from gang violence and being shot."

Indeed, Weber's band hall became a refuge from Harvey's gathering storm of murder and crack cocaine. As happens in so many schools, his band hall became a separate world and occupied kids for hours after classes ended. Many could not practice at home, in cramped houses or apartments, so band hall lasted often until nine at night. A lot of kids joined band who had no interest in practicing but just wanted a place to be away from the rest of the school.

Weber's kids were, or became, different simply by staying in band. The act of physically holding an instrument and preparing to play requires focus, training, attention. It is hard to do two things at once—like misbehave with a horn in your hand. You have to choose. In time, Weber's band hall combined seriousness of intent with middle schoolers' naturally scattered goofiness.

Weber had the boxes of tapes of brass band music, classical orchestras, funk, and solo instrumentalists. "He made it available and just got out of our way," said Christopher N. Davis, the trumpet player. "He allowed us to be curious on our own."

Weber's kids lived near a world-class city, yet they remained isolated from it all. Race tensions in Chicago were fierce and confining. Plus, most of their parents worked, and Harvey kids had little access to public transportation. It pained Weber to think of what his students hadn't seen or done.

Like any tuba player, he had a minivan to accommodate his instrument. Through the years, he took his band kids to see Miles Davis, and Maynard Ferguson, and the Chicago Symphony, and the Canadian Brass quintet. And, in the evenings after practice, to the McDonald's on Sibley Boulevard, which became almost a tradition. He drove Chris Davis, a trombone student, up Michigan Avenue north of Chicago to a tuba and low brass conference at Northwestern University. "That was the first time I'd been on Michigan Avenue in my life," Davis told me. Davis now plays trombone in Switzerland and returns to Northwestern periodically to teach. "The reason I knew he loved us," Willie Clark told me, "is because he would take us places and nurture our questions, showing us that there's more out there."

This practice continued long after his students left junior high. Chris Davis, the trombonist, was among the high school students Weber took to see the Chicago Symphony at Grant Park in downtown Chicago. At that show, Davis told himself he wanted to be sitting up there one day. "Fast forward twenty-five years," he said, "and I was. There's a whole lineage of Weber kids. It's a huge lineage and we're all over the world."

In 1986, Weber took Willie Clark, his brother Anthony, and Eugene Campbell down to Disney World, with their parents' permission, in his minivan. Weber didn't have to drive much because Willie and Eugene had licenses by then. They wandered the park for two days. Every corner seemed to have another brass band. They went on almost no rides. They were enthralled by the sight of people making a living playing music. So many were tuba players, more than Willie Clark had ever seen in one place.

LONG AFTER WILLIE and Eugene had left Harvey and were out in the world, John Weber would tell his band students of Brooks' two greatest players, who once sat where they were sitting and were no different from them. "They conquered the 'hood," said Landon Fuller, the band's eighth grade tuba player in 1986. "They ignored the gang stuff, drugs, the economic decline, and they became something that was so much better."

Part of that lore was to tell how Willie and Eugene had one day in 1986 played "Flight of the Bumblebee" by Nikolai Rimsky-Korsakov on the National Public Radio station up in Chicago.

By the time they got their hands on the sheet music for "Flight," Willie and Eugene had already formed their own small world after school in Weber's band hall. They took on duets meant for piano and violin just to push each other to get better.

There was a time when Weber and Willie were sure Eugene was living on the street. He was wearing the same shirt for days. One day, as they discussed this, Weber and Willie hopped into the teacher's minivan and drove the town looking for Eugene. "We came upon him on the west side of Harvey," Weber said. Wan and unwashed, "he didn't look like Eugene."

For a bit, Eugene stayed with the Clark family. Eugene was the funniest kid Willie had ever known. He was also guarded about his family life. "He was a complicated individual and had to deal with a lot at home," Willie said. "Looking back, I can see that now."

The boys met mainly over music, each recognizing in the other a superior talent and work ethic. They played constantly. Didn't want to do much else. Waiting for the commuter train to a youth orchestra rehearsal in Chicago, they would take out their horns and play. Harvey was falling apart around them. A half dozen kids they knew were murdered. Others were incarcerated. But Willie Clark had his tuba, his basement, and a solid family behind him. Eugene may literally have saved himself through the euphonium—that's how Willie saw it later. Anyway, Eugene was always playing. His skills were otherworldly, with a musicality to match, nurtured first through Weber's Check Off system in junior high.

The day they performed on WBEZ, Weber drove the pair into Chicago. He couldn't find a parking spot and double-parked outside the station. He turned on the radio and sat in his minivan as his former pupils blasted the piece across Chicagoland NPR.

Back in Harvey, the Brooks Junior High band listened as these two older kids, whom they watched every day, played this impossible music on the radio. Weber's kids practiced harder than ever after that. No one considers it a coincidence that Brooks was selected a SuperState Concert band by Illinois music educators that year.

A few months later, Willie graduated from high school and went to the University of Illinois on a tuba scholarship. He returned the next summer to tutor younger kids. In 1989, he auditioned for a job at Disney World, won it, and drove to Orlando, Florida, to begin his professional life. Weber told him he could keep the mighty Miraphone 186 that Willie had borrowed from him.

Meanwhile, no one stood taller in the minds of Weber's band kids coming up than Eugene Campbell, this fellow who played a euphonium better than anyone else, who was humble, not terribly brash but funny, and who was almost on the street for a while. In his last years of high school, he dropped by Brooks often to teach the youngsters. Weber's system relied on the collaboration of older kids returning to help those coming up. To those kids, Eugene "was a legend within the community, a hero of sorts," said Landon Fuller.

Yet the day after Eugene graduated from high school, he wanted out of Harvey. He turned for help to John Weber and asked him to drive him to the U.S. Army recruiting office. Weber also drove him to basic training at Fort Knox, Kentucky, a few weeks later.

Eugene returned a time or two to Harvey to mentor Weber's new kids. Then he was sent to Stuttgart, Germany, where he married a German woman. Weber went over and stayed with them once and watched Eugene march in an Army band.

His last contacts with Eugene are a source of sadness for the teacher. Eugene and his wife once came to Chicago and asked to stay in Weber's upstairs unit. But Weber was embarrassed at the unit's filth and clutter and instead paid for a motel room for them. Later, Eugene asked Weber to send him the euphonium he used to play. In a moment out of keeping with his personality that he later tried to understand and could not, John Weber figured Eugene had money to buy his own, so he sent him a trombone. Eugene sent it back.

Weber never heard from Eugene again. Nor did anyone else in Harvey, it appears.

"He was this mystical guy who left his mark," said Landon Fuller. "Everyone in that band was affected by this guy—then he vanished. People spend the rest of their lives wondering what happened to Eugene Campbell."

Chapter 17

H. E. Nutt III

"He did everything he would have expected of us."

In the summer of 1981, H. E. Nutt was reaching the end of his life.

He was ill with prostate cancer and was no longer living in the apartment at VanderCook College of Music. He was in a wheelchair now, and living with his wife, Thelma, in a nursing home.

As VanderCook's summer session was ending, a graduate student band traveled to that nursing home and assembled on the lawn.

The several dozen musicians in the band had spent previous summers at VanderCook getting master's degrees in music education. For many, these summers involved deep, sometimes daily conversation with H.E., conversations that began with social niceties but quickly dived into the details of the "8 Teaching Points," the importance of studying mimes for facial

H. E. Nutt, the "messianic evangelizer" of band directing, with his mentor H. A. VanderCook. Courtesy VanderCook College of Music.

expressions, and H.E.'s *Directing Etude #1,* that short exercise he composed years before to train students in all they would need to conduct school bands.

H.E. had stopped running classes. But he still used to sit on a bench outside the apartment within the school where he and Thelma lived, and talked with students who came to sit beside him, and in this way he spent his last years at VanderCook, and those summer students didn't forget it.

Rolando Zapata was among them. In June 2024, I met him at the Dunkin' Donuts in Brownsville where so many of the town's VanderCook band directors had started their mornings decades before. Zapata is dapper, with gray hair, a thin mustache, and an easy way of speaking. He is in his seventies and many years retired.

Yet he remembered his talks with H. E. Nutt over four summers getting his master's degree. He remembered that they discussed whether all students had the same innate ability, whether they could all be taught music, as H.E. insisted. Zapata, too, believed that they could, but in south Texas he had also seen how a lack of resources kept kids from learning. They also talked, of course, about conducting and proper baton motions and the like.

That summer of 1981 was Zapata's last at VanderCook. He played saxophone and was in the band that visited H.E.'s nursing home. It was a sunny day, Zapata remembered. In the audience were residents of the home, VanderCook teachers, and alumni. Friends wheeled H.E. out to the lawn to hear the concert.

H.E. was unresponsive. He sat through the forty-five-minute performance slumped in his chair, and it seemed to those in the band that he was barely aware of his surroundings. "It was very hard to see him that way," Zapata told me.

For the concert's finale, the director announced the band would play H.E.'s *Directing Etude #1*. Generations of VanderCook students were required to perform it in class. Many of those in the crowd and every musician in the band knew it by heart.

"They wheel him to the front of the band. He's slumped over," Zapata said. "Then they put the baton in his hand. I thought, this is not going to turn out well."

Then suddenly, somehow, sitting in his chair, H. E. Nutt snapped to attention. He raised the baton, and with that he set the band off, conducting *Directing Etude #1* one final time.

"He did every cutoff, every entrance, every rest," Zapata remembered, "everything he would have expected of us."

The exercise is not long, and three minutes later, it ended. Nursing home residents made up most of the crowd and understood neither who this man was nor the moment. They politely applauded. Meanwhile, the band, VanderCook faculty, and alumni leaped to their feet and roared, tears in their eyes. H.E. bowed his head and smiled.

He sat up as people came to congratulate him, but he soon grew exhausted and slumped back in his wheelchair. After a bit, they wheeled him inside the nursing home.

H. E. Nutt died a month later, an independent, creative American spirit if ever there was one, yet known to few beyond the generations of band directors whose lives he shaped. He was eighty-four. His teachings were most profoundly felt off in the Rio Grande Valley of Texas, in Brownsville, and eventually up in tiny Roma.

VanderCook, meanwhile, had an excerpt from *Directing Etude #1* printed on a glass wall in his honor.

SECOND MOVEMENT

Chapter 18

The Man Who Made the Tuba Dangerous

"Sing well, it'll be the last time."

Late on May 16, 1992, on the outskirts of Culiacán, the capital city of the Mexican state of Sinaloa, a convoy of what appeared to be police pulled over two SUVs.

Riding in one of the SUVs was Chalino Sanchez, a singer at the height of his underground popularity.

Chalino sang badly and knew it. Nevertheless, he had fashioned a career composing ballads of drug smugglers and shootouts from the dusty villages of his youth outside Culiacán—villages that formed part of Mexico's first drug lands. He had done this not in Mexico, but in suburban Los Angeles. Now he was back in town after many years away.

At fifteen, Chalino killed a man who had once assaulted his sister, then he fled to Tijuana, where his brother was a *coyote*, an immigrant smuggler. When his brother was also murdered, Chalino went to live in Los Angeles. He had begun writing songs about the people in those villages back home. Mostly, the songs, known in Mexico as *corridos*, were about how they died. He packaged these tunes in rudimentary tape cassettes that he recorded.

His corridos caught fire in Mexican Los Angeles. Mexican radio didn't dare air his songs. That was okay, because kids with stereos in their trucks blasted his music across the tiny suburbs of Downey, South Gate, Huntington Park, and others southwest of Los Angeles. These towns were once populated by White GIs returning from World War II. But in the 1980s, industrial jobs and the White population left. Mexican immigrants moved in from downtown Los Angeles for the now cheap housing. Chalino spent the last years of his life there.

These immigrants, and many of their children, bought his cassettes where he sold them—at swap meets, bakeries, and car washes across southeastern L.A. County. They came from Mexican villages where murder was part of life. Family feuds lasted decades. Chalino's innovation was to sing the great tales these villages produced. Even the poorest man had a story like a movie, and Chalino found that others like them wanted to hear it.

Everyone had enemies in these villages. That's why so many folks left, fleeing north as Chalino had. In the United States, they found better-paid work and relative safety under the rule of law. Turned out, though, they still wanted to be reminded, safely, of their dangerous youth back home. His corridos found their first market among them.

To the amazement of many, including Chalino himself, his shows were soon mobbed.

That night, after the show in Culiacán, he and his brother and cousins and some girls jumped into a couple of cars and were at a traffic circle when they were stopped by a convoy of men dressed like police. Everyone understood these guys were not cops but *madrinas*, criminals hired to work on behalf of the police.

Culiacán was a dangerous town for someone with enemies. But the club paid Chalino a lot of money to come sing—$20,000, it was said. He walked on stage, three women on each arm, a trademark pistol in his waistband. During the show, someone in the crowd passed him a note. Something to the effect of "Sing well, it'll be the last time."

The convoy drove off with Chalino that night. His body was found the next day, dumped near an irrigation canal outside town, two bullets in the back of his head.

His murder was never solved.

Over the next few years, Chalino became far more famous in death than he ever was in life. Hundreds of singers followed his lead. Chalinillos, they were called (little Chalinos). They sang off-key. They dressed like him, which is to say like drug traffickers, so-called Sinaloa cowboys: ostrich-skin boots, dark blue Levi's 501s, belts with big buckles, sharp-creased blazers, and cowboy hats. The style became known as the Chalinazo—the Big Chalino.

Chalino Sanchez was among the most influential musical figures to come out of Los Angeles during a vital period for underground music. In the late 1970s, White kids found in punk music an alternative to overproduced corporate rock. They recorded their own 45s and put on their own shows in warehouses and Hollywood dives. In the mid-1980s, Black kids in Compton used drum machines to create a new form of hip-hop—gangster rap—to tell stories of the crack-and-gang streets they grew up on.

A few years later, in those suburbs southeast of Los Angeles, Chalino renewed the traditional corrido. The Mexican corrido had always been reserved for famous generals, revolutionaries, or bandits. Instead, Chalino wrote corridos of poor, unknown men from those wild towns in Sinaloa, as they discovered they could make a better living growing marijuana than tomatoes or lettuce.

Many of his records used *bandas*. These were bands playing Mexican dance music with marching band instruments: clarinets, trumpets, snare drums, and, bolstering it all, tubas. Chalino's home state of Sinaloa was as much a center of banda music as it was of drug trafficking.

Banda was corny parents' music to the Mexican kids growing up on cutting-edge gangster rap in Los Angeles. Until Chalino appeared. His cheerful polkas beneath lyrics of village shootouts and heroes going to their death made this old music hip, and the tuba dangerous.

I wrote the story of Chalino Sanchez while I was living in Mexico. I included his story in my first book, his picture on the cover, and returned to Southern California in 2004 to take a job with the *Los Angeles Time*s. Chalino's image was a fixture of Mexican L.A. by then. The "narcocorrido" he helped popularize was raging. His photo was on T-shirts, and singers could boost sales by simply referring to him on their CDs.

As his postmortem fame rose, Chalino took the tuba with him. Perhaps for the first time ever, girls loved guys in trucks blasting tubas. Mighty sousaphones grew into the centerpieces of Mexican immigrant backyard parties. Large and glistening golden brass, tubas were part of poor migrants' American Dream. The horn they could never afford at parties back home was in Los Angeles a sign of their prosperity now that their true talents and energies were freed.

To a Sinaloan narco, hiring a banda with a tuba and throwing cash tips into the bell showed everyone he was top dog. He wanted everyone to see he had freed himself from poverty, at least for the night.

The tuba as symbol of Mexican liberation was an unexpected idea. For if in America the instrument had been constrained by the beliefs of what it and its players could do, in Mexico the horn was positively incarcerated. Bandas were dictatorships. Banda leaders could not fathom more than the most limited role for the horn. Those low expectations straitjacketed the musical imaginations of most *tuberos*.

Their horn itself embodied the scant opportunities that migrants left Mexico to escape.

A FEW YEARS after Chalino's murder, another event rocked the banda tuba.

It involved a soft-spoken young tuba player named Alfredo Herrejón. He had played trumpet in a family of musicians. He was uncommonly fluid on the horn. He found tuba work in Sinaloa with an outfit named Banda Tierra Blanca, run by a leader named Tomás Sandoval. Sandoval was one leader who

Alfredo Herrejón. "He changed the sound of the tuba."

didn't limit his musicians. "He gave you freedom," Herrejón told me. "They let you play what you wanted. That was important. They let you be who you were."

Herrejón had the chops to use this freedom. He put in the time, working out ideas for bass lines that even to him were offbeat. In 1997, Banda Tierra Blanca entered the studio to record "Mi Gusto Es" ("My Pleasure Is"), a classic ranchera song. The tuba line Herrejón chose for the tune was actually tame by any other standard. But to Mexican tuba players, it was every bit the revelation that *Bill Bell and His Tuba* had been to youngsters in the 1960s.

"He changed the sound of the tuba. It was brighter," said one player I spoke with. "All tuba players began playing that way. [The tuba] was no longer an accompaniment. It was like, 'Here I am, here's the tuba.' "

"Mi Gusto Es" freed Mexican tuba players from their chains. It also expanded the tuba rage that began with Chalino Sanchez.

"*Tuberos* want to put out more of their own ideas and stand out," said Rigoberto Santos, a tuba player from the Mexican state of Jalisco I met who was living in L.A.'s San Fernando Valley. "Only those of us who knew the music could hear it. The public doesn't know it's happening. All they need is that the tuba be up front and loud—that's sufficient."

"*Tuba salvaje*," this new style was known as—"wild tuba"—loud, fast, braying. A traditional trio lineup was accordion, bajo sexto (a lower-register twelve-string guitar), and bass. In Los Angeles, the tuba replaced the bass. Now a family could have a tuba at its backyard party without the cost of a twelve-piece banda.

Tuba players grew into stars. Olvera Music in Los Angeles began coloring the brass. A tuba could be cherry red, jet black, or royal blue, engraved with the name of the banda, or, most amazing of all, the name of the player himself.

Soon Alfredo Herrejón had his own signature mouthpiece—the Herrejón. So did Carlos Soto, aka El Jokoki (Sour Cream), the tuba player from Banda el Recodo. Soto, who died in 2014, was said to be the first to raise the bell of his horn. Now he could be seen and admired. Before that, the banda tuba player was identifiable only by the green stain that spread across his forehead every night, created by the copper in the horn's brass covering his head down to his nose as it mixed with his sweat from the ceaseless playing.

In Los Angeles, tuba players found the freedom that Herrejón's bass line implied. A good *tubero* could now charge triple what trumpeters made. I met trumpeters and trombonists who took up the tuba to cash in. In Los Angeles, they met musical influences from across the world. One player told me, "Back in Mexico, you think that you know all the music of the world. You get here and you realize music is just immense. You grab something from here or from there. That's what makes your style different. There's a musician who's doing something I like, I listen to him. I'm learning a little from everyone. That's how I grow."

This fellow told me he once played trumpet but found little work and had to take a day job in a sewing factory. Only when he switched to the tuba, practicing for a year every night after work, he said, did he realize what America could mean in his life. The tuba's new freedom was America to him. "That's when I saw the change," he told me. "They began to call me and offer me more money." He quit his sewing job. He freelanced, open to new tuba work and new musical ideas. On the side, he bought tubas and sent them to his hometown, where he charged a healthy markup.

That was the story of the banda tuba's explosion of popularity after Chalino Sanchez and Alfredo Herrejón, and I wrote about this for the *Los Angeles Times*. The story appeared on the front page. I got phone calls that morning.

The first was from Ruben Gonzalez, the band director at South Gate High School. Was I aware, he asked, that thieves had been stealing high school tubas?

Sure enough, their new popularity had created a tuba black market. Thieves seemed to know which school horns were worth stealing. But they stole only sousaphones—no trumpets, electric guitars, or computers. Eight of the huge horns were taken from a Compton high school.

Thieves broke into Huntington Park High School twice. With many instruments to choose from, the band director said, "they just took the tubas." Now the school had none.

I wrote about that as well.

Saturday Night Live's "Weekend Update" with Seth Meyers did a bit saying that Los Angeles high schools were seeing a rash of tuba thefts. In a related story, people in Southern California had found a new way to smoke marijuana—using a tuba.

But it was serious stuff to these schools. Each horn cost thousands of dollars. South Gate High lost five tubas with a combined valued of $30,000. At a marching band competition, I spoke with one youngster who told me, "I was playing one; they stole it. I switched to our second tuba. They stole it. Now I've got this one. I played it for the first time yesterday."

Who stole all those tubas? Who knows? No one put together a Tuba Theft Task Force to investigate.

At one point, a person called me, blaming an ex-relative. The ex-relative, this person told me, was stealing the horns to buy cocaine. This ex-relative had deep connections to the Mexican tuba world. Then the ex-relative died. The thefts stopped. By then, the value of the tubas stolen likely exceeded $150,000, lost to schools that could least afford it.

"We still have three tubas left," Ruben Gonzalez told me, last I spoke with him. "But we have more players than instruments. We're going to have to find a way."

Chapter 19

Arnold Jacobs II

"Singing in the head is all important now!!!!!!!!!!"

In the spring of 1977, a seventeen-year-old farm boy named Stacey Dunn called telephone information in Chicago and asked for the number of Arnold Jacobs.

Years before that, Dunn, the son of a machinist and a beautician, had badly wanted to play in the high school band of his rural town of Poplar Grove, Illinois. He worked on a horse farm and would have to balance band with his job. But first he faced a bigger problem: His family couldn't afford an instrument. Then a band teacher found a forgotten tuba in a school closet.

So Stacey Dunn and his beat-up horn joined band. Trumpet and flute players awed him, as if the instruments they played meant they must come from money. As a poor rural kid, he found kinship in his pugnacious horn and its low standing that mirrored his own. "It spoke to me," he said. "It said, 'Hey, I'm like you. I understand you.'"

No tuba teacher lived anywhere near Poplar Grove. Anything Dunn learned on the horn was up to him. Years later, he would say that his band director helped him see the broader world beyond but told him that accessing its opportunities was, like playing the tuba, up to Dunn and his effort alone. Toward the end of high school, Stacey Dunn developed a chip on his shoulder common to both a tuba player and a rural kid—the kind that often leads to startling acts of bravado.

He decided he simply had to take lessons from the world's greatest tuba player. So that day, Stacey Dunn kept calling all the Arnold Jacobses in Chicago, until on the fifth try he got *the* Arnold Jacobs.

"Mr. Jacobs, I'm a high school tuba player. I want to take lessons from the best tuba player in the world."

Jacobs, startled, said he didn't take high school students. Couldn't Dunn look elsewhere?

"There's no lessons out here, sir."

But Jacobs was about to travel with the symphony for six months. Six months later, Dunn called again. Jacobs had a soft spot for persistent youth, so that Saturday, Dunn took a train into Chicago and lugged his school tuba around downtown until he found the Fine Arts Building on Michigan Avenue. Up a few flights, he came to a small studio. "I'm from a little old country town. I open the door and walk in and there's Mr. Arnold Jacobs, the greatest tuba player in the world! It was surreal."

For a year or so, Dunn would haul his horn to Chicago every few Saturdays to sit with the master. "I didn't do anything right. But I had the ear. I could hear what I wanted to play, though I was doing it poorly. He liked that, and the tenacity I showed."

Jacobs was like a Zen master. His lessons were less about the notes on the page than about the philosophy and physiology of creating music—about breath and the brain. "The real instrument was inside me, in my brain, in my ear," Dunn told me. "The instrument was not the tuba. The tuba was a microphone. The tuba would do whatever I heard."

To no one else in the life of Stacey Dunn would this encounter, nor the name of Arnold Jacobs, mean a thing. But out in Poplar Grove, it spurred Dunn to dream of a symphonic career, and of all the places the tuba could take him. If his persistence had resulted in lessons with the great Arnold Jacobs, why couldn't he achieve that dream as well?

More than anything else, in fact, that's what Dunn took from it all: that he could determine his own future. His high school band director had first stoked this view, and every visit to Jacobs' studio confirmed it. It was an intoxicating idea for a farm town kid, and one that, as years passed, Stacey Dunn did not forget.

As it happens, something like this vision is what Arnold Jacobs was teaching his students by then.

Brass playing is almost as punishing to the human body as some forms of athletics. The Chicago Symphony had a pension policy allowing its brass players to retire at fifty-five, when their bodies usually began to break down. Jacobs was rumored to have only one lung. That was untrue, though the story was typical of the mythical status he held. He did suffer from asthma, and the factory smoke trapped in Chicago's low cloud cover tormented him.

Arnold Jacobs in 1968. *"A new kind of orchestral tuba sound."* Image provided courtesy of the Rosenthal Archives of the Chicago Symphony Orchestra Association.

So Jacobs studied how to make the most of each precious breath.

"Part of his legend," said Peter Schwendener, a jazz pianist and journalist who profiled Jacobs for the *Chicago Reader* weekly newspaper in 1984, "is that he was born to be as economical as he could be with his own breathing. Stuff that he inadvertently discovered by necessity, he turned into the foundation of his teaching strategy."

A dapper youth with a thin mustache and a baritone voice, Jacobs made a sideline of understanding how the body produces the column of air that rushes up from the diaphragm, past the tongue, and across the lips. Beginning in the 1940s, he embarked on a study of human anatomy. Casual interest grew into an obsession. He audited classes at the University of Chicago. He learned about how lungs work, he once said, not from studying brass or woodwinds but rather studying "defecation and childbirth—the study of what happens with breath pressure."

He spent time at the university's Pulmonary Function Lab. He purchased the Thin Man—this was a 5-foot laminated map of the male torso that hangs from a stand, with overlays of the torso's organs, bone structure, and circulatory system.

As his curiosity grew, he filled his home studio with contraptions that he used on his students. Jacobs adapted a thing called a Spirometer, a large and complicated device with lie-detector-like needles graphing lung capacity, and followed that with a more efficient gadget called the Inspiron. He used pneumography bands, strapped across the student's chest, to measure proper breathing. He adapted draft meters, used by heating and air-conditioning technicians to measure air leakage in attics and basements, into devices to measure inhalation and exhalation. It wasn't clear whether this was pure science or his attempt to quantify things that might not always have been quantifiable, at least by him in his studio. Yet he kept at it.

He studied hyperventilation, believing that it tended to create hunger pangs and thus had something to do with why some tuba players are overweight.

As we age, our lungs lose elasticity, and with it our ability to draw air. Jacobs measured his own lung capacity through his life and found that it dropped from 4.7 liters of air as a young man to 3.7 liters in his midfifties. He dilated his lungs before a concert and found that his ability to breathe was greater after the show. He urged doctors to use wind instruments to treat asthma.

By the 1970s, Jacobs was moving away from the technical and physical aspects of playing and toward a more philosophical approach. The hundreds of books he left reflect his evolution. The older books were on the body; the newer ones were on psychology and the mind.

In the summer of 1978, a French horn player named Paul Schwendener, whose brother Peter would later write a profile of Jacobs, sought the master's guidance. Paul Schwendener felt tense while playing, so his teacher put him in touch with Jacobs.

In that first lesson, Jacobs had him play a symphonic solo through his mouthpiece, without the horn attached, while marching around the studio. "It was crazy stuff, but he had authority, so I did what he said," Paul Schwendener told me. Jacobs' goal was to get him to loosen up, to unwind. "You are about as tied in knots as anyone I've ever seen," Jacobs told him.

Schwendener was living near Lansing, Michigan, and for the next year took a train into Chicago to see Jacobs. "He let me know in a nice way that he really liked to have a certain type of cookie from the coffee shop downstairs. So I brought him a cookie and coffee at the beginning of every lesson. He was always very happy about that."

Schwendener remembers a studio filled with gizmos. But Jacobs' most important exercises, Schwendener felt, were low-tech. Jacobs had him put the mouthpiece to his lips and pretend he was blowing out a lit match in front of him. He aimed to create a funnel of air up from the diaphragm. He gave Schwendener exercises to visualize the sound he wanted to create on his horn. Jacobs was trying to get his students to forget they were pressing their lips against a hunk of metal. Sing the note in your mind, he said.

Jacobs came to focus on two ideas: wind and song—respectively, the air you use to physically play the instrument, and what you hear in your head that you use that air to express. Imagine your body as a lovely open tube, Jacobs would say, through which air flows and allows you to express your own vision, your own song.

"It was immensely liberating to me," Schwendener said. "It's inspired that he used such a simple word as 'song.' He was getting at something well advanced, a whole mental and spiritual concept which today we would probably think of as visualization. Psychology, or sports, teaches you to visualize what you want. The power of your mental image is strong enough that your body will, on its own, adapt to making that come true."

Jacobs' approach was intended to help musicians find the unity that comes when preparation meets musicality, technique meets soul, and they forget their instrument and are transported almost euphorically to another place in a harmony of body and spirit, so that what is in their mind is instantly expressed on the horn.

Schwendener's tensions ebbed. He mastered pieces he once struggled to play. His body became an instrument to be played upon by the wind. "He could clearly see I was not a top talent," Schwendener told me. "Yet he brought so much out of me. He was always very focused on making me a better horn player, and wanting me to succeed."

Paul Schwendener's French horn career never was what he had hoped for. He went on to produce classical music television. Still, there were times, years later, when he thought about what he learned from Arnold Jacobs.

He'd come to see that the master's teaching went far beyond how to play the tuba, or the French horn, for that matter. It was connected to ancestral ideas, even to the Hebrew Bible's book of Genesis, Schwendener thought.

In Genesis 1:2, the Hebrew Bible uses the word *ruach*—life-giving breath: "God's breath hovering over the waters" is one translation of the verse. Something like this was what Jacobs meant by "wind," Schwendener felt—a force that led to creation when nourished and strengthened.

As I spoke with Schwendener, it occurred to me that Jacobs aimed for the exact opposite of what I'd been writing about for the last dozen years. Overdosing on opioids, the brain shuts down the lungs. Wind stops, song ends, the person dies.

After years of reporting on this grim, enslaved search to extinguish this life-giving energy, I felt freed to be writing about what could happen when it was nurtured. This was not unlike, I suppose, an addict in recovery, or a tuba player in a big hall hearing the horn's sound reach its full, free measure after being so long confined to a tiny practice room.

To those devoted to musical creation, Schwendener said, wind and song were inseparable: "Song is the creation, the creativity; wind is the breath. If you're a teacher of tuba or anything else, I don't think you could think of two more inspiring pillars of creativity than 'breath' or 'wind'—wind blowing across the waters—and the creative impulse, which is the 'song.'"

Schwendener took down Jacobs' sayings. "Visualize excellent tone," read one. "Clear mind as you take deep breath." "Singing in the head is all important now!!!!!!!!!!"

"Only play as fast as you can excellently." "Be a child. Think only on the stimulus that's going to make you play—such as the most beautiful note I can think of."

And finally, "Paul: if you aren't able to play with love, put down the horn and go love and be loved."

Paul Schwendener occasionally rereads those notes. He is still struck by how Jacobs' ideas apply to any craft or creative endeavor.

The German composer Paul Hindemith wrote that inspiration was like the flash of lightning at night, briefly illuminating the landscape. "There were some of those moments with Mr. Jacobs when I saw into the reality of things and had a glimpse of what it's like from the mountaintop," Schwendener said. "I'm not a genius, so these were just glimpses. [But] those moments are what makes life memorable."

Chapter 20

The Perfect Tuba

Sine Waves

"We ought to be able to figure this out."

From World War I to the early days of World War II, the Japanese used "war tubas" to warn of approaching enemy aircraft.

These were massive curved tubes, dozens of feet tall, with wide bells pointed at the horizon. They were monitored by men with earphone stethoscopes, listening for airplane engines. British and French forces also used them to listen for German zeppelins. The deployment of radar early in World War II made them obsolete.

But Bob Carpenter, a century later, turned to the story of the "war tubas" to remind himself of something about tuba bells. They did more than just broadcast sound, vibration, energy. They were a lot like antennae. They picked up sound as well. This was not a strange idea. Metal cones have long been used to both receive and broadcast sound. In orchestras, tuba players at times get great gusts of energy coming backward into their bells from the nearby pounding of kettledrums and other percussion.

But the thing about an antenna is, it needs to be made of really hard metal to function properly. War tubas were an example of that. They picked up sound frequencies from miles away. They had to have terrifically hardened metal to work so well.

All this got Bob Carpenter thinking about why his big Holton tuba was functioning poorly. Holton was a respected brand going back a century. The horn was big. Bigger than that old York tuba Carpenter had purchased on eBay in 2007. Yet, Carpenter was beginning to realize, in certain situations the Holton just faded, or it upset harmony like a grating dinner guest.

Years later, in fact, he would think back and count the signs that his big Holton was disruptive. It began when one day the case strap broke and the horn dropped, denting the bottom. Trauma can fundamentally change a tuba—altering the way it vibrates and sounds—in the way trauma can change the human brain.

The first person to notice something amiss was an Orlando recording engineer Carpenter worked with. Carpenter's Holton was emitting weird vibrations, the engineer said. To deaden them, he took to covering parts of the horn with duct tape.

Carpenter had been given a second York tuba. This was literally found atop a trash heap, baking in the sun, with 2 feet of tubing cut out of it. It had been used as a birdbath. (Careful readers will note that this is the second York tuba in this book to have been used as a birdbath once its playing days were presumed to be over. That earlier horn I mentioned in a previous chapter was refurbished by Kevin Powers and brought back to playing life.) Carpenter had it fully retooled and brought it to the recording studio instead of the Holton. Immediately the engineer said, "Yes, that's better!"

Then there was his Orlando Philharmonic Orchestra conductor who, during rehearsals for Verdi's *Requiem*, kept giving Carpenter and his Holton "the hand." A motion Carpenter took to mean "play softer," until the conductor said, "I just need you to go away right there."

The Holton was loud when played solo, but it disappeared into the orchestra. Where did its energy go, and why?

About that time, Carpenter met Tom Treece. They spoke often. The Holton was somehow fighting itself, Treece thought. The sound was dulled before it emerged. The tuba's many feet of tubing required precise tapering—from a small diameter at the beginning to one larger than a human head. Maybe the tapering was the issue?

The braces on Carpenter's Holton were weak. Braces are tiny metal reinforcements soldered between the tubes. They hold the many feet of tubing sufficiently still to allow the vibrations to move through the horn on the way up to the bell. Too many braces will stifle vibrations and dull the sound. Braces that are too few or too weak will dissipate the force of the vibrations before they get to the bell—part of what Carpenter was feeling. So the braces might be the problem.

Whatever the case, Carpenter thought, "We ought to be able to figure this out."

Perhaps a spectrum analyzer would help. A spectrum analyzer takes a sound and breaks it into its component parts—similar to the way a prism divides light into its elements. It graphs these sonic parts, leaving a visual display of what is in a sound. There are apps for this now, but at the time it required a large computer program, which Carpenter had. All they needed to do was play tuba notes through a microphone connected to the software and see what it showed them.

They cleared Treece's dining room table, and over the next two weeks, they played notes on more than fifty tubas into the microphone. Treece was still doing some freelance baking consulting, so the smell of low-fat Pop-Tarts accompanied them as they played.

On many tubas, the overtone graphs were uneven, wobbly—meaning the overtones within each note were weakly delivered or out of tune with the original note. Carpenter's Holton produced such a scribbly graph. But the two Yorks that Carpenter now owned were different. The notes graphed high overtones like upward-pointing arrowheads, "like little soldiers, like they're drawn with a ruler," Treece said. They were strong and in tune with the others.

Hidden within the tuba were all the notes of the orchestra—from the lowest register to the highest. Listening to music, our brains take such overtones and recombine them with the original note. The effect then is to strengthen and enrich the deepest bass sound that the brain perceives. Good high overtones add to this fullness. Scientists have long known this is true. However, watching these York horns reveal such enriching overtones, graphed in real time, was not something Treece or Carpenter imagined they would ever witness. Knowing it could happen did not lessen the miracle when it did.

Carpenter began bringing tubas to Orlando Philharmonic rehearsals, switching them during the breaks. The idea was to test these sounds, these overtones, with a real orchestra. With the Yorks, the core of the orchestra was in tune with every other instrument, binding the symphony into one strong community. The Holton's effect was to make everyone feel slightly out of tune.

Treece held that the Holton's bell was the culprit. Carpenter was coming to agree. But if the Holton bell was about the same size as others, why did it behave so differently?

That's when Carpenter remembered those "war tubas." Brass can be worked—rigorously bent and beaten—into a harder state. If the Holton's bell was not broadcasting well, perhaps it needed to be replaced with one made of more hardened brass.

This returned Treece and Carpenter to their long-held hunch about recreating the sound of the Chicago Yorks: that it was the nature of the brass that mattered. This was a new insight, though. As far as the two engineers knew, none of the companies that had copied the famous horns had spent time analyzing the brass they were made of. Perhaps this was because cutting pieces of the Chicago Yorks' brass for laboratory analysis might damage the horns irreparably. Maybe these companies were also understandably focused on copying the horns' physical measurements; to keep costs low, they used brass that was plentiful and cheap.

Yet it gradually occurred to Carpenter and Treece that York artisans a century before must have figured this out. Alone in the industry, they must have discovered a specialty brass that, when worked to greater hardness, yielded that powerful, unifying sound that emerged as the hallmark of the company's prewar tubas, and achieved its most exalted expression in the two custom Yorks now owned by the Chicago Symphony.

Brass is an amalgam of copper and zinc. Which brass did York use? How much copper, how much zinc? And how did York artisans figure that out? "God knows, but they knew what they were doing," Carpenter said.

To test their hunch, Treece and Carpenter first needed a bell made of harder metal that they could attach in place of the Holton's original. Let's see how that changes the sound, they thought.

With that, they moved almost without thinking to another phase in this strange project: the search for someone in America who could build them a tuba bell. If they could find someone to do that, it might bring them closer to understanding the sounds of the two Chicago Yorks. Maybe, they thought, they were even on the cusp of finding a way to remake the great horns, as so many companies had tried to do.

All they had to do was find the right kind of brass and, especially, someone who could make them a tuba bell.

Tom Treece, a baking consultant, had often retooled factories with large metal tubs and cauldrons. He knew some metal experts. He called them. He called the Copper Development Association, inquiring about various forms of brass and who might make such a bell.

No one had a clue about the brass. That was to come later. But everyone told Treece that there remained in America only one guy who could build what they had in mind.

He was out in Anaheim, California. He was a peculiar man, prickly, a rebel in his own way, with a life spent following his craftsman's instincts and curiosity. Doing so led him to do what no one else had tried in a long time: He had formed his own brass instrument factory just as that industry was consolidating into conglomerates that roamed the land stomping out tiny competitors like him.

His name was Zig Kanstul.

Chapter 21

The Perfect Tuba

Zig

"He . . . was much nicer than he let on."

For decades, Zig Kanstul stood as a lone wolf among U.S. brass instrument makers.

No corporation owned Zig. In the United States, there remained a handful of boutique brass makers, producing a few horns a year, but two companies dominated the market: Conn/Selmer and Yamaha.

Into an industry so consolidated stepped Zig Kanstul in 1981 to create a factory employing dozens of workers whom he trained to make hundreds of horns a year. He did it in America and in high-cost Orange County, California.

Kanstul Musical Instruments was no more expected than a new car maker might have been at the time. Nor did he start the factory to introduce some radical new version of the trumpet or French horn. Zig Kanstul did it because he was sick of corporate finance guys from out of town, knowing nothing, telling him what he could and could not do.

A sturdy, tight-lipped man, Kanstul was one of the country's best brass instrument artisans, knowledgeable about the most intricate details of trumpets, his main product. "He was one of the few people in the world who could make every part of the instrument and set up the whole factory by himself if he had to," Robb Stewart told me.

Stewart was among the top brass repairmen in Southern California, perhaps the country, until his retirement a few years ago. He has a fascination with antique brass instruments, mainly trumpets. His office is almost a museum of trumpets, bugles, and cornets from the mid-1800s by America's first brass instrument artisans, most of whom were in New England. These instruments are gorgeous, strange things, with tubing like mountain roads, designed and built long before the Industrial Revolution made bending and binding metal an easier task.

Stewart himself is a slender, soft-spoken fellow who got to know Zig Kanstul over the years through buying parts from the Kanstul factory. "Zig Kanstul," Stewart told me, "was the modern equivalent of these makers from the 1800s."

Kanstul grew up in Minnesota. Effectively orphaned when his mother died and his father abandoned him, he was shunted from foster home to foster home, thrown out of one school after another. "Zig was never good with authority," one friend said. A local chief of police and his wife took him in and raised him along with their own kids. Still, Kanstul seemed stung by life.

After serving in the Air Force in World War II, he worked as an instrument repairman. But seeing little future in that, in 1952, he applied for a job in Southern California with a manufacturing firm called F. E. Olds & Son, run by a legend in brass making, a man named Foster A. Reynolds.

F.A., as Reynolds was known to everyone by then, had apprenticed for a year at the York Company in 1902 while it was emerging as a leading brass maker. Four decades of honing his craft followed, innovating new trumpets and opening his own line of horns before Reynolds retired in the 1940s. He was recruited out of retirement in 1948 to come to Southern California to run Olds & Son, which he did like a dictator.

A few years in, he hired Zig Kanstul, who arrived from the Midwest having never made a horn. Reynolds put him to work assembling French horns. Kanstul threw himself into the job with the urgency of the desperate. Soon he was producing more than other workers, who then had to match his output.

Reynolds saw Kanstul's talent and attention to detail. He mentored the young man, helping him understand each job in the production line in ways Kanstul's resentful co-workers would not. Reynolds became the father figure Kanstul never had. Soon, Zig Kanstul ran things in Reynolds' absence. At night, after work, he stayed and produced his own line of bugles, as bugle corps were just then gaining popularity. He also worked some nights for Benge, a renowned trumpet maker.

Zig spent years this way, working with Reynolds and the Olds factory by day, Benge by night, and focused entirely on making brass horns.

Up to then, Kanstul's life had been about limitations. He never went to college because his adopted family couldn't afford to send both him and their biological children. More than that, no one had encouraged him. He couldn't imagine that his talents could result in anything so tangible as a fine musical instrument.

So he relished the faith Reynolds placed in him and loved living up to his expectations. Zig gave Foster as the middle name to his youngest son, Mark. Designing brass instruments was now all he did, all he ever wanted to do. His sons remember watching television with him when they were young, while Zig, with a piece of graph paper and a pencil, was busy sketching some new horn design.

During his years at Olds, he read widely on the science of acoustics and found he could understand it. As his skills sharpened, he could imagine any new horn, and its detailed measurements, in three dimensions. Years before computer programs were created to perform this function, Zig could tell what would work and what would not. Meanwhile, he could teach workers how to assemble instruments with the speed he had learned from Reynolds.

Yet for all his talent as a metal workman, Zig lacked just as much in personal skills. He was not given to socializing; he could be crusty and irritable. Most every worker in the Olds plant respected his knowledge, but no one liked him. He loved making instruments and hated having to sell them. It annoyed him to have to schmooze horn players who'd come to the factory to see the products. This required a salesman's finesse, and Zig Kanstul just didn't have it.

Dale Olson is a trumpeter, and back in the 1960s he was a salesman for the Olds company, where he met Zig Kanstul. Kanstul was a grating personality at first, until you got to know him, Olson told me when he and his wife, Diane, met me at their home in Orange County, California. Zig and the Olsons became friends and remained so throughout Kanstul's life. Dale Olson, a slim, energetic fellow now well into his eighties, told me that Zig once all but threw Chet Baker out of the Olds factory when the legendary jazz trumpeter, broke from his heroin addiction, came asking to borrow an Olds horn. "Zig had a sense of humor, but only to a select few people," said Dale Olson. "He was extremely generous, but not to people who wanted things from him."

"He was brilliant," said Steve Ferguson, a trombonist and horn retailer in Pasadena, "and much nicer than he let on."

Eight years into Kanstul's time at Olds, in July 1960, F. A. Reynolds collapsed on the factory floor and died of a heart attack in his assistant's arms. Kanstul never quite recovered.

He ran Olds' research and development for several tumultuous years. Instrument companies were bought up into conglomerates. Now directives originated far from the factory floor from people who knew nothing of fine instrument design and production. Zig grew to despise corporate finance guys. It didn't seem to matter to them what their factories produced.

One day in 1970, a new boss came in from Chicago. Kanstul offered to show him the plant and the new models. "I don't need to see the factory," the Chicago guy said. Zig Kanstul resigned that afternoon. Olds lasted another nine years.

Zig went on to work for larger companies—King, Conn, Benge. At one point, one of these companies bought the other. Zig was offered a vice president's position with the firm in Ohio. He accepted. But on the day he was to fly to Ohio, the story goes, he stood at the gate, looked at the plane, and decided against it. He walked out of the airport and remained in California until he died.

Shortly thereafter, he opened Kanstul Musical Instruments. He loved his factory. He loved its solitariness, working at a bench, his mind entirely focused on the instrument before him, puzzling out the details, escaping the glad-handers. This setting offered more fulfillment than he had expected from life.

He and his wife separated. He moved into the factory in Anaheim and fashioned an apartment for himself, with a hot plate and a microwave. He didn't leave the plant much after that. He woke each morning at four. At six, he unlocked the doors and turned on the lights as workers arrived; every night, he locked the plant. He often spent Sundays in the factory at a bench. Living for decades in sunny Orange County, he was always pale white. His machines, his sheets of brass, his mandrels and lathes, they became his life.

Through all this, his friend Dale Olson came to believe, Kanstul was competing with a memory—the company his mentor F. A. Reynolds expanded that was then taken over by finance guys from out of town, who ran it into the ground. "Zig would tell me, 'Olds used to make thirteen kinds of trumpets. I'm up to sixteen.' I heard that many times from him. Same with French horns and everything else."

Zig drank. Smoked for many years. Didn't eat too well, mostly what he could microwave. He played poker with buddies on Wednesdays and watched an occasional Sunday football game with a friend or two who dropped by. But he could sit for hours at a factory bench and work out issues with the latest trumpet or French horn.

Zig would move his hands up and down a new horn's tube, like a Hindu mystic looking for chakras, before that tube was bent into shape. As a worker blew into it at one end, he would feel the length of it for vibrations, noting each on the horn with a red pen. "He knew where it should vibrate and where it shouldn't," said Charles Hargett, a long-time Kanstul sales manager. "That's as much as I know, but Zig knew these things."

It was what this prickly man was made for.

Problem was, that was only half the job description of the owner of an instrument factory. The other half was to go to sales conventions, to meet with buyers, band directors, music store owners, and musicians. Telling the same story dozens of times a day about, say, what made his horn's bell superior to those from other companies. Telling of the legacy of horn making passed down through the centuries. That his knowledge traced to the legendary York Company, where Foster Reynolds had apprenticed.

Zig hated all that. It meant socializing at large tables over dinner, often with people who didn't know the trade the way he did. He had a stiff, uncomfortable smile around people who seemed so naturally sociable. What do you say to such people? Zig Kanstul's impulse was to retreat. At one convention, he left the table in mid-dinner and was later found asleep in a bathroom stall.

Meanwhile, no sales manager could ever do the job well enough for Zig Kanstul. He fired several, including his son, Jack. He never saw his sons as inheritors of his skill. "The second generation always screws things up," he groused. He had that wrong. It's usually the third generation that botches the business. Either way, though, he didn't prepare any of his three sons to succeed him, and in any case none wanted the job.

For years, Kanstul was a beloved name in horn making. The company produced great trumpets and one of the best flugelhorns on the market. The early 2000s were especially good years. Money flowed through the economy and made its way to Kanstul sales.

Then the 2007 recession hit. Cheaper horns from China also arrived about then, eroding Kanstul's sales to school districts. In response, Zig strengthened his professional line of brass horns—for studio and orchestra musicians. He built pro-grade trumpets, French horns, and that fabulous flugelhorn, and he got into trombones.

But in all those years running his own factory, the one brass instrument Zig Kanstul had never made, the one horn he would come to believe he now had to have to offer a full line of professional horns, was a top-quality orchestral tuba.

Zig knew the York sound. He, too, was absorbed with how it might be recreated. On his factory floor were several disassembled old Yorks that he was studying in his off-hours. His artisan's curiosity drove him. He hadn't thought much yet of how one went about selling top-line tubas. However, adding a York copy might complete the transformation of his company into a pro-line instrument maker. With that as his niche, he might not have to worry about Chinese competition for student horns.

In the fall of 2009, with recession still lingering, Zig received a call from a guy named Tom Treece, a tuba player in Orlando.

This man Treece had a strange question for him: Would Zig, if they paid him adequately and provided him the measurements and found him the proper brass, make a bell for a concert tuba?

Zig responded in the way you might imagine of a beleaguered business owner:

"What's in it for you?"

and ties for boys. If Roma's band was to play better, Cortinas felt, it needed to look better. This was also something he learned from Roberto Botello in Crystal City.

Thing was, a good number of boys didn't have ties, nor fathers at home who had to wear them for work and knew how to tie them. That became another skill that Cortinas and the other men on the team imparted. Every concert, they would tie the ties of boys who stood there with throats exposed looking off into the distance.

At first the boys didn't like the idea. Other bands had no dress code. But to Al Cortinas, ties would help his boys lift their gaze. "He'd sit us all in the van and say, 'Loop it this way, then around,'" said Lizardo Hinojosa. "He would show us how to do it. I borrowed ties many times from him."

The boys came to feel sharper at performances when they wore ties. Other Valley bands followed their lead.

Cortinas never threw away a tie, and his closet grew into a museum of necktie fashion. There were ties from the 1970s, baroque and wide, there were black ties, blue ties, ties squared at the end and ties that pierced like an arrow, striped ties, slim silk ties, woolen ties. Well over a hundred of them hung in a corner of his closet, ready to be of use to this borderland band director as a recital approached, when he invariably would ask some mop-headed ninth grader, "You need a tie for the show?" and the answer was often a furtive nod yes.

MEANWHILE, THE BAND system Al Cortinas set up at Roma High School relied on competition as motivation.

The third French horn chair could challenge the second chair, and if she played better, she moved up and the second chair musician was demoted. This made everyone feel that the next chair up was theirs for the taking, and, conversely, that their own chair was in constant jeopardy. In either case, best not to rest on laurels.

No kid had private music lessons. Each started from zero in sixth grade. They were from similar neighborhoods and churches, with parents doing similar work. The band was therefore imbued with a sense of merit: Those who moved ahead did so largely because they worked harder. It was no secret. You could see them practicing in the band hall, which was open to everyone.

Saturday band competitions, too, were new. Roma began traveling to other schools to compete. Kids saw new standards to reach for. Waiting to perform, said Rudy Barrera, "we'd sit with them and watch other bands. You could see the sparkle in their eyes when they could hear the difference now."

Then, in 1997, a Roma student was selected All-State in his instrument for the first time. This achievement belonged to trumpeter Daniel Rentería, a sophomore by then.

Rentería had been like a lot of band kids, eager but untutored. Rudy Barrera saw a middle schooler who didn't know how to practice a musical phrase but could make a solid tone. So Barrera worked with him, shaped his attitudes as well as his fingering, scales, and arpeggios. "He would focus on fundamentals," Rentería told me, "and that's what took me to the next level."

By the end of that first year under the Cortinas system, Daniel Rentería felt himself part of the middle school generation coming up to energize the high school band. By his sophomore year, no one was practicing harder. "My mentality going in was that nobody—nobody—was going to come close to my playing," Rentería told me. "I would practice with this in mind. At home, I'd practice in the laundry room, to not be a nuisance to my mom. Sometimes I would lose track of time. One time, I did five hours straight. Sometimes it was holding one note until my breath gave out. Then doing it again."

Rentería was remarkable for his poise when playing with the band. He never missed a note in his solos. Except once, during a rehearsal. He stumbled over a phrase, and the band stopped, amazed.

Texas All-State student musicians each year form an orchestra and play a concert after a week of rehearsals. Up to that point, Roma's pre-internet isolation meant that its student musicians almost never saw higher-caliber musicians and could remain satisfied with their own progress. At All-State band rehearsals in San Antonio, however, Rentería met players from the rest of Texas who were the best he had ever heard.

When he returned at the end of the week, the news of his All-State selection was all over Roma's newspaper and television. Rentería walked taller on Roma's campus, now with a broader view of the musical world. His selection energized Roma's band. Practicing became the new standard of cool. Kids competed with each other to get better. "From that point on," he told me, "things were never quite the same."

But Rentería's achievement was part of a gradual improvement of the band already under way by then. Cortinas remembers it beginning during the 1995–96 school year, his second at Roma. Walter Watson and Eloy Vera had found the money the band needed for new instruments. They began coming in boxes: tubas, trumpets, trombones, snare drums, clarinets.

This prompted Cortinas to propose to his teachers that the band perform *Carmina Burana* at a regional competition that year.

This was a daring idea. The band was two years removed from musical illiteracy. *Carmina Burana* is a dramatic, thrilling piece of music, anchored by the tuba and other low brass that propel it. The German composer Carl Orff wrote it in 1936, setting to music a collection of Latin poems written by medieval Austrian monks. The monks' poems are vulgar, charitable, violent, beautiful, drunken—a wide spectrum of human emotion that kids in Roma were most likely to hear in the Mexican corridos that were so much a part of border life.

This is what we'll be doing next, Cortinas told the students when he played the piece over the hall speakers. That first rehearsal of *Carmina Burana* with new instruments, he said, "we hit the first note and the kids just heard what they were capable of" and it was on. Roma's band room filled with clarinets and French horns, tubas and thunderous bass drum, training hands and minds on the musical phrases of *Carmina Burana*.

The Roma band played excerpts of *Carmina Burana* that spring in its first regional competition. They weren't perfect; their sight-reading needed work. But it was a startling moment. This piece composed sixty years before by a German, based on poems by thirteenth-century monks, all of it so far from this

A retired Al Cortinas. "Just don't tell them it's hard."

town overlooking the Rio Grande, left them mesmerized and showed them that this, too, was theirs.

The following fall, in a regional marching competition, Roma earned a 1, announced that day as rain drenched the band. In the spring, they earned a 1 in sight-reading and another in concert band. This trifecta in one school year is known in the Texas band world as a Sweepstakes.

The Sweepstakes of spring 1997 was the greatest moment in Roma High School band history up to then. A junior, a class clown of sorts, sobbed at the news that day—just stood there, his body quivering, as he cried uncontrollably. The clarinet teacher, Claudina Anderson, a single mom, had a young daughter in the band who wanted to be a doctor. After Sweepstakes, she told her mother, band is what I want to do. And she did.

Over the next three years, Al Cortinas assigned the kids some of the most difficult pieces in the wind band repertoire. They played "Movement for Rosa," about Rosa Parks, by composer Mark Camphouse, whom Cortinas called one day, asking him about the piece, and who in turn wrote a letter to the kids that Cortinas posted in the hall.

Cortinas had them try a long, complicated four-movement piece by the composer Vincent Persichetti, a work known as *Symphony No. 6*. He played it for them. "They got excited. 'Do you think we can do that, sir?' I'd say 'Yeah, sure,' " and Cortinas noticed many were no longer looking down when they spoke.

Carmina Burana, though, was the first step. "After that, I could put [any kind of music] in front of them and they would get it done," he told me. "Kids will rise to the level you set. If you set it low, they'll get there. If you set it high, they'll get there—you just don't tell them it's hard."

Chapter 23

Rio Grande Valley

All-State

By its third year, Al Cortinas' band experiment at Roma High was already emerging as a success. Daniel Rentería was an All-Stater on trumpet, and the band was scoring high in regional competitions.

Folks at the Texas Music Educators Association in Austin took notice. The TMEA holds an annual conference in February attended by thousands of music teachers and students. That year, they invited Cortinas and his team to present a session describing what they were doing out there on the border.

That morning, the hall kept filling until audience members had to stand at the back and along the sides. Cortinas had printed five hundred handouts explaining the band's curriculum and gave out every one of them.

"This was probably the first time people had heard that there was a school and town named Roma and that there was a band there," said Daniel Carrera, the school's euphonium teacher.

Each Roma instructor spoke for a few minutes.

What they described was band as a team system. Teachers traveled daily between the middle school and high school, each teaching a specific instrument to kids from sixth on up to twelfth grade. Sustained attention through high school was necessary to train kids without private lessons on the fundamentals of tone, lip flexibility, sight-reading. But the middle school years were the most important. Get them young and they'll learn anything. Competition was essential to moving kids to practice and improve. All this required the support of top administrators, who cut costs, even other programs, to keep their commitment to band.

The program the teachers described was unheard of in Texas. Ten band directors for one tiny district? Teachers working together in both middle school and high school? The crowd sat entranced, Cortinas remembered. "They were shaking their heads, wondering 'Why didn't I do this?' or 'Can I do this?' or 'How am I going to do this with only two band directors?' "

His team was mobbed with questions. For weeks after the conference, music teachers wrote to Cortinas asking for copies of the Roma band curriculum handout, which he reprinted and sent them.

BY NOW, UNDER the Cortinas system, the youngsters from middle school were moving into high school with a foundation in fundamentals and a bolder sound.

It wasn't that no one ever quit band. But teachers and students alike sensed a new energy in those who stayed. Practicing now became a mania. It was born of excitement after Daniel Rentería earned All-State, and of the elation after the band won its first Sweepstakes. Skills slowly built upon skills; confidence grew.

"Slow makes fast; fast makes slow." This was Rudy Barrera's motto. Practice something slowly until your mind develops the facility for it so that you can then play it fast and cleanly. If you only play something fast, you will forever stumble.

It helped, too, that band, unlike football, provided space for dozens of kids to participate. Both activities required a lot of work—band probably more than football, in fact. But band was egalitarian. A kid didn't need to be big or fast, just willing to work.

The number of All-State musicians from Roma High grew. After Daniel Rentería in 1997, there were four All-Staters the next year, then a dozen the year after, then eighteen, then twenty-two after that. No school in the entire Rio Grande Valley—and few in the state of Texas—achieved such excellence.

"I think they were expecting the band to get better by the time we were seniors, once everyone there before us graduated," said Lizardo Hinojosa. "But it got better way before that. Everyone could tell. Not just at the school, but the whole town."

Hinojosa was *the* tuba section in ninth grade. He was joined the next year by a freshman named Jose Garza. He had known Garza in middle school. Garza then was a beginner on the horn. He arrived at high school as the superior player.

"How did that happen?" Hinojosa asked. "He was like, 'I just practiced three times a day, didn't miss a single day.'" Garza lived across from the town's middle school and Rudy Barrera opened the band hall for him each morning.

Now in high school, Hinojosa said, "We were practicing every morning, every lunch, and any time our teachers let us leave class early, then more in the evening." Without intending to, they pushed the rest of the band to a higher level. Cortinas would scold the flutes: "This is the only band I've had where the tubas play faster than the flutes."

With two strong tubas, the band could reach new heights, try new music, and become what Cortinas imagined it could be. Part of that was the excitement these two young tubists felt for what they now saw possible.

Yet there was another element to the tuba section's improvement. Out there somewhere in the Rio Grande Valley during those years, I was told, was a tuba savant who had materialized unexpectedly in one of the dusty Valley farmtowns. He was a youth whose playing was beyond anything ever heard on the horn in the Valley. His playing spurred Roma's tuba players to heroic effort in hopes of beating him in area competitions. Younger Roma players remember watching Jose Garza in his senior year practicing ferociously to beat this kid. The first people to tell me of this boy did not know his name. But he was out there, he really existed, they said. Maybe he was from Brownsville, one suggested; the town's bands were always so good.

It was now almost twenty-five years later, but I set out to learn what had become of this mystery tuba player. One thing led to another, as they do, and a few months later I was knocking on the door of a tiny, worn wooden house with thick-curtained windows in a neighborhood north of downtown in the ranching burg of Harlingen, about ninety miles downriver from Roma.

Chapter 24

Rio Grande Valley

J.R.

Julian Ray Treviño, known to all as J.R., was now forty-two.
He was the oldest of two children born to Joseph and Mary Treviño, an older car washer / flea market vendor and his younger wife.

Joe and Mary had no background in music. Yet their son would become the greatest teen tuba player of his time in the Rio Grande Valley. Harlingen then had a population of forty thousand and the limited cultural opportunities of any farm town. But J.R. could play almost six octaves above the lowest C note on the instrument. He had a fluidity and a soul to his playing that had advanced far beyond his peers by his early teen years.

He was a tiny child but grew into his horn. By high school, he stood 5 feet 11, with thick glasses and an awkward manner. He seemed to lose himself in the horn when he played, for the tuba was more than an instrument to J. R. Treviño.

The first time he ever saw one, he told me, was in third grade at Zavala Elementary School down the street from his house. The son of the school janitor brought in his sousaphone to show the kids and asked who might want to try to make a sound on it. As J. R. Treviño remembered years later, he made a noise on the big horn.

"Good job," the tuba's owner told him. "You did it!"

The man probably didn't give much thought to the comment. But it changed the life of then tiny J. R. Treviño. "To be one who could make the noise on it made me extremely happy," he told me. "He made me feel like I had done something. It was really, really special to me."

As it happened, this moment came two or three years after J.R. had been molested—"tortured," as he put it—by a neighborhood youth. He said it happened more than once, and he never spoke of it until he was well into adulthood. J.R. also stuttered and patted his head and hummed a lot without realizing it. Kids thought him odd, called him names: "Re-re-re-retard." He learned that the world was a threatening place, and that people could be cruel without warning.

For the next three years, as he buried the memories of his abuse, J.R. thought about that third grade tuba moment. He eagerly entered sixth grade, the year band class started in Harlingen schools. That summer, he went through the first half of the school's music book in anticipation. He was that rare kid who on the first day of band just knew he wanted to play the tuba. He played his first solo on the tuba for the PTA that year, "Variations on Jolly Old St. Nicholas."

Immediately, he began lugging the instrument home. Neighbor kids laughed at him, but he didn't care. He just wanted that tuba near him. "I played it all the time. I bothered my parents. They'd want me to mow the lawn or whatever, and I just wanted to play the tuba."

He often had crippling migraines. The tuba's vibrations flowed back into his body and transported him from the pain. "It was another thing that motivated me to keep playing."

At school, as he went through the next few years and into high school, he was mercilessly bullied. Mocked for his thick glasses, his stutter, his tuba. He froze up trying to speak to others and had no friends. He never told his parents. They were so proud of his tuba talent. He didn't want them to know that in the school corridors, he walked along the walls, edged away from the minefield that was the packed center of the hallway, where he might be at any moment hit, taunted, laughed at.

The tuba was his oasis. "The gloom, the sadness, the pain was always there," he said. "The relief was the new thing, relief through the tuba . . . I would play to make myself feel good. When you're playing the tuba, it feels like a body massage. Your whole body vibrates and it feels fantastic. You can feel it, literally, in your heart. It, like, was a form of self-soothing. It soothed the feeling of the bullying. I would block everything else out. It's one of my favorite feelings, and it was right away."

His high school's horn was a Miraphone 186 B-flat, a massive thing, the school's best tuba. He loved its deep dark sound. He never went to it reluctantly, kicking and screaming. He sought it out with perfect focus and desire and felt the world's threat recede as he cradled it. His family could never afford private lessons. But J.R. played that horn so much through high school that he rubbed the lacquer from it.

"We had a relationship," he said. "I want to say it was a mask, but I think it was a way to express myself, to make myself known. It made music for me. It was how I could communicate a musical feeling. I could tell a story. I didn't have, like, any close friends, but I was super close to that horn in high school. It was my best friend."

He rarely went to the lunchroom, where he knew he would eat alone. Instead, he ate outside, then snuck into the band hall to be with his tuba and to play it. "It was like my medicine. Because of that, I did it all the time. I got really good. I would play all the time to make myself feel good. It fixed something that was broken."

Above all, the note he loved most to play was the horn's middle A-flat. It enthralled him for reasons he can't explain. It just felt *so* good to play that A-flat. Some people see musical notes in color. J. R. Treviño is not one of them, but in his mind's eye he did see that A-flat in a deep maroon.

When he played Ralph Vaughan Williams' *Concerto in F Minor for Bass Tuba* with a local orchestra at a church in McAllen, he could sit in front of a crowd without fear or nerves because he had his tuba in front of him. Then he was barely aware of the world beyond. The audience was there to hear him, but he didn't play for them. People would tell him how much they loved his playing, and he did not intend arrogance when he responded, "I know, I love it so much, too." Finishing the piece left him empty. "It's like ending a good book," he told me. "You're done and you got to find another one."

During his junior year, he was chosen to play in a Washington, D.C., honor band of high-schoolers from around the country. Before he left, the principal went on the intercom: "Let's wish

J. R. Treviño good luck as he goes off to represent our school in Washington, D.C." He still remembers students' mocking laughter that followed the announcement.

That week was the longest he had been away from home. Homesickness made him physically ill. But it liberated him to be far from Harlingen. For a time, he became someone he was not back home. A bit cooler. He would never see these honor band musicians again, "so I wasn't scared to say what I thought. I hid behind the fact that no one knew who I was."

At a region-wide orchestra competition in McAllen in 1998, he sat near the front. The Roma High School tuba players were competing, too, sitting toward the back. J.R. began to play, coaxing sounds that neither Lizardo Hinojosa nor Jose Garza had ever heard from the horn. "I looked up and thought, 'What the *hell* is that?' " Hinojosa told me. "That was the first time we heard a really good tuba player."

Treviño was part of the exposure to the world that Roma band students were getting for the first time. Hinojosa and Garza sat in awe. Then they copied how Treviño sat, how he held the tuba. The next years were spent practicing with J. R. Treviño in mind. "I almost beat him my senior year," Hinojosa said.

It's probably not an exaggeration to say that J. R. Treviño was one reason why the Roma tuba section grew strong and powered the band as it began to compete statewide. Little by little a higher standard was set that other Roma tuba players had to meet, and the whole band got better because of it.

J.R., meanwhile, played and he played, and he played through the years. In school, he daydreamed off into his own tuba world, imagining the fingerings he would use to play this musical passage or that. At times the music of his daydreams would take him and he would begin dancing. "I know you're Mexican," his Spanish teacher told him, "because Mexicans don't need music to dance."

He played at lunch and at home, in front of the TV. His Miraphone seemed to oscillate the TV screen like a sound wave. People next to him wouldn't see it. He realized he was being moved, that the horn was sending the vibrations through him, not through the TV; his body was resonating, like the tubes of the instrument itself.

In time, it seemed, his body, his mind, and the horn became one. As I got to know him through visits and phone calls, he seemed like a human version of those legendary Chicago York tubas. He was the perfect vessel, lovingly channeling breath, focus, and desire through this metal funnel, in tune with whoever accompanied him. This was not something he tried to achieve, nor was even aware of. It was rather just the result of years of coming to the tuba eagerly, tenderly, yearning for the way it made his body feel, how it soothed his wounds.

"When I play, I play mainly for myself . . . but every time I've said that I've left something out. I know it was to self-soothe, but I got there so easily. It's something I loved to do. That love comes from God. I put in all the work, but it was so easy to do. I'm playing for, like, God, too. Every time I play, I thank God. You don't need a special teacher, or a band director pushing you, you just need to love it. That's all it was. That's interesting. That's why you're writing about it."

The last week of his senior year, he had to turn in his Miraphone 186, as it was, in fact, not his. He mourned. Later, he returned to the school to ask if he could play it. Most of all, though, he missed playing the music in his head, the orchestral parts, the études from *70 Tuba Studies* by the late Russian tubist Vladislav Blazhevich.

J. R. Treviño may have been the greatest high school tuba player the Rio Grande Valley ever produced. But he was limited by his almost complete inability to be around others.

In high school, he had to attend class, though he dreaded it. In college, he didn't have to attend class. He spent four years pretending to be a sophomore at the University of Texas in Brownsville in order to be close to a tuba. He played it constantly. He was not enrolled but showed up anyway to play in the ensemble, and everyone assumed he was an official student. Eventually, though, that had to end.

He left college without a degree, yet at the peak of his musical skills and sensitivity. At UT Brownsville, he had felt musically alone though he was surrounded by music students. Now he didn't even have that accompaniment.

Alone, he turned to music of rebirth. He found a 1988 recording by the Chicago Symphony, guest conducted by Leonard Bernstein, of the legendary Russian composer Dmitri Shostakovich's *Leningrad*, written during the Nazi siege of that city and finally its liberation. The recording took over his life for a time. The ending, which builds and builds, like the city rising from the rubble, pulverized him. "Sometimes I'm left whimpering," he told me, "it's just so beautiful."

He got that same feeling from a 1988 New York Philharmonic recording that Leonard Bernstein also conducted of Gustav Mahler's *Resurrection* symphony, about death and rebirth, reflecting the composer's belief in the afterlife. J.R. grafted his own story onto it, for "when I started to lose myself in the tuba, if I wasn't dead, I was dying. In a very real way, I did become alive to a new world. The horn would make me feel better than what other people thought of me. Maybe that's why this symphony affected me so much. It would take my breath away. You can feel that resurrection and become like a new creature."

The album's liner notes described similarities between Mahler and Bernstein: "Both were subject to tremendous mood swings that could be all but incapacitating. Most important, though, is the fact that both Bernstein and Mahler distilled their joys and sufferings into art." There was also some of J. R. Treviño in that description, it seemed to me.

His playing became meditative. He reworked his lips and relaxed his breath, kept from hardening his diaphragm. Band directors had taught that you had to force the air, push hard. He no longer believed that. He no longer forced air through his lips and into the mouthpiece. Opening the throat to the column of air and exhaling caused the air to vibrate the horn, and the resulting sound felt to him deeper, easier.

These were ideas Arnold Jacobs had expounded, though J.R. came to them alone, needing them. He found Jacobs' tuba sound more like a spotlight, piercing and unsettling. Bill Bell's was like an embracing floodlight, and this comforted him more. "Arnold Jacobs was a philosopher, and everyone loves a philosopher. You can fall in love with someone like that, the way he would explain things. But as far as the best sound, I think it's Bill Bell."

J. R. Treviño now needed exposure to the tuba world beyond the Rio Grande Valley. He needed the best players, teachers, and orchestras, people who had opinions on Shostakovich, Mahler,

J. R. Treviño and his tuba in church. "It was my best friend."

and Bernstein and who knew the names Bill Bell and Arnold Jacobs. Harlingen, Texas, offered none of that. "Looking back," he said, "I was playing virtuoso level solos, and had a huge range. But there's definitely a higher level I could have reached. I never really got there."

J.R.'s relentless desire for the tuba had grown in Harlingen partly from his fear of its people and how they treated him. That fear of people now kept him from leaving Harlingen. His father had just died. The family had no money. He took a part-time job as tuba instructor in the schools. His tuba playing was ready for a new stage yet found no such nourishment.

Perhaps it's no coincidence that his health now declined. He had high blood pressure and took his medicine erratically. He quaffed quantities of Diet Coke. He began to retain fluid. He bloated to 380 pounds and could hardly move. Carrying his tuba was out of the question, much less playing it. He had to quit the teaching job. Went on disability. His kidneys failing, doctors gave him the choice of hospice or kidney dialysis.

He put the tuba aside. "I needed to get better. That became the most important part of my life because I was dying."

Now forty-two and on disability, J. R. Treviño has end-stage renal disease, from which people can die quickly or live for twenty more years. He lives in the old wooden house he grew up in, near Zavala Elementary, with his mother. His mother was diagnosed with acute kidney injury. Each a terminal patient, on dialysis on alternate days of the week, they care for each other.

He sees a therapist and plays a tuba he borrowed from his college and hasn't yet returned. He leaves it at his church, as he finds it too cumbersome to move; he plays it only on Sundays.

His life now revolves around kidney dialysis three times a week. He has lost the weight and walks seven miles every day he's not on dialysis. He takes medicine for his depression and talks to a counselor every two weeks.

"All that replaces the tuba," he told me. "The tuba gave me my life for a while. It was a lot of things, and everything to me for a while. When I played the tuba, sometimes I thought that was all that I needed, honestly. It wasn't everything I needed. It was a substitute for things that it probably shouldn't have been a substitute for. But in general, at least for me, the tuba was a good thing."

Chapter 25

Orlando I

Willie and the Mouse

In 1989, Willie Clark arrived in Orlando, Florida, from Harvey, Illinois, to join a new tuba quartet formed to play full time at Disney World. He was now twenty years old.

The Tuba Fours—two tubas, two euphoniums—dressed as paperboys of the Little Rascals era, with knickers and suspenders. They played for park visitors, especially near the longest lines to distract customers from the wait.

Clark received health insurance and the fabulous annual salary of $60,000 to play the tuba, twenty minutes on, forty minutes off, five times a day, five days a week.

The first song they ever played was "Mr. Sandman." Clark would play it a half dozen times a day for ten years. Decades after leaving the job, he still remembered the fingering. They ran through "Chattanooga Choo-Choo," "In the Mood," and other swing and Disney tunes, and as they did, Willie Clark thought he'd died and gone to heaven.

In fact, he only later realized his even greater luck: He was part of a trail of migrant tuba players traipsing into Orlando.

Disney was hiring. Had been since at least the early 1980s, when the company added EPCOT Center, then its Disney-MGM Studios, now known as Hollywood Studios, in 1989. Now there were bands, and tubas, all over the Disney parks: the Future Corps, Kids of the Kingdom, Voices of Liberty, Hollywood Hitmen, a Moroccan band, a fife and drum corps. Some thirty tuba players eventually landed in town to work for Disney.

No American city so small had acquired so many tuba players so quickly as Orlando, Florida, population 163,000. They formed a tuba scene that lasted a decade—playing constantly, drinking often, challenging each other to improve. "I learned more there than I could have learned at any university," Clark told me.

In Orlando, being a tuba player no longer meant being alone, or hanging out with trombonists. You could play or talk tuba all day long. The phone tree was almost magical. A call would go out and soon two dozen tubists would appear at the Ale House to drink Guinness until the wee hours. One pub had a wall of names of those who tried ninety different beers in ninety days. A dozen young Disney tuba players were up there.

Several times a month, "tuba hangs" took place at the home of Claude Kashnig, who had arrived to work for Disney in the mid-1980s. Kashnig's neighbors were a stripper who worked nights and a deaf musician. With no one around to complain, his house on Glasgow Avenue became an after-hours tuba center.

Kashnig made endless margaritas and had bunches of bananas ready to give out when his guests left early in the morning. By the time the night was rocking, there'd be fifteen or twenty tuba players, drinking or playing their tubas in Kashnig's back room. Others would be repairing an old horn or two.

"It was miraculous," Kashnig said. "The only time you'd run into that many tuba players anywhere else was at an audition."

Kashnig always cranked tuba tunes at these affairs. He wore out one copy of *Bill Bell and His Tuba* and bought another. "I'd just play it in the background," he told me. "Or if someone was working on Hindemith's *Tuba Sonata*, you'd throw on Roger Bobo's recording of it."

They staged Thunder Domes—competitions among tuba players. "You do whatever you need to do," Kashnig said, "to be the one person leaving the Thunder Dome."

A bootleg record scene thrived. Players came to tuba hangs with five-packs of blank cassettes, ready to copy albums others might have already pirated. Sometimes they were copying copies of copies of the latest cool tuba record. Often, they were recording things no one could imagine a tuba playing. *Kind of Blue* by Miles Davis, for one. Occasionally someone suggested "Stairway to Heaven."

But that was the liberating point of the Orlando tuba scene in those years. Tuba players were free at last. "Blow the box apart," Kashnig said. "We were fixated on how we were going to create ourselves. This was a continual creative process that allowed people to develop beyond what their imaginations had allowed. The world is whatever you want to make of it."

They caroused hard but were as serious about their craft. They held mock auditions, judging each other. During one audition, Willie Clark was told to play an A-flat above middle C on a C tuba. I'm told this is a stretch for most players. He couldn't do it at first. His judges kept at him until eventually Willie hit that A-flat. To Clark, that was the Orlando scene. A tuba family pushing you beyond your limitations. "This was Orlando as a tuba hotbed," said Bob Carpenter, who returned from college to his hometown as that hotbed expanded.

For those who lived it, Orlando's Disney tuba scene took the place of traditional routes to music. In fact, this is what made the horn vital, and made its players rambunctious and independent, more likely to rebel at musical orthodoxies. Almost all were from non-tuba families. They found strange roads to the horn. Early tubists were trained in the circus. Many others still came from marching bands. The Orlando generation was fired in the crucible of a Disney amusement park.

I'D SEEN THIS kind of thing before.

For an earlier book, I remember speaking with neuroscientists to understand addiction. Like the tuba, brain science was relatively new. Neuroscience rules were still being written. Many neuroscientists I met were the first in their families to go to college, let alone to study the brain. "With the brain," said one, "it was, what do you feel like studying? It was wide open. It allows you to be creative in a way that most scientific disciplines don't."

Years before that, I spent a lot of time in the Mexican border town of Tijuana, which in its way reminded me of the tuba as well. Tijuana hasn't the beauty of Mexico's colonial cities. It is chaotic, potholed, and grimy. Its beauty lies instead in the absence of entrenched hierarchies stifling poor people's chances. Tijuana offered some of the life-changing opportunities that Mexican migrants hoped to find in the United States. Many stayed, and their optimism further energized the place.

I realized amid my tuba project that the horn enjoyed some of this freedom from hierarchies. The actual horn itself was being reinvented in real time. Its size and lung requirements meant that players rarely took up the instrument before the age of thirteen or so, when other musicians were already playing Mendelssohn concertos and grooming for music conservatories. The path to a tuba career was less governed by prestige and conservatory training than was, say, the trumpet or the violin.

The tuba's function in any orchestra or band is to provide the basis for everyone else to sound good. The tuba economy, however, fought against that harmony. Tuba players far outnumbered decent-paying tuba jobs. Grim hardship, isolation, and fear of competition were part of tuba life. Except, that is, in Orlando in the 1990s. Free from economic desperation, the tuba in Orlando achieved its purest form as a community enhancer.

This insight occurred to me when I spoke with Boston Symphony tubist Mike Roylance, who fondly described the Orlando scene's camaraderie. For years, Roylance played in the Future Corps, a drum and bugle outfit at Disney World. Seven shows a day, beginning at eight fifteen in the morning. Then he played Dixieland jazz in a bar until midnight. Years of this equipped him with a remarkable physical endurance, "chops of steel." Dozens of tuba players went through this common fire, he said. They urged each other on, drank together, bonded over the years. No hierarchies, no pecking order.

This harmony relied, of course, on Disney's socialist equality. Every player received the same health insurance and steady salary, which was enough to buy a house in Orlando at the time. Most were young and single and for one shining decade, they found a tuba wonderland in Orlando, Florida. They could share their mania for the big bass horn without fear of helping a competitor.

The French philosopher Jean-Jacques Rousseau imagined a garden where man was free of the economic dog-eat-dog and his natural benevolent state could emerge. For end-of-century American tuba players, that garden turned out to be a Florida amusement park where they daily jammed "When You Wish upon a Star" while parading by sunscreened tourists. They just had to not mind dressing in lederhosen, or futuristic tights, or Revolutionary coats and powdered wigs.

Willie Clark found this kind of mystical exaltation in the Tuba Fours. Through years of "Mr. Sandman" and "Chattanooga Choo-Choo," the quartet melded into one mind. Each knew where the others were going with every breath, every pause of a phrase. The songs never varied, yet Willie Clark felt every day might hold its own surprise, its own indescribable connections. He arranged "Flight of the Bumblebee" for the quartet, bringing it in at under a minute.

And this is how things were, and it seemed they would never end.

Until one day in May 2000. Clark was summoned to Disney offices and told it was over. The Tuba Fours were laid off, given two weeks' severance pay and five minutes to clean out their lockers.

He felt as if he'd lost a limb. He didn't expect to make millions from the tuba. But he had come to need those moments of musical clarity and connection. In Orlando, the tuba repaid his love and years of study with these instants of bliss, very much like that moment in sixth grade band playing the *Star Trek* theme. That was enough for Willie Clark.

Walt Disney protected his park bands. He knew that the Magic Kingdom needed that alchemy of brass and wood and breath and muscle to remain magical. But Walt was gone, and Disney finance guys didn't see it his way. Elaborate musicals were what audiences wanted. Marching bands seemed dated. Technology allowed for high-quality recorded music. Remaining a Wall Street darling brought Disney cost pressures. "Before, there wasn't much talk about stock prices," said a band director who worked at the park for years. "Then it was, 'What's our stockholders say?'"

At Disney World in 2000, close to three hundred musicians were downsized until about thirty remained. "Walt Disney would have said, 'What have you done?'" the director said.

The tuba scene dissolved. Players left town. A few stayed behind, and every so often one or two showed up to sit on Claude Kashnig's porch and reminisce.

But the scene had prepared them for this. Despite a bias against Disney musicians in the classical music world, with "chops of steel" they won jobs at some of the best U.S. orchestras. Seattle, Detroit, Cincinnati. Mike Roylance wound up in Boston.

Claude Kashnig taught at the University of Central Florida. Willie Clark won the tuba chair in the U.S. Air Force Ceremonial Band.

Yet wherever they landed, they were alone again. None of those I spoke to had stopped missing the Orlando tuba scene. Years later, Willie Clark would say that he'd never again found the unified musical spirit the Tuba Fours had created.

"The Mouse put an end," he told me, "to ten glorious years."

Chapter 26

Orlando II

Willie and Sam Rivers

"It's sort of like the universe: The more you see out there, the more there is."

In the early 1990s, and well before that downsizing of the Disney World bands, however, an unexpected event occurred in Orlando that would help shape the town's robust tuba scene. An avant-garde jazz saxophonist named Sam Rivers came to town from New York.

His Orlando story was one of the strange, little-noticed episodes in the history of both second acts and American jazz.

Rivers grew up in Chicago playing the saxophone and went on to play with Miles Davis, Wilson Pickett, and other big names. In the 1960s, he departed from straight-ahead jazz and moved off to follow the more liberated muse in his head, encouraged by the decade's cultural changes. By the mid-1970s, Rivers and his wife, Bea, were pillars of the growing free jazz movement in New

York City. Their Studio Rivbea was a hive of jazz musicians and improvisation.

The Riverses were seat-of-the-pants jazz entrepreneurs and possessed fertile imaginations, which they matched with an energy for the daily efforts required to turn their ideas into reality. They set up at 24 Bond Street in east Greenwich Village. They filled a space with old sofas and thrift-store chairs, igniting what became known as the "loft jazz" scene. Others followed their lead, opening "clubs" in abandoned buildings with nominal cover charges.

New York's Lower East Side was going through hard years. The Bowery was next door, with alcoholics sleeping in doorways. In the late 1960s and 1970s, wrote the poet and jazz critic Amiri Baraka (known until 1965 as LeRoi Jones), the Lower East Side was a place "where no one lives but poor and new Americans and artists." The city was going bankrupt. Cops were on the take. The Mob controlled the construction industry, unions, waste management, and dope. Heroin was everywhere. Times Square theaters were Triple-X rated.

These were the years of Frank Serpico, the French Connection, *Dog Day Afternoon,* and Lou Reed's *Transformer.* Rents were cheap. It was a good time for fringe music. The legendary club CBGB opened in 1973 and by the end of the decade was the breeding ground for the first punk bands—the New York Dolls, the Ramones, Talking Heads, the Dead Boys. But punk rock was predated by the loft jazz movement, from which it borrowed a DIY spirit then the rage in New York City arts, and partly pioneered by Sam and Bea Rivers.

Strange new jazz began to flow from those abandoned offices and factory floors. It dispensed with commonly understood ideas of melody, rhythm, and song structure. Instead, the music stewed up bleats and blats of horns and drumming earthquakes and long-tailed saxophone lines. These pieces could sound like a hurricane; they achieved at times a similar rage. Musicians cared little for cultivating a popular audience, but instead were intent on establishing their credibility as artists. It was an attitude shaped during the 1940s bebop jazz movement in Harlem—a movement that the journalist A. B. Spellman called "the first expression of the black ego" in America. Bebop musicians soloed with their back to the audience, wore dark glasses, and played for themselves as much as for the crowd. The 1970s free jazz movement updated those attitudes with a post-assassination civil rights militancy.

The New York's loft jazz scene lasted about as long as those cheap rents, which began to rise by the middle of the 1980s. Crime fell. The subways cleaned up. Times Square went G-rated and chubby Mafia dons went to prison.

Studio Rivbea closed in 1979 but Rivers kept at his music. He toured with trumpeter Dizzy Gillespie for a while. The *Guardian* newspaper later wrote, "It was on tour with Gillespie in Florida in 1991 that he met a group of jazz-devoted musicians from Walt Disney World who knew his earlier work and invited him to reconvene the Rivbea band in Orlando."

Sam Rivers was now in his seventies, but age hardly slowed him. A thin, wiry man of seemingly boundless energy, he was the avant-garde jazz kindred spirit to H. E. Nutt at VanderCook College. Rivers composed music every day, in a curtain-drawn room, with strange creations flowing from a driven brain. Why would he retire? "I have so many more ideas," Rivers told National Public

Radio in 2009. "I have so much more knowledge. It's great, it's sort of like the universe: The more you see out there, the more there is."

Orlando at the time had a limited jazz scene. "It was either Dixieland, or bebop, or fusion," one saxophonist told NPR. "Sam came to town and broke everyone's conception of what was acceptable and commercially viable in town."

To most musicians, his compositions were close to incomprehensible. They were in Rivers' scratchy handwriting, with bizarre time signatures. His works were meant to be forms for near-constant improvisation, usually over what are known as thirteenth chords. The thirteenth chord, in fact, jars most ears. It appealed to Rivers because it includes the first six notes in any major scale and a flatted seventh note—the entire overtone series, in other words. Thus it allowed for the widest improvisation.

Rivers moved to Florida for the weather, like so many New Yorkers—but also because of Disney. Probably in no American town outside New York, other than possibly Los Angeles, would Rivers find so many competent musicians to recruit. Though he was known for free jazz, Rivers was looking for players who had learned the rules of musicianship that he would ask them to break. In Orlando, he could mine a stratum of musicians formed by years under the daily pressure of playing "Mr. Sandman" and Sousa marches.

Sam Rivers also loved the tuba. He had recorded albums of tuba trios in the 1970s during his New York loft days. He always wanted a tuba in the orchestra and his presence coincided with Orlando's tuba scene.

Sam Rivers appeared in town as tuba players with good Disney salaries, health insurance, and a community of peers were interested in just getting better. By day, they played "It's a Small World After All" and "The Chattanooga Choo-Choo" to tourists. By night, they could also hone their divergent musical instincts navigating the works of Sam Rivers.

"When I tried to get through a Sam Rivers chart, and tried to figure out was going through his mind," said Claude Kashnig, "many times I walked out and could not find my car. I had mentally melted down."

Sam Rivers was to some of the players in Orlando's tuba scene what Bill Bell had been to the early 1960s generation of tuba players. He forced them to reimagine their limits, extend themselves beyond what they thought they could do. He was one more unexpected influence they could absorb on their renegade instrument.

Rivers started with a rehearsal band of twelve to sixteen musicians assembled one night a week to try out his latest composition. But in time, Rivers found a home to perform publicly.

Will's Pub stands in what's now known as the Mills 50 district. That's a hip brand for what in the 1990s was a weary but hopeful Orlando neighborhood, attracting urban pioneers and immigrants who started small shops and eateries on the cheap, then worked like hell to make them go.

Will's Pub belongs to a man named Will Walker. I was in Orlando one afternoon and called. Walker told me to drop by. Walker's musical tastes run to punk rock and death metal, and his pub reflects that. It's a dark cavern of a place, with the irremovable smell of old beer and perhaps the most graffitied bar bathroom in America. A few years ago, Walker told me, he began getting gifts of velvet paintings—lions, eagles, droopy-eyed dogs—so he put them up on the walls. I had once written a long story that told the history of velvet painting on the U.S.-Mexico border. I had interviewed many now-retired velvet painters, including the last one in Tijuana to paint Elvis on velvet. So we talked about that for a while, and I later sent him my second book, *Antonio's Gun and Delfino's Dream*, which contains the piece.

In one corner of Will's Pub are framed posters of Sam Rivers' extended engagements ("The Summer of Sam," reads one), which make the bar at least a footnote in the history of American jazz.

Walker had heard of Sam Rivers, was aware of his stature in jazz, but knew little of his music. At the time, beneath the amusement park surface, Orlando had a daring music scene that attracted large audiences. One place they were going in those large numbers was Will's Pub. Walker offered Rivers the pub on Wednesday nights for a couple of months at a time. He extended the stage to make room for sixteen seated musicians. For several years, Will's Pub became a weekly gathering spot for punks with green hair and other fringy Orlando folks who were drawn to Rivers' galloping sonic cavalry.

It was an informal thing. Rivers would at times stop the band to instruct them on a certain passage. And there was no money in it. But Orlando's tuba players were making their livings at Disney. "A lot of people rag on Disney," Walker told me that afternoon, "but it did create a scene of really skilled local musicians. I think [Sam] appreciated that."

Mike Roylance was one of them. His Disney day job was playing in Future Corps. But at night, he played with Rivers for several years, hungry to learn. The band toured Portugal and played Lincoln Center in New York. "Of all the things I played in

Orlando," he said, "that was the thing that made me grow the most, that band."

Willie Clark was another who volunteered for the Sam Rivers challenge. Reading Rivers' music was nerve-racking. Clark missed a third of the notes. "It was trial by fire," he told me. "His music sounded like the most beautiful New York gridlock. I loved that cat and his musical energy ... I was young, with maybe a little fear. He had played with Miles and you're almost overwhelmed at what type of musician he was. But it was the perfect learning environment. He appreciated the tuba, which isn't always the case with these composers. People wanted to [play with Rivers] because of his energy and his belief in you and his belief in the music. Stravinsky is enormously complex to play, but after a while you get it. [There's] nothing quite like playing Sam Rivers."

Sam Rivers died in 2011 at the age of eighty-eight. The *Orlando Weekly* music critic Matt Gorney wrote that when Rivers came to town, "the jazz players were let out of the barn, free from the grumbling, Sansabelted jazz police, unmediated within Sam's orbit. Post-punk, punk and funk bands became more experimental and far-reaching having interacted with him."

Willie Clark felt lucky that he could spend ten years playing "Mr. Sandman" and "Chattanooga Choo Choo" and once a week head to the edge with Sam Rivers.

Likewise, if the story of the tuba in America is about people extending their capabilities beyond what they and others believe possible solely for the love of creation, then Sam Rivers' years in Orlando marked the far extreme of that idea.

THIRD MOVEMENT

Chapter 27

The Man Who Built a Tuba Hall on His House

"The tuba needs space."

Sometime around the early 1990s, the idea gripped Jim Self that he should build a concert hall on top of his house in the Hollywood Hills that was long enough to contain a tuba's sound wave.

Self was in his fifties. He was doing well playing the tuba on movie soundtracks—more than fifteen hundred of them when I spoke with him years later—and taught the horn at USC for what would be forty-eight years by the time he retired.

Yet he had always played tubas in small practice rooms where only a trumpet's sound wave would fit.

"The tuba needs space," he said.

He and his wife, Jamie, had purchased an 800-square-foot hillside home in 1975 and expanded it through the years. At some point, Self realized he could remove part of the hill and extend a second story to his house back far enough to have room for the 36-foot sound wave of a B-flat tuba, the lowest-register horn.

When it occurred to him this might be possible, doing so became his obsession. In the Hollywood Hills, people added tennis courts and swimming pools to their properties. In 1992, Jim Self set out to build a tuba-friendly music hall atop his house.

He had once taken tuba lessons from Harvey Phillips. Phillips believed the horn's marginalization had crippled its players, too. They had to lose their sense of shame for their own horn, step out and try bold things. Only then, Phillips believed, could tubists become fully formed musicians.

Jim Self remained in Phillips' orbit for decades, and thought him the most influential tuba player who'd ever lived. So there was something of Harvey Phillips in this tuba hall that Self conceived.

It took him four years in the design and execution. The best acoustics, Self learned, are produced by rooms twice as long as they are wide. An architect cousin drew the plans. The property was too narrow for an earthmover, so workers dug away at that hill with shovels. Los Angeles building inspectors crawled all over the project. Self had to build a retaining wall to protect against an earthquake. The project's $150,000 estimated cost doubled.

But then it was done, a tuba's natural habitat—38 feet long, 19 feet wide, 19 feet high—where even the lowest-register horn's sound wave had room to prowl. Finally, now, Self had a space for the kind of fully formed tuba player Harvey Phillips imagined.

Self had come to Los Angeles to nurture the spirit that could conceive a project like this.

In 1973, he helped Phillips organize Tuba Woodstock. There he played in perhaps the first tuba quartet ever to perform in public, premiering "Lament," an experimental composition on the death of Bill Bell by Gunther Schuller, the classical and jazz composer. "It sounded like mud," Self said, "but it opened people's ears to lots of stuff that day, including mine."

Thus inspired, Jim Self left the security of a professorship at the University of Tennessee and headed to Los Angeles. The city supported that kind of daring with a smorgasbord of studio work on soundtracks, TV shows, and commercial jingles.

Furthermore, Los Angeles had two players who were transforming the horn.

Tommy Johnson was a big man, a former USC basketball player who played the tuba and dominated the Hollywood soundtrack scene. His father was Black and mother was White. He made the tuba a creative business while training hundreds of students as a teacher at USC. He rarely took weekends off, playing cartoons and films, including the tuba solo on the sound track of the movie *Jaws*. The legendary composer John Williams wrote tuba music he knew only Johnson could play. When Johnson died in 2006, ninety-nine tuba players assembled onstage to play tribute to him.

The opposite of Tommy Johnson was Roger Bobo. Bobo played with the Los Angeles Philharmonic for twenty-five years, then fled to become the tuba's first solo performer. His first solo recital, at Carnegie Hall, inspired the novelist John Updike to write a poem titled "Recital." Bobo's first solo record in 1969 had about the same effect on young musicians as did *Bill Bell and His Tuba*. (Bobo as a boy had pictures of Bell on his wall.) He followed with experimental music, playing with harpists, rock guitarists, avant-garde composers. In 1985, he played "Carnival of Venice" and was interviewed on *The Tonight Show Starring Johnny Carson*, which then dominated late-night television, making the moment a landmark in U.S. tuba history. Bobo spent his last years teaching, eventually in Oaxaca, Mexico. There he conducted village bands until his death in 2023. His family needed a GoFundMe site to cover his burial expenses.

Angelenos both, Johnson and Bobo were friends and competitors from adolescence. As youths, they played duets at Bobo's house every Sunday for more than a decade. As adults they presided over the L.A. tuba world. Each, by his example, shaped half the mold of one fully formed tuba player: someone both technically expert and professional, while testing the borders of tuba acceptability.

In 1974, at age thirty, Jim Self arrived. He took lessons from Johnson, who introduced him to the world of Hollywood studio musicians. Johnson gave Self his first gig, playing with Quincy Jones.

Two years later, Self subbed for a vacationing Tommy Johnson on a recording session for Steven Spielberg's *Close Encounters of the Third Kind*. Spielberg and conductor John Williams were playing around with an idea: that alien visitors might not be threatening but simply curious and that music was a universal enough language for humans and aliens to communicate through it.

With two oboes and a contrabassoon, Self played what are perhaps the tuba's five most famous notes—which the film's scientist uses to communicate with the alien mother ship. John Williams is said to have proposed some three hundred versions of the musical phrase before Spielberg chose one in the key of A-flat.

Close Encounters is sweet science fiction. Hundreds of millions of people worldwide have seen the film. Those notes made Self's studio career. From then on, he was called to sessions constantly.

Meanwhile, he grew creatively productive to an intense degree. He learned jazz improvisation, played clubs, composed and produced his own CDs through a label he formed called Basset Hound Music. He has owned some twenty basset hounds and may have inspired other tubists to an infatuation with the low-slung pooches. Gene Pokorny owns four. The Portuguese tubist Sergio Carolino has included his basset hound, Sparky, barking on a record. Like tuba players, basset hounds "are used to low music," Carolino told me. "They like their own voices. My dog likes himself when he makes a sound. He enjoys his own voice."

Self had an artisan build him a tuba looking like an engorged flugelhorn (supported by a tripod). He calls it the Fluba.

He and Johnson started a Monday night tuba class at USC's music school that became a place for students to play in ensembles and explore new ideas on the horn. It is still going, though Johnson has passed away and Self is retired.

Above all, Self organized small tuba festivals, tuba ensembles at USC, and the third international tuba symposium in 1978. In time, that hall on top of his house became a tuba community center of sorts. Self used it for social gatherings and for concerts by USC student tuba quartets and by chamber music and jazz groups.

Years later, Self was recording a series of oral histories of tuba players from early Hollywood. One of these was George Boujie. In the 1930s and 1940s, Boujie was Hollywood's best tuba player and played in the MGM orchestra, a job he won based on a nightclub act that included him playing "Flight of the Bumblebee."

At MGM, Boujie recorded "Tubby the Tuba" with the actor Danny Kaye. "Tubby the Tuba" is the story of a tuba yearning to play the melody and finally getting the chance. It expressed tuba players' dissatisfaction with their lot—the founding manifesto, if you will, of the tuba civil rights movement and the first prominent tuba solo in American culture. It also associated the instrument with a cartoon and obesity, which it has had trouble shaking.

When Self interviewed him, Boujie was in his late eighties and bedridden. He had a York tuba that he had purchased direct from the company in 1940, the end of its great tuba decade. It was an elegant silver horn. Self asked him his plans for his tuba. Boujie wanted to sell it. Self paid him $2,000 for the York and an older tuba.

The older horn was unplayable, but the York was a revelation. It was one of the great handmade Yorks, a smaller brother to Arnold Jacobs' Chicago horns. It was fragile and needed repair, yet still a jewel. Self had heard awed stories of the sound of these York horns, and of Boujie's in particular. Roger Bobo had always wanted that horn.

"Then I got home from George's," Self said, "and I understood."

Up in the hall, Self took out the York for the first time, put it to his lips, and blew. It produced a sound that filled the room, a sound Self had always imagined possible.

It was an unexpected encounter, atop a house in the Hollywood Hills. A classic horn, in the hands of a skilled player, in a hall built for both.

It was his own perfect tuba.

"I felt, 'This is me,' " Self said.

Chapter 28

The Perfect Tuba

Zig's Bell

*"If you care a lot about what things cost or
how much time they take, you don't do anything
that's fun or interesting."*

Years after they had met Zig Kanstul and become friends, Tom Treece and Bob Carpenter would both insist they had no intention of talking him into getting into the tuba business.

All they'd really wanted was to get a tuba bell made, affix it to Carpenter's Holton, and see how that changed its sound.

Tom Treece took it as a reflection of how American manufacturing had so profoundly changed that the only person left in the country who could do it was Zig out in Anaheim.

We'll pay you for your time and materials, Treece told him when they first spoke.

But why would you want to make such a thing, Kanstul asked him, the wheels in his mind churning to detect either a scam or an opportunity.

"Well," Treece said, and he went on to explain the project he and Bob Carpenter had begun into how the sound of those legendary Chicago York tubas might be recreated.

Zig was agreeable. Let's try it, he said. "I think Zig was obsessed with the York sound, like we are," Treece said. "He was way ahead of us, in fact. Zig was already tearing Yorks apart and figuring out how they could be made before anyone mentioned any of this to him."

Yet no one knew what kind of brass the Yorks were made *of*. Brass is actually a family of metals, all made with different amounts of copper and zinc. The more copper, the more malleable the brass.

Both Treece and Carpenter had scoured the country, talking with metal experts. They learned only that most tubas are made with brass that is 70 percent copper, 30 percent zinc. That's why they didn't want to use it. The Chicago Yorks are not most tubas. They produce an elite sound. The York Co. must have used another kind of brass.

One metal consultant suggested something called Naval Brass, used in ships and bullet cartridges. Naval Brass is 59 percent copper, 40 percent zinc, one percent tin. Carpenter and Treece paid to have some shipped to Kanstul in Anaheim. They discovered, however, that Naval Brass doesn't endure the spinning, the bending required to make a tuba bell and harden it. The brass fell apart on the lathe and almost killed Kanstul's worker.

Slowly the thinking of Treece and Carpenter shifted. Maybe answers wouldn't come from metal experts. Instead, they hit upon the idea of autopsying old York tubas for their brass makeup.

A medical examiner during an autopsy tests a corpse's bloodstream for substances it contains. In a similar way, Carpenter and Treece now endeavored to find out what kind of brass York used by cutting up old beater Yorks from before World War II. Again, it was unclear whether anyone replicating the Chicago Yorks had tried this.

Nevertheless, Carpenter and Treece found three old, unplayable Yorks and cut chunks from each horn's bell. They sent these samples to a company that analyzes metals. Weeks later, Treece returned from a trip when he found a letter from the company. Each horn's bell, it reported, came back as an alloy known as C43600, which is 80 percent copper and 20 percent zinc.

This happened to be a stunning moment for Tom Treece and Bob Carpenter. The brass was not the kind used to make most tubas. Perhaps this helped explain the Yorks' sound.

Problem is, no one in America makes, may ever have made, C43600 brass except on special order that is too expensive for a consumer product like a horn. Where did York find this brass in the 1930s? I still don't know. A workshop in Michigan, I've been told. Or a place in Gary, Indiana, or a foundry near Paris, France.

As it turns out, though, Zig Kanstul had stocks of a brass that was 90 percent copper and 10 percent zinc. The last company to make this brass in the United States had sold it to him cheap before moving to China.

This brass was not exactly what tests showed the Yorks were made of, but without any other option, it was close enough to try, they figured. So Zig Kanstul had a bell spun from this stock of brass. He shipped the bell off to Orlando. That was in October 2009.

The Orlando Philharmonic was rehearsing *Symphony No. 5* by the Russian composer Dmitri Shostakovich that month. Carpenter and Treece brought the bell to a rehearsal. Treece sat in the empty hall with a recorder. Carpenter played the first part of the rehearsal with his old Holton that had given him such problems, the horn that no one wanted to record.

Then, during a break, he removed the Holton's original bell. To the horn, he affixed Zig Kanstul's newly spun bell.

Now the orchestra resumed rehearsing. Immediately, Tom Treece felt the orchestra gather a startling power. The band seemed to blend, achieve a new unity. At one section in the symphony, the orchestra hit a low A, and to Tom Treece this sound was just enormous.

It is not in Treece's nature to display wild signs of elation. No frantic fist pumper he. But his eyes opened wide. The sound gave him goosebumps, and he simply said, "Oh my!"

Later that day, Carpenter emailed a group of tubists interested in this tuba Manhattan Project: "New bell is clear, dark, beautiful, unselfish . . . Success."

Onstage, Carpenter remembers feeling the way he did when he hit a golf ball perfectly—when the club doesn't shudder but connects soundly with the ball with a concise *tok*. The horn vibrated as never before, a sign that the new bell was broadcasting the sound and not dissipating it. And though more sound than ever now came from this old tuba, for once the conductor did not give Carpenter "the hand." The orchestra effortlessly roared and, as he had for a moment in seventh grade playing Schubert's *Unfinished Symphony*, Bob Carpenter felt in control of the world.

At the next break, musicians came over.

"I have a solo while you're playing," said a flute player, "and it changed. It was different. What are you doing?"

"Whatever you did," a bassist said, "it's more in tune."

This was a moment neither Treece nor Carpenter ever forgot. The new bell, made of proper brass, aligned the horn's overtones with the rest of the orchestra.

Out in the hall, as the rehearsal continued, Tom Treece sat listening. So much of his life seemed to culminate in what he and Carpenter were doing. They had no corporate R&D funding. They were simply a couple of engineers / tuba players hashing out in their off hours how a perfect York tuba might be replicated. They had measured tuba sound waves, autopsied horns to analyze the brass, sought out Kanstul, and spent months and tens of thousands of dollars to see if they could come up with, of all things, a better-sounding tuba bell.

Treece called Zig Kanstul with the news. Zig's bell had turned Carpenter's Holton into a tuba that gloriously sang.

In an era when people spent so much on pleasure of one kind or another—bigger houses, cars, vacations—he and Carpenter had done all this to satisfy their curiosity. Others might take that as strange. But Treece had done similar things with lacquer, and chocolate, and bass-bow resin, and it always worked out well. He had lived his life like this, not waiting for permission but just doing it, ever intrigued by how things worked.

Listening to the rehearsal that day, he remembered that York horn he had borrowed for part of a summer as a teenager in

1960. He knew immediately it was different, just like this new sound coming from Kanstul's bell. "From 1960 to 2009 that sound haunted me. York bells produce a different sound than anything produced on the planet that I've heard. I just wanted to know why that was.

"If you care a lot about what things cost or how much time they take, you don't do anything that's fun or interesting."

Chapter 29

Rio Grande Valley

Juan and Frank

"Awards for being mediocre? Life isn't like that."

On his first day of sixth grade band class at Roma Middle School, a tiny kid named Juan Guerrero decided he was meant to play the trombone.

It was 1997, and Al Cortinas, the district's head band director and its tuba instructor, tried to persuade Juan that his mouth better fit the tuba. But Juan stuck with his decision and never made more than a honking sound on the trombone.

In seventh grade, he switched to the tuba. This did fit him better, but now he was a year behind everyone else. Roma Middle School had three bands. He filled the last tuba chair in the school's lowest band.

Over the next year, Juan Guerrero came in early to practice on a Miraphone that seemed literally to consume him every time he wrestled it onto his lap. He stayed late. He took the horn home on weekends. He sat on his family's porch for hours playing slowly as neighbors and quizzical dogs wandered by, and his tones wobbled down the sidewalkless street.

At school, he now challenged for higher tuba chairs. He won the first one—so no longer was he the school's last tuba player. Then, like a racehorse gaining on the pack, Juan Guerrero gradually surpassed one tuba friend after another. When he saw that he *could* do it, he realized that he *wanted* to do it. The more he practiced, the better he got. He cracked the school's top band. By the end of eighth grade, little Juan Guerrero sat in the second tuba chair of the top concert band—right next to Frank Moreno.

Frank Moreno by then was devoted to the tuba. His first day of sixth grade band, he'd wanted to play the sax, but the section was full. Maybe trumpet? Al Cortinas told him he didn't have the mouth for it. Trombone didn't interest Frank, nor did the euphonium. Moreno was about to leave when Cortinas took him down a hall to the tuba room, with enormous sousaphones clamped to school chairs. To get out of there that night, Frank just signed up for tuba.

He quickly got notes out of the horn. "Something about the big sound and being a really small kid," he told me, "made the sound cool to me."

Rudy Barrera was his middle school instructor. Frank Moreno loved him. Rudy B was often stern, insisting his kids sit straight when they practiced. He started them over and over when they made mistakes. But Frank felt Barrera was full of the joy of music, and gave free rein to his kids' desire as they came to feel it as well.

Before long Frank felt that joy, something he hadn't known possible from an instrument. "I went after school every day to practice not because we had to, but because we wanted to."

New creative possibilities occurred to him. He wanted to make his tuba sound like a cello. So he learned Johann Sebastian Bach's *Cello Suite No. 1 in G Major* on the tuba, and made the horn soar into the high registers at the end of the piece.

At school, he said, "they would call us band freaks because that's all we talked about. All we listened to was brass band music: Canadian Brass and Wynton Marsalis, Drum Corps International. We lived, breathed, and ate it up."

IN JUNE 2000, AL Cortinas retired as director of Roma High School's band and Rudy Barrera took his place.

Cortinas was fifty-four and had been teaching for thirty years. He'd recently married and had a toddler daughter. An unprecedented six of his band kids accepted scholarships that year to study music at Texas A&M University at Kingsville, a hundred miles north.

If Al Cortinas had insisted on standards, Rudy Barrera took that to a new level. Excellence, perfection, endless études.

Barrera had been more approachable when directing middle schoolers, maybe smiling a bit more. As high school director, he became someone else. The way he saw it, Roma's students had to work harder than anyone if they wanted to compete with kids from wealthier schools across Texas.

Doing that could mine Roma's hidden competitive advantage: kids who had lifelong exposure to music in Mexico. In

Mexico, they had grown up in a world where every gathering, every party, seemed to include musicians, with endless repertoires of ranchera songs. These kids came from families who understood life to be inseparable from hard work.

"There was so much talent in Mexico," Barrera told me. "They didn't have any musical instruction before. But as the band program took fire, they started flourishing. It was a pearl waiting to be harvested."

Coming up in the Roma band were the Diaz twins, Alberto and Roberto. They had spent most of their non-school lives in Ciudad Mier, across the river in Mexico. But their family had U.S. visas, so they went to school in Roma. The twins were the first in the family to join band, both taking the trombone. Eight younger cousins followed them on the trombone.

Alberto Diaz loved Barrera's discipline. "We come from a culture and a time where if the director would get after us, our parents would say, 'What did you do that he got mad at you?' They would scold me because I must have done something to make him mad."

As these kids improved, Rudy Barrera had them play *Symphonic Metamorphosis*, by Paul Hindemith, a German composer who combined the physics of the overtone series with music composition. They performed the "Rolling Thunder" march, a dizzyingly fast piece of circus music, intended to accompany horses and elephants charging around the circus ring.

Students didn't know they were too young to try anything like these pieces. Yet their isolation combined with musical rigor and all that turned the Roma High School band into a kind of expectation-shattering musical petri dish. Off in this secluded part of Texas, poor Hispanic kids, who had never even been to the Gulf of Mexico or to San Antonio, were playing the "Rolling Thunder" march and études written by New York Philharmonic musicians because their teachers one day told them they were going to.

Meanwhile, it thrilled them to watch how they were improving the more they worked. "This was the first thing we were good at," said one student.

Years later, when Rudy Barrera was kind enough to invite me to his home, he expressed dismay that some former students might remember only his discipline. He wished now he had been lighter, more joyful, perhaps, but he was trying to move the band to a level it had never reached.

Too many American parents tried to shield their kids, hover over them, and demanded that schools do the same. Participation trophies, endless praise, self-esteem classes, keeping children from not just pain but disappointment—Rudy Barrera wasn't having it. "Awards for being mediocre?" he said. "Life isn't like that."

To him, this corroded the point of high school band, which was to extend the limits of what kids thought they could achieve. Barrera's kids needed to expect to exceed the world's demands. To weaken that was especially dangerous to kids from remote, poor areas like Roma, Texas, where the hazards outside band hall they might fall into—drug trafficking, gangs, teen pregnancy—were so unforgiving. Against that, they needed bulwarks of defense built with band's values.

Barrera felt vindicated in 2001. With this discipline as its foundation, Roma High went to the state band championships for the first time. The band marched across the field at Baylor University's massive football stadium. It didn't make the final round. But Roma band kids left Baylor and returned home buzzing with anticipation for the next time they could compete, which would be in 2003.

FRANK MORENO, MEANWHILE, soon was the Valley's best high school tuba player, now that J. R. Treviño had graduated down in Harlingen. The standard that Frank's skills set among players throughout the Roma High tuba section upped its sound and power.

Roma's tuba section had gone from one player in 1996 to eight by 2003. "It was a great feeling to be part of that team, that tuba section," Juan Guerrero told me. "It felt like we were doing extraordinary things."

Juan and Frank became great friends, despite their competition. Juan often challenged Frank for that first tuba chair. He never won it, though he improved in the effort. "There was a substantial gap between where I was at and where he was at," said Juan. "Sound-wise we were about the same, or I'd like to think so. But his fingering was smoother, more fluid. His range was crazy, way better than I ever got."

In 2003, their senior year, Frank Moreno again made All-State, the top chair in the tuba. Roma's tuba section was larger than ever. Players were motivated and practicing hard. That year Roma went to the final round of state band championships, up against bands from Dallas and Austin. This was a landmark moment for the school, and I'll tell you more about it later.

Yet that was precisely the moment when Frank Moreno quietly had had enough. He didn't speak of it, but he had lost the joy of music. Sick of metronomes, sick of the discipline, the constant drilling, sick of the études over and over, of not having time for anything but band.

Juan Guerrero thrived on Rudy Barrera's discipline. When Juan dropped a new tuba, bending the bell, Barrera busted him down to fourth chair in the school's lowly third band. Juan spent the next week winning his way back to the top.

Frank Moreno, though, longed for that feeling of the enormity of the tuba sound that enthralled him in middle school. Rudy Barrera then was more willing to let kids' excitement for music play out. Now that he ran the Roma high band, the disciplinarian was all Frank saw. Others were dying to play tuba with his skill. To Frank Moreno, it felt like a job.

Before one recital, Barrera asked him and other students to play études. Moreno said he asked not to play. During the performance, Barrera called on him anyway. Moreno stood up, played one note, then sat down, to the consternation of his bandmates, his parents, and Barrera himself.

Moreno kept studying the instrument to get a degree at the University of Texas in San Antonio, believing it to be his ticket out of the Rio Grande Valley. But his heart wasn't in it. He tanked auditions to allow others to win ensemble spots. He graduated, moved to Austin, formed a rock band, toured, and never again played the horn on which he was the Valley high school standout. He doesn't own one now.

Juan Guerrero, in effect, took the tuba with him. The tuba had been a guidepost in life, training he never forgot, though he never played it again after high school. He joined the Marines, went to Iraq for a year—Al-Anbar province, where he was the radio man for his combat unit. He returned to civilian life and studied to be an emergency medical technician, and now works an ambulance in Starr County.

Band exposed him to new places, to people who were not Hispanic, to challenges he didn't think he could meet but did. Being part of something bigger than himself was fulfilling. "You're in the tuba section," he said, "and everybody's counting on you to do your part." Combat required the same accountability. So did his work as an EMT. "There's no room to be selfish," he said. "I've never thought about it—that I'm inclined to that kind of environment."

It all seemed rooted, he figured, in what he learned playing tuba under Rudy Barrera.

Frank Moreno now teaches music to second graders at a private school in Mexico. He feels reconnected to his love of music, eager to impart it to his students, and he sounds like Arnold Jacobs when he talks about it: "I teach that your first instrument is your voice. If you can hear it in your head, then you can play it."

He uses the techniques and, yes, the discipline that Rudy Barrera taught at Roma High School. "It does work," he said. "I'm Mr. Rigor now."

I met Juan Guerrero at the Rio Grande City Starbucks twenty years after he last played the tuba. The day before, he told me, his daughter slouched on the couch practicing her violin for her middle school mariachi program.

Sit up, he told her: The way you practice is the way you play.

"Anyone who was in band with Mr. Barrera and now has kids beginning to play music," he said, "their inner Mr. Barrera comes out."

Chapter 30

Rio Grande Valley

Roma Gets Ready

"It snowballed into something good."

In 2003, two unrelated events took place that would rock the town of Roma, Texas.

The first was that Osiel Cárdenas Guillén was arrested in the border city of Matamoros after a fierce firefight with Mexican soldiers. Cárdenas Guillén was the leader of the Gulf Cartel, whose main theater of trafficking operations was in the Mexican state of Tamaulipas, across the river from the Rio Grande Valley in Texas.

The second event was that Roma High School advanced to the finals of the state band championship for the first time.

Following the band's trip to the championship preliminaries in 2001 at Baylor University, a buzz had formed around the band. Josué Alanis had been a freshman euphonium player that year, and he was not at first clear on the importance of state championships. But by later that weekend, when they were headed home having missed the finals, Alanis was all in and wanted nothing more than to get at it again. We're going to come back and do some damage, he thought.

The Mighty Gladiators jelled after that into something resembling a family, Rudy Barrera believed. Teachers, staff, students, parents—all in and pulling together. The kids coming up from middle school had solid musical chops. They dreamed of getting to high school and earning All-State on their instruments. That was the attitude.

More and more Roma parents viewed band as a healthy, exciting thing in general, and as a place kids wanted to be. For Roma, 2002 was an off year. But by the beginning of the 2003 school year, expectations were running high in tiny Roma, Texas.

The arrest of Cárdenas Guillén earlier that year would, meanwhile, ignite the cartel wars that scar Mexico today. Cárdenas Guillén had recruited Mexican Army special forces deserters as his bodyguards, known as the Zetas, as he climbed to the top of Gulf Cartel leadership. His arrest set off a ferocious fight within the cartel. The Zetas became their own organization and warred with their former Gulf employers. Joaquín "El Chapo" Guzmán, the notorious head of the Sinaloa cartel on the Pacific Coast, had escaped from prison a second time and, on the loose, he too saw an opening in Cárdenas Guillén's arrest. He sent his gunmen to Tamaulipas, the first of several power grabs Guzmán attempted along the U.S.-Mexico border. The Zetas turned back the Sinaloans. But the violence that began on the south side of the Rio Grande soon spread, and Mexico disintegrated into sadistic cartel wars.

Life on both sides of the Rio Grande roiled after that. America's ban on the commercial sales of assault weapons ended in 2004. Some of those guns now for sale flowed to the warring factions in Mexico. In 2005, the new police chief of the Mexican city of Nuevo Laredo, a crucial border entry for legal and illegal cargo, lasted six hours in his job before he was murdered.

In the Mexican town of Mier, a few miles from Roma, one band student's father was detained by dozens of gunmen who took over the street leading to the main plaza. The father was well known and was allowed to pass. The next day, though, the entire extended family moved to Roma and still hasn't returned. Much of the town of Mier did the same in the next couple of years.

Cartel violence would disrupt the lives in Mexico of many Roma High school band kids just as the band itself was stretching for new heights. One of these was a youngster named Orlando Herrera. His father, an oil refinery worker, had been murdered in a bar in Mexico when Orlando was young. His mother was raising him and two siblings. They lived in Roma, where his mother worked two jobs as a cook. In sixth grade, Orlando signed up for band, opting to play the euphonium because the school owned the horn and he didn't have to rent it.

For years, though, Orlando spent any day there wasn't school with extended family across the river in the Mexican town of Miguel Alemán, where he had a web of cousins, aunts, uncles, and grandparents. "I loved going over there," he told me. "You couldn't go to a party or get-together without old-timers bringing out guitars and accordions and playing."

As he grew past middle school, Orlando began hanging with kids in Mexico who were under the influence of a streetwise older boy. This kid introduced a friend of Orlando's to drugs. Orlando said he stayed out of that, but in time the group was doing things that he would describe later as "bordering on criminal"—small stuff, for which Orlando was often the lookout.

Meanwhile, Roma's marching band began to excel. "They were developing student musicians like nobody's business, and it was very competitive," he said. "These kids were making amazing leaps from one grade to another. With eighth graders being so advanced, seventh graders had to keep up, and it snowballed into something good." He, too, started practicing hard.

In eighth grade in 2001, Orlando watched the high school band go off to Baylor for the state championships. He was eager to join the program. "We came in as freshmen the next year, and the upperclassmen were like, 'You better not mess up this thing we got going.' It was aggressive, but in a good way."

By 2003, seventeen Roma band members were All-Staters on their instruments. That fall, Rudy Barrera had the band travel to marching competitions hours away. The school that a few years before couldn't march on a football field now won one competition after another throughout south Texas.

Orlando Herrera felt lucky to be part of it. Band took up so much of his time now. The Mighty Gladiators practiced well past dusk, and Orlando and his euphonium stayed with them each step of the way. He stopped going to Mexico as much. He just couldn't go. He was torn, but his high school band was now poised to do something great.

He wanted so much to be part of it.

Chapter 31

Rio Grande Valley

Lopez High

"Results, Not Excuses"

Through all this, Roma's rival in the Valley was the band from Lopez High School, a hundred fifteen miles away in Brownsville.

Rudy Barrera made sure his band felt Lopez's presence. "Lopez is going to eat your lunch," he never tired of saying, and the rival band loomed in the minds of Roma's kids.

The Lopez area, it turns out, was a lot like Roma.

The school, built of burnt-orange brick, had opened in 1993 on land donated by the Lopez family, owner of a chain of markets. The school's enrollment area encompasses the poorest part of Brownsville. It sidles up against the Rio Grande, across the river from the Mexican city of Matamoros. The area is ranchland of sparse houses on large plots with roosters, horses, goats, dusty pickups, and twisting mesquite.

Brownsville's development and tax dollars went more often to the northern sections of town. The Lopez area—connected to the rest of Brownsville by the aptly named Southmost Road—is the starting point in America for many from Mexico. Few other townspeople have reason to go that far south. South Brownsville was easy to neglect. When it was built, the new high school itself was a recognition that south Brownsville locals believed was long overdue. But it's also true that its residents, coming from Mexican poverty, were driven by a work ethic that didn't have time for victimhood.

Like Roma, the Lopez area was drenched in the promise of America and the customs of Mexico. And like Roma's Mighty Gladiators, the Lopez Lobos grew into a band eager to show what it could do.

As it happened, Lopez's band director was Stacey Dunn, the tuba player from rural Illinois I told you about several chapters ago.

Stacey Dunn was far from Arnold Jacobs' studio in downtown Chicago. After his lessons with Jacobs, he entered VanderCook College of Music, where he studied conducting under H. E. Nutt while still hoping for a symphonic tuba career.

Dunn's first night at the school, H.E. was cleaning up late and began to ask the young student about tuba playing. Dunn took him for the janitor. It was only the next day that Dunn saw that the janitor was also his conducting instructor.

In time, H.E. was to Dunn's conducting education what Arnold Jacobs had been to his tuba playing—a mentor and fountain of practical ideas of how to improve. But it's also true that the years Dunn would spend at VanderCook taught him, more than anything, how much he had to learn. "Your real education is just starting," a professor told his graduating class in 1983.

With that in mind, that fall, Dunn followed others to a job in Brownsville, Texas. When it came to high school band, the town by then was almost a VanderCook mecca, a place of intense learning by doing, of adherence to the methods of H. E. Nutt, and led by band teachers on that path for years. "It's almost like a Buddhist thing," Dunn said. "You're trying to capture and learn all these things from these elders."

Dunn expected to stay for five years, while he auditioned for symphonic tuba jobs elsewhere. He was asked to train a lowly second band at Oliveira Middle School. His kids were the poorest Dunn had ever known. But they were willing to dig in, and he worked them hard and they didn't complain.

At the end of that first semester, he took them to a small band competition. They played there that day, then hung around outside the hall until someone posted the results. The band earned 1s in performance and sight-reading. It seemed a minor thing to Dunn. Yet, crowded around the posting, his kids exploded in cheers, hugging each other, running about. Some of them burst into tears at the recognition. One trumpeter told him, "Nothing like this has ever happened to me."

As a poor Illinois farm boy, Stacey Dunn had once seen himself in the marginalized tuba. He became its advocate, its fierce defender, devoted to the horn. In a similar way, at that competition that day he came to see himself in the lives of his kids. "I was every night preparing for symphony auditions, but that was the moment I said, 'You know what? I want to be a band director.'"

Dunn put aside his professional tuba dreams without regret. He had come to Brownsville to stay for five years; he stayed for seventeen.

In 1993, the district opened Lopez, the southernmost high school in Texas, and named Dunn its band director. One of his assistants was a young conductor named George Treviño. Treviño came from a middle school fifteen miles to the north, but another world away. His middle school students were largely Mexican Americans, who listened to rock and hip-hop. At Lopez, most of the kids were from working-class families, the children of welders, grocery clerks, custodians, and homemakers. A few came from *colonias*—the shantytowns of old trailers and plywood shacks with dirt floors that were what amounted to affordable housing for workers along the Texas border with Mexico. Some weren't legal U.S. residents. Lopez kids dressed in classic Mexican ranchera style—cowboy hats and boots, tight jeans, large belt buckles—and listened to norteño corridos and banda. At Lopez, Treviño felt he had crossed the border into Mexico.

Dunn and his assistant directors went class to class that first year at Lopez High, recruiting kids for band. They came up with only twenty-six. Most of them had no background in music. But the group was small enough so that following the afternoon band practice, the directors could give weekly private lessons for each kid, four to six a night, until eight thirty, then wait until the last of them had rides home before locking up about ten. On the wall, Dunn posted one of H. E. Nutt's mottoes: RESULTS, NOT EXCUSES.

They began by training the kids on all that went into playing one note well, and with that, the "8 Teaching Points" of H. E. Nutt settled on that portable classroom at Lopez High. Start, sustain, release. One note. As kids played that note, Dunn and his assistants dissected their body position, their breathing, worked on their counting. It was an entire process of making sure the note was produced the right way and it lasted a whole semester.

Visitors found Dunn's pace agonizingly slow. But no one told the kids they were going slowly. So they dutifully followed. It helped that there was nothing else to do after school. No violin or tennis lessons. If kids had anything after school, it was a job. Otherwise, band was it. By Christmas break, the entire class had the foundation in tone production they would need from then on and were ready to move to the B-flat scale and other basics.

Yet the idea was never to stop working on fundamentals, like a basketball player practicing free throws. So every day until they graduated, Dunn put his students through the warm-ups they had learned in those first months—intentionally, carefully playing one note.

Over the years, teachers asked the advanced kids to tutor the beginners. The older kids took that trust seriously and emerged as leaders.

Two years into this process, in 1995, the best Lopez band had only thirty-one members, tiny by any Texas standard. But "they were solid rock," Dunn remembered. About to perform, "I'd look at them, and they'd look at me, and with their eyes they'd say, 'Mr. Dunn, don't worry about a thing. We got you covered.'"

That year the Lopez Lobos vied with a dozen other 4A high schools for the title of Honor Band—the best performance band in Texas. Lopez came in second, and that was a thrill.

Per state rules, the band could compete only every other year. Each time—in four competitions over eight years—little Lopez

High came in second, in 1995, 1997, 1999, and 2001, runner-up each time to suburban high schools near Houston, Dallas, Dallas, and Dallas, respectively.

This was still an immense achievement considering the competition Lopez faced from these northern bands. Yet down on the southern tip of Texas as years passed, second place gradually lost its shine. Dunn's kids began to rebel. Like, why should we even compete? They won't let us win against those rich schools. It's a joke. Stacey Dunn felt this, too. "That was a wall that had to come down," he said, "but even to acknowledge it was an excuse."

He created a year-end award, the band's highest honor, and called it the Persistence and Determination Trophy.

In 2000, Dunn retired as Lopez head director, and his baton passed to George Treviño. Yet through his time at Lopez and until he left, Dunn pushed his kids not to wallow. He pointed to H. E. Nutt's motto on the wall: RESULTS, NOT EXCUSES.

"We don't walk away from this," he told them. "A circumstance like this is what makes us *not* stop. We're competing with kids who take lessons from the symphonies of Texas.

"We keep knocking at this door until everyone up there says, 'They got it.'"

Chapter 32

Weber's Kids

Roosevelt

"The Greatest Band Director in the World"

Among John Weber's band kids in Harvey, Illinois, one young tuba player in particular remembered how he spoke of his prized students.

By the 1990s, Willie Clark and Eugene Campbell were long gone. But to Roosevelt Griffin in junior high, it was as if they were still there. Roosevelt was a tuba player in Weber's band. In his mind, Willie and Eugene grew to mythical stature as Weber told of their great talents. That Willie, once chosen for McDonald's All-American High School Band, was now at Disney World making his living with his tuba. That no one ever equaled Eugene. That they had played "Flight of the Bumblebee" on Chicagoland radio.

"I never even heard them play," Griffin told me later. "I'd just hear stories."

These were dazzling tales, but Griffin found them hard to inspire his own musicianship on the tuba.

It wasn't until he had left Brooks and was in ninth grade that he found that inspiration, and from a different source, though as with so much of this story, it involved "Flight of the Bumblebee."

Weber was no longer his teacher. But Roosevelt kept in touch, returning to Brooks Junior High every so often, as so many Weber kids did. One day Weber asked Griffin's mother for permission to take her son, along with some other students, to see the legendary Canadian Brass quintet.

That day, Roosevelt and four others drove in Weber's minivan an hour north of Chicago to Ravinia, the summer outdoor performance theater of the Chicago Symphony Orchestra. It was an experience that years later Roosevelt Griffin remembers as almost cinematic.

He, Weber, and the other kids sat far off on the venue's grass. The Canadian Brass were tiny figures on the stage. Then Charles Daellenbach, the group's tuba player, took the lead with "Flight of the Bumblebee."

Griffin sat transfixed. The piece required a manic display of technique, yet Charles Daellenbach was fluid and precise, and to the boy sitting on the grass, the musician seemed improbably at ease. Roosevelt spoke not a word all concert long. Instead, he felt transported to the stage. The crowd faded behind him and Roosevelt Griffin was alone together with the musicians, enthralled by their skill and by the revelation that a tuba could be used this way.

He wanted that show never to end. But when it did, he knew he didn't want to do anything else but play the tuba like Charles Daellenbach for the rest of his life.

From then on, Roosevelt Griffin was on a tuba crusade, practicing endlessly, as Willie and Eugene had, grounded in the fundamentals learned from John Weber's Check Off system. By his senior year, he was selected the top high school tuba player in Illinois.

"I became one with the tuba and I was able to speak through it," Griffin told me. "Because I didn't have formal lessons, I approached it with no limits. Nobody told me you can't do this, can't do that. I couldn't sing. The tuba allowed me to express myself, as a voice."

By his freshman year in college, Roosevelt felt free, that he could do anything he wanted with the instrument.

Years passed and he remained in touch with Weber. Roosevelt was studying now to be a band director. In 2004–05, Weber was planning on retiring. He brought Roosevelt Griffin in to student teach and take over when he left.

In June 2005, on the last day of class, John Weber left the school that had been his post for almost his entire adult life. There was a small party, a thank-you-very-much. He left his stuff in a closet. The Check Off sheets, the CDs and tapes and videos of operas and brass ensembles, all those band trophies. After thirty-three years, and thousands of kids, Weber got in his minivan and drove home from Brooks Junior High for what he thought was the last time.

Roosevelt Griffin took his place that fall. Griffin kept using Check Off, with kids competing publicly with one another to get better, afraid of having the least number of checks. Administrators later did away with this method of training. But in his time at

Brooks, Griffin found that the system pushed students to reach beyond what they thought they could do.

Weber, meanwhile, went on about life. He played tuba gigs here and there around Chicago. He was now mostly alone, after years surrounded by the roiling energy of youth. That first fall in retirement, he found himself walking the Chicago streets with nothing to do. It struck him how many people were outside during the day. Don't they work? he thought.

Griffin threw himself into his new job at Brooks. He found in band the kind of fulfillment that the tuba had given him. Soon he didn't have time for the horn. He gave up gigs, having no time to practice. He was married now, with children. His band kids replaced the tuba as the focus of his professional life.

Yet through it all, it bothered Roosevelt Griffin how the district had treated John Weber upon his retirement. "They didn't do what they should have done to honor a man who shaped the entire city," he told me.

Friends and schoolmates Griffin met around Harvey inquired often about their former teacher, who for years had been a fixture at school functions, at concerts, and in his minivan driving kids to McDonald's, but who had now vanished.

So Griffin began to plan an event to bring him back. It took Griffin a year of contacting Weber kids across the country and coordinating schedules.

Then one evening in 2017, twelve years after Weber had retired, Griffin invited his old teacher to what was now called Brooks Middle School. Some forty former students were there waiting for him in the school cafeteria, some from far away.

Atlanta, New York, Texas. Some were grandparents by now. Others were just beginning their professional lives. The school cafeteria made food.

One after another, Weber's kids stood and told him how much he had meant to them. What Check Off had helped them achieve. The trips to Indiana Dunes, and to McDonald's. The competitions against bands far from Harvey. John Weber broke down in tears. He was seventy-two and had trouble remembering some names. Much later, he told me, in his spare style, that it was "very nice to see them and find out what they're doing."

They stayed around laughing and reliving memories, as these kinds of events often inspire people to do. They signed a poster thanking him. At the end, they took photos and presented him with a plaque.

The plaque read that for enhancing the lives of children in Harvey, Illinois, John Weber was, to them, THE GREATEST BAND DIRECTOR IN THE WORLD.

Chapter 33

Tuba Fats in New Orleans

In Love

*"He was the leader of the band—and he was
a tuba player, not a trumpet player."*

In New Orleans, twenty years on, they still tell stories of the man whose name was Anthony Lacen, but whom the whole city knew as Tuba Fats and most people just called Tuba, for the instrument he loved and whose size he resembled.

For years, he ran a jazz band of the town's best musicians on Jackson Square, the center of New Orleans' French Quarter. It was his domain, playing for tourist tips and feeling the crowd's love up close. He could play the songs he had grown up on, the money was tax-free, and he could sing when he wanted. Like Bill Bell in another tuba world, Tuba prized his oaken baritone voice as much as he did his horn playing.

You needed a half hour to walk a French Quarter block with Tuba because he was constantly hailed, prevailed, detailed in conversation.

The most famous a tuba player in America has ever been was likely the two decades when Tuba Fats ruled Jackson Square. "He ran that square like a king," said one musician I spoke to.

Yet he remained gentle in temper, never raging or frantic. No one I met could remember Tuba Fats angry. He was instead a comforting presence, with that voice that matched both his horn and his peaceful soul.

He was like the Mississippi. The mighty musical currents of New Orleans flowed through him and out his bell: traditional brass band, jazz, blues, uptown parades, rhythm and blues, old gospel, new soul and funk. He played folk songs like "She'll Be Coming 'Round the Mountain" or "Little Liza Jane" and could make them swing like "Blueberry Hill."

The more I heard people talk about him, the more Tuba Fats took shape as a tuba folk hero—a John Henry of the horn. He was said to have once picked up and moved the front end of a car that was blocking a band bus.

Another time, in 1975, during one of the city's frequent jazz funerals, Tuba invented a riff on his sousaphone so infectious that it propelled the young Hurricane Brass Band for a full five miles, as drums, trumpets, trombones wailed over it and hundreds of second liners—marchers with the band—chanted the title to the classic rave-up "Hey Pocky A-Way."

Five decades later, that riff is known simply as "Tuba Fats," and played every week by brass bands throughout New Orleans.

In neighborhood parades, kids poured from the houses when he played his riff. "They knew it was Tuba Fats coming down the street," said Benny Jones, a veteran New Orleans bass and snare drummer, and leader of the Treme Brass Band. "These young guys, all of them wanted to play like Tuba Fats."

In him, tuba and man—flesh, bone, and metal—fused into myth and legend.

But he was real.

He was about 6 feet 5, a Black man with beautiful dark chocolate skin, somewhere well above 300 pounds, with size 16 extra-wide shoes, or maybe they were size 22. Hands the size of baseball mitts. His sousaphone bell high above made him even larger, but the horn itself seemed to shrink in deference as it circled his body. In his hands, a euphonium seemed downright petite.

He was born bow-legged, his family said, and he had both his legs broken in order to straighten them. His people doubted as a boy that he'd ever amount to much on that horn. Yet from that humble seat on Jackson Square, Tuba transformed the horn into a monument for the city, of the city—the first local tuba star in a town growing economically dependent on the instrument. He infused the horn with an independent spirit it hadn't known. "He revolutionized the tuba in New Orleans," said Mark Braud, a trumpeter who played with him in the Treme Brass Band and at Preservation Hall. Perhaps that was because that bass horn was all Tuba Fats had to make it in the world. Maybe it was all he ever wanted.

For hours a day, Tuba played his horn for people—yet he was always broke. He was occasionally without a horn. His life fitted into a suitcase. Sometimes he slept on the Square. He was a "man with very few ambitions, very few possessions, who moved from house to house," said John Richardson, a British piano player who lives part time in New Orleans and toured the United Kingdom with Tuba. "He didn't have anything. He didn't bother about not having things."

His horns were raggedy at times, missing parts, held together with tape. He was missing three front teeth, yet played the tuba with power. At a gig one night, the veteran trombonist Craig Klein felt a funnel of air hitting his back. Tuba's tuba had a hole in the tube. Only Tuba could play a tuba with a hole in the tube. Trumpeter Mark Braud remembered him playing a horn with two of the three valves broken off. Tuba still made it work.

He loved children but had none of his own, though he had helped raise stepchildren in a first marriage. He had a ten-year-old's appetite for food in its less healthy forms, his sisters told me. He was a big-pancake man—pancakes big around as the plate. He loved to barbecue and cooked a great shrimp casserole with mirliton, a squash known in Mexico as chayote. He was also diabetic, and had the heart condition that killed his father.

He was country and city, downtown and uptown, in the same man. He was afraid of heights and the dark, and wouldn't sleep near an electrical outlet for fear it would suck his hair away. "He knew something about everything," said Gregg Stafford, one of New Orleans' great trumpeters. He could hunt and fish, knew cars and plumbing, discussed local politics and politicians in depth, and despite his size, "he could go through water like a dolphin."

That's what his friends remember, twenty years on.

They also remember the day Linda Young walked onto Jackson Square from out of town, sometime in 1989, and asked to sing.

She was a big woman, pretty, confident, and in charge, too. "Everybody looking at her. She's a complete stranger," said Gregg Stafford, who was playing in the band that day. "We start to play 'Just a Closer Walk with Thee.'"

> I am weak but Thou art strong;
> Jesus, keep me from all wrong.

Her voice soared over Jackson Square, mesmerizing the crowd and the musicians playing behind her, Stafford told me. "It almost sounded like Mahalia Jackson." And sometime not long after that first verse, Tuba Fats was irrevocably in love.

ANTHONY LACEN WAS born in segregated New Orleans in 1950, the second child and first son of Johnnie and Leola Lacen.

Johnnie Lacen had moved from rural Georgia for the city's plentiful dock-loading work back when its port was booming and known as a place Black men could get hired. Twenty years later, though, containers and cranes were replacing men as ship loaders. Longshoreman work faded. Other cities remade their ports to handle the huge metal boxes. New Orleans stumbled and lost its port advantage. Shipping business and union jobs went elsewhere. Eventually, so did a lot of oil jobs and White people.

To fill the void, entrepreneurs saw gold in what had been simple, organic parts of the city's mixture of working-class cultures: its rich food and especially its music, with the tuba as its foundation. No town became more associated with the tuba, nor more reliant on the music it powered.

"Here you have a million people raised with the habit to celebrate," the veteran jazz banjoist Danny Barker once told the author Tom Sancton. "Most people, when they give parties, they go on till six o'clock in the A.M. Somebody going to jail? Give 'em a party. This is the only city in the world where they bury a person with a brass band."

Tourism went from sideline to NOLA mainstay. Club owners touted Bourbon Street's all-night bad behavior and "big-ass beers." Preservation Hall opened to sustain traditional jazz of a much earlier era, keeping it going amid the bacchanalian bray outside. The Jazz and Heritage Festival (Jazz Fest) began in 1970, featuring Mahalia Jackson, Duke Ellington, and Fats Domino, and attended by 350 people; it now attracts hundreds of thousands over eight days.

The Lacen family reflected the city's changes through those years. Johnny Lacen worked for longshoreman wages that allowed the family, in 1947, to buy the modest duplex it still owns. Four decades later, his son would play for tourist tips on Jackson Square, moving from rental to rental.

Growing up in the Tenth Ward, where jazz funerals and second lines were part of neighborhood life, Tuba was enthralled by brass bands. As a child, his sisters remember, he "played parade," using a piece of hose to lead them marching around the yard. At eight, he joined his school band wanting to play the trumpet. But he was a big boy, so naturally his elementary school band director, Clyde Kerr Jr., guided him to the bass horn.

The family attended Greater St. Stephen Full Gospel Baptist Church a couple of blocks away, where Tuba heard the songs he played for the rest of his life: "His Eye Is on the Sparrow," "Lord, Lord, Lord," "Just a Closer Walk with Thee." As an older kid, he snuck into the nearby Dew Drop Inn, where Ray Charles, Bobby "Blue" Bland, and other R & B acts played.

His father died when he was sixteen, and from then on Anthony was the leader of the Lacen clan. By his late teens, he was that rare thing, a youngster gigging in uptown brass bands of men old enough to be his grandfather but over whom he towered. He was twenty, with years of playing in brass bands, when his friend, Gregg Stafford, asked him to join the Fairview Baptist Church Christian Marching Band in 1971.

Danny Barker, the jazz banjoist, had joined the Fairview Baptist Church. Its pastor asked him to form a traditional brass band with neighborhood kids who were playing instruments. The older musicians were dying. These kids needed a place to play and improve.

Barker had grown up in the traditional New Orleans jazz styles and took on the task with zeal. He had spent years in New York playing with Cab Calloway, Jelly Roll Morton, and various swing bands, and had married Blue Lu Barker, a blues singer. Fairview was his remarkable second act.

Barker recruited twelve-year-old Leroy Jones, whom he spotted practicing trumpet in the Jones family garage near the church. Jones was already an accomplished player. He assembled some other kids and Barker held rehearsals in the Joneses' garage, teaching them traditional brass band blues and gospel tunes from records on the Jones family stereo. A year or so later, Gregg Stafford joined, and he brought Anthony Lacen, whom Barker may or may not have dubbed Tuba Fats. These two were the older guys brought in to help the kids.

The band grew to more than thirty youngsters, and soon every church wanted the kids from Fairview Baptist playing their Sundays. This was music from deep in the city's history, what New Orleans had created with the brass marching bands of John Philip Sousa. Brass bands were typically made up of much older, more staid musicians. With Tuba Fats on the bottom, the kids gave the music new life. "It captured me and a lot of youngsters who would get out there and dance," Jones said. "There was something about the groove. We didn't think about it as being an old man's music. We sounded just as powerful as some of the older bands. We were getting hired for gigs they were getting hired for."

The older bands were unused to the competition. "The brass band leaders got together," Tuba told an interviewer. "I think that was the first time that they ever agreed on something—to break that band up." They alleged that Barker was exploiting children.

Barker dissolved the band in 1974. Many youngsters then joined Leroy Jones, who, at Barker's urging, formed the Hurricane Brass Band. Jones would later go out on his own to Europe and Asia, leading his own jazz quintet.

That Fairview Baptist band had infused the city's aging brass band world with new energy. Its kids grew into the next generation of great New Orleans musicians. Branford and Wynton Marsalis were in the Fairview band for a time. Leroy Jones is now one of the city's premier trumpet players. Gregg Stafford is another. Drummers Herlin Riley and Shannon Powell, and the late saxophonist Darryl Adams and the late trombonist Lucien

Barbarin, were among those who grew from Fairview into long musical careers.

Danny Barker died in 1994 at the age of eighty-five. The city holds a springtime music festival in his honor. His great accomplishment was to turn tuba-powered music into something kids made their own. They were listening to the intoxicating soul music of the 1970s: Marvin Gaye, Stevie Wonder, Curtis Mayfield, Al Green, the Temptations, Earth, Wind & Fire. Fairview Baptist trained these kids on their instruments and together they found a path to a future in old music, infusing it with soul and funk. Jazz funeral parades got a jolt that made them again the rage. Parade tempos and dancing got more frenetic.

All this dovetailed with a band directors' scene, not unlike the one in Brownsville, Texas, of conductors devoted to teaching music to children. As New Orleans desegregated its schools and music formed its economic as well as cultural heart, it was that rare city where band directors emerged from anonymity to become actual public figures, almost stars.

Clyde Kerr Sr. and Jr. taught in schools for a combined seven decades. At Bell Junior High School, Donald Richardson was legendary for his instruction and his discipline. He directed his blue-and-white Marching Crusaders on the school grounds from the building's second-floor fire escape, had them practicing turns down neighborhood streets, then sent them home exhausted every night. Richardson died in 1995 of a heart attack at fifty-three. By then, he had molded a generation of brass band leaders and school band directors. The late clarinetist Joe Torregano, who himself became a band director, told the *Times Picayune* newspaper, "Watching Donald Richardson and other educators,

I realized teaching was like becoming a priest. You had to prepare for a life of service."

At St. Augustine High School for boys, Edwin Hampton ran the "Marching 100" for more than fifty years. He declined university offers to leave the school and stayed at St. Augustine because, he said, he "just wanted to do something different." Walter "Doc" Harris taught at Carter G. Woodson and John F. Kennedy high schools and was, wrote one former student, "Father figure, role model and the best definition of a real Man I've ever known."

Yvonne Busch, for decades at George Washington Carver High School, was the city's lone female head band director, a great jazz musician who switched paths. She was "a lot like jazz," said drummer Herlin Riley, one of her students. "She was intense, but relaxed. She had rules, but she would give you the freedom to explore. She stressed discipline but encouraged self-expression."

Resources were scarce, so these directors shared equipment and musical arrangements. Under Jim Crow, Black marching bands couldn't perform on the streets. By the 1970s, though, Donald Richardson, Edwin Hampton, and the others were turning out some of the best marching bands in Louisiana, insisting that kids keep up their grades if they wanted to march.

The city produced huge numbers of skilled youths beginning their careers just as New Orleans musicians were moving from the neighborhoods to regional and national renown. Wynton Marsalis and his brothers, Branford, Jason, and Delfeayo, are the best known of these, but there were many more.

One in most local demand was Tuba Fats.

He spent a few years with the Olympia Brass Band, run by Harold "Duke" Dejan, the dean of the city's brass band world.

Soon, though, he formed Tuba Fats and the Chosen Few. "There were quite a few [older] tuba players who didn't like me," he told an interviewer. "They were scared that I was going to take their positions—because I was young. I was able to walk longer, blow longer. But there was room for another, for a young traditional brass band. That's why I formed the Chosen Few."

He kept doing other gigs—parades, funerals, Preservation Hall—but Jackson Square became his real stage, where it's likely Tuba Fats and the Chosen Few played for millions of people before he was done.

"He was the leader of the band," said Kermit Ruffins, a prominent trumpet player, who played with Tuba on the Square for years, "and he was a tuba player—not a trumpet player." Imagine that.

As a bandleader, Tuba mined the vast musical talent found casually on the streets of his city. "He was always into things that were live, in the moment, and he was like that his entire life," said Jerry Brock, who, among other things, founded WWOZ radio in 1980, which broadcast the music that the city was discovering could be an economic force. "His first vocalist was an eighty-year-old guy we all called Steamboat, who used to sell joints outside the Caledonia sitting in his long beige Cadillac, and who was a great blues singer."

On Jackson Square, Tuba Fats and the Chosen Few were like the city's house band. It was a tight unit, with Freddie "Shep" Sheppard, who had played with Ray Charles and Fats Domino, on sax, Robert Harris on trombone, Mari Watanabe on piano, Jerry Anderson or Shannon Powell on drums. Top New Orleans musicians, back in town after gigs elsewhere, dropped by to see friends and make some tax-free cash. "Musicians came from around the world who knew they couldn't get a gig in the clubs but knew they could get a sit-in with Tuba Fats in the Square," said Jerry Brock.

The city relied on Tuba Fats and the Chosen Few to create the kind of musicians New Orleans was known for. Young musicians could come try their chops. But "when you played, you better impress," said Julius McKee, a tuba player coming up in the generation following Tuba's.

McKee, now fifty-seven, was a teenage sousaphone player when he came to the Square for the first time in the early 1980s. He had grown up in the city's Ninth Ward, across a canal from the rest of the city.

Taking up the tuba in junior high, McKee heard that somewhere off in the city was a mythical mountain of a man called Tuba Fats, who had created a parade riff that bore his name. One day, McKee on tuba, with a friend on mellophone and another beating a box with a beer bottle, marched through the ward playing the Tuba Fats riff, replicating the jazz funerals and second lines across the canal. "People would come out of their houses," he said. "They had to call the police to break up the crowd for three middle school guys playing Tuba Fats."

Years later, McKee went to Jackson Square with his horn and saw Tuba Fats for the first time. Tuba didn't know him, didn't know if he was worthy. So McKee sat there all day. Happened a few times. "I remember when that day came, and they let me play a song or two," McKee told me. "He took a break. I seized the opportunity. They saw I could play."

Once in, young players learned from the master how to entertain an audience. Tuba beckoned children to sit on his lap as the band played. He sang. He charmed the crowd. Knew when to pass the bucket. It was the new work for New Orleans.

"Entertaining the people—I think that's very valuable to the city," said trumpeter Mark Braud. "To go to the Square and hear native New Orleanians playing the music of New Orleans, and somebody like Tuba Fats representing that."

The street music that revolved around Tuba delighted tourists. It was exactly what they expected to see, what the New Orleans travel posters depicted. He posed for endless photos. But to the musicians on the Square, it was deadly serious. Tuba had a work ethic like no other, and insisted his musicians come early—nine o'clock every morning, playing off and on until the city's live music curfew at eight.

Tuba drank and smoked marijuana. Friends caretaking his memory don't welcome discussion of what else he might have consumed. The streets of New Orleans were and remain famously rife with harder drugs. Yet to whatever extent substances were part of the life of Tuba Fats, they never fundamentally changed the peaceful, gentle giant.

He relished, in fact, his role as a keeper of peace. He was a parade musician above all else, and he walked interference, his horn and body naturally moving people out of the way of the oncoming musicians. Once, he had to lower the bell on the head of a second-liner who wouldn't move, but that kind of thing happened rarely.

His reign was a time of peace and prosperity on Jackson Square. An ecosystem of musicians, artists, and merchants lived from tourist money, and knew and cared for one another in whatever way they could.

Among them was the musical duo of David & Roselyn. He is White and plays guitar, she is Black and plays mandolin. They married in 1959 in California and raised a family playing music on the streets. I remember them playing daily at UC Berkeley in the early 1980s when I was at school there. I never knew them but never forgot them. Turns out they moved to New Orleans and played Jackson Square for years, they told me when I met them for the first time, now in their eighties, at their home in the city's Bywater neighborhood.

David and Roselyn's own love story is itself a powerful one, set against antimiscegenation laws, and a way of life that obeyed no established marital norm. They raised four kids on income from street performing, sent them all to college, and did well at Jackson Square when Tuba ran it.

Perhaps all that is why, despite fading memories, the couple remember when Tuba found a sweetheart.

THERE WAS LITTLE conventional about Linda Young. She had grown up singing in her father's Baptist church in a small Black community in the solidly White Appalachia of southwest Virginia. As a girl, she traveled with him often, singing at churches in the area. Yet she was also hard of hearing, diagnosed later in life as legally deaf, heard only certain tones, and needed hearing aids. The first time she wore them, a plane flew over and Linda jumped out of her skin.

She was big in every sense. Talkative, loud, the energy in every gathering. She sang constantly (and in tune, though legally deaf).

Tuba Fats and Linda Young: "Who said I can't play melodies?" Courtesy of Casper Schadler, Sabella Music, Good Morning to Heaven.

She left rural Virginia to study theater at the University of Miami, then dropped out at age twenty for Broadway, where she understudied, then toured with a theater group for several years. She returned to Florida, married, had two children, worked as a social worker, divorced. In her thirties, she had a boyfriend her family barely knew and didn't trust; he turned out to be controlling and violent. The couple left town quickly in 1989, quietly, just disappeared one day—leaving her car at the bus station and her children with her ex-husband, in a story her siblings never fully understood.

"I'm not sure there's a sweet story behind it all," said Hal Nester, a private detective from Missouri, who in frequent visits to New Orleans formed an unlikely, yet close friendship with Linda. "We never talked about her children. I think it was something she hated to think about."

Linda showed up in New Orleans, singing on the streets. The money rained down when she sang, she reported to her older sisters back in Florida, who found this hard to believe. But they knew she was a belter, filling the room whether she sang gospel or blues. You could hear her two blocks away. She was a woman, in other words, with a voice to match Tuba's horn. She ditched the violent boyfriend, and a while later she met Tuba.

"She came along and they fell for each other," David said. "That was something new for him—to be in love with that woman. They liked each other a lot. They spent time with each other. It was nice."

David and Roselyn watched, from their seats on the Square, this tuba love story that married these two people—his instrument, her voice. Tuba's T-shirts were less likely now to be gravy-stained. "She was good for him," said Roselyn. "He was cleaner. She washed his clothes. They were doing good, the two of them, playing on the streets together. They were like a team. It was the best thing that happened to both of them."

Along the way, Linda met another couple, whose story was about as strange. Ronda and Walt Rose had lived on the road, making money at the shopping malls of America, tying balloons into the shapes of wiener dogs and other animals. Somehow this made good money. They settled in New Orleans, now making rag rugs as a way of funding their first love, which was living in the French Quarter and hearing great music every day.

"She lived with us for six months and that's when she developed a relationship with Tuba," Ronda told me. "She was the only person I've ever known that every morning when she woke up, she was happy."

Linda and Tuba played Jackson Square, and night gigs at Bourbon Street clubs. They got gigs that neither could have obtained alone. Linda auditioned for a theater group to work in city schools. She reconnected with her children in Florida.

Their life wasn't what you could call stable. They stayed for a time in the now closed Hummingbird Hotel, where many musicians found weekly rates. But there was harmony, as if each found it natural to be with the other.

"I'd never seen him so in love," said Leroy Jones.

Among street musicians, this love story involving their captain found easy acceptance, and who knows, maybe it renewed the faith some of them had in affairs of the heart.

Soon the couple were touring Europe, invited by folks who saw them perform on the Square. Linda sent postcards to the Roses, addressed to "Ma and Pa," from Copenhagen and Venice. "We went on an island cruise and 100 dolphins appeared," she wrote from New Zealand. "They were almost hypnotic to view."

Tuba and Linda visited her sisters, who lived traditional middle-class lives in West Palm Beach. Linda was always shaking things up, living on the edge. So they were not shocked when she showed up with this enormous, quiet man she called Tuba, the most famous tuba player in all New Orleans, with stories of making music on the streets. She filled her tales with a cast of crazed, talented, driven musicians and artisans who seemed to have shaken loose from somewhere else, rolled down into New Orleans, and found one another in Jackson Square.

"She'd always talk about Jackson Square, singing in a troubadour style," said Bryan Boysaw, her nephew and a West Palm

Beach personal injury attorney. "We enjoyed hearing about that different life."

Tuba and Linda married in 1993. NOLA musical royalty played in the band that day: "It was like no other wedding," said her sister, Trula Vereen. "People from other countries. People from all over. We just didn't understand how popular they were." In England in 1995, the couple recorded an album of gospel songs Linda grew up singing around the house—*Good Morning to Heaven* it was called—with a photo of them together: "Mr. and Mrs. Anthony Lacen."

For those few years, Linda and Tuba lived content and unconventionally, immersed in their music, the Square, and each other.

Until, on tour in Germany in 1996, Linda took sick and was diagnosed with something as wretchedly unoriginal as advanced colon cancer.

She was thirty-nine.

Chapter 34

Tuba Fats in New Orleans

At Rest

"I'm just a lonely tuba player"

It is the conviction of many who knew Tuba Fats well that he never got over the death of Linda Young. His heart was broken—that's how they put it.

"Now when he'd sing 'Am I Blue,' it sounded to me like he was saying this is the real thing," remembered Seva Venet, a guitarist who played daily with the Chosen Few in those years. "It felt like that every time he sang the song."

Tuba and Linda were playing in Germany when a doctor there diagnosed her with colon cancer. She came home to New Orleans but then moved to Florida, where her older sister, Mary Boysaw, took charge. "Bohemian life is nice when you're healthy and doing well, but it's not at the end of life," said Bryan Boysaw, Linda's nephew.

The cancer moved quickly. She grew gaunt. She went into hospice and died in March 1997. In New Orleans, they held a jazz funeral for her. This time Tuba walked behind the coffin without his horn.

"He was very, very lonely after Linda died," said David Leonard, of David & Roselyn.

By then, the New Orleans brass band music had been hitting worldwide.

The Dirty Dozen Brass Band, made up of veteran New Orleans musicians, created a sound that they took far beyond the city. Tuba player Kirk Joseph started out at Bell Junior High under band director Donald Richardson. At Bell, Joseph heard the Ohio Players' funk hit "Skin Tight" and thought about how it might be played on the sousaphone. He kept rethinking the instrument, eventually electrifying it.

The Dozen recorded modern jazz and old gospel standards and toured with rock acts—Widespread Panic, Elvis Costello, the Black Crowes. "We did three hundred gigs a year for fifteen, sixteen years," said Roger Lewis, the band's co-founder and baritone saxophonist. "It took us all over the world." Younger bands formed. Rebirth Brass Band, propelled by Philip "Tuba Phil" Frazier, followed the Dozen to its own fame and a Grammy.

Brass bands were how young, Black New Orleanians made it out of the ghetto.

Yet this seemed to pass by Tuba Fats. First Linda, then his mother died. He gradually stopped caring for himself. He could be the same sweet Tuba, but his clothes looked shabbier than ever. His heart problem got worse.

In mourning, this prince of New Orleans had no safety net. His years of busking in Jackson Square had left him little backup other than that ecosystem of French Quarter artists and merchants. Walt and Ronda Rose offered him a place to live in a small apartment behind their house. Ronda tried to cook nutritious food for him, but she'd find candy, cookies hidden around the apartment.

On the Square, the Chosen Few began to grow. Tuba hadn't the energy to keep it a tight unit. Maybe he needed the companionship of musicians. By each afternoon during tourist season, two dozen musicians would be playing, all expecting a share of the bucket.

"But no matter how sprawling the band was, he'd sit here, three times as big as I am," said guitarist Seva Venet. "Kids would come up, take a picture on his knee. The moment the band started to fall apart, he'd play as many notes as it took, two or three notes, so that everything got locked back into place."

The larger the band, though, the more squabbles interrupted the music—mostly over CD sales from some artists that siphoned tips from others. These conflicts pained Tuba, but he didn't know how to stop it. "He just didn't have the energy," said Venet. "He'd fall asleep in almost every set. Doctors gave him different medication, so he wasn't falling asleep, but he didn't have the same energy."

In 2000, at a studio across the river, the English piano player John Richardson assembled musicians for a session with Tuba singing. The man loved to sing, Richardson told me, and "there was nothing of him singing."

Tuba had a court date that almost led to canceling the session, but District Attorney Harry Connick Sr., father of the jazz pianist and singer, intervened. The band that day included Craig Klein on trombone, Mark Braud on trumpet, Freddie Sheppard on sax, Walter Payton on bass, Bob French on drums, and John Rodli on guitar—all top NOLA musicians. Above it all, Tuba sang with his sweet, gravelly baritone: "Am I Blue," "Lord, Lord, Lord," "His Eye Is on the Sparrow."

"He picked the songs that moved him," said trumpeter Mark Braud. "These were songs he had heard all his life. I'm not sure he knew all the words to every song, but it's in the spirit of true improvisation. His delivery would send chills through you."

John Richardson gave Tuba copies of the CD. "Sell it on Jackson Square," Richardson told him. "You'll sell hundreds." Richardson never knew whether Tuba tried to sell those CDs or not.

The album was never properly released. It is known only as "Tuba Fats"—a joyous, raw recording that captures a moment in the city's time and is a final testament to the man. It is among the greatest records I've heard in decades of listening to New Orleans music. I've been listening to it while writing this story.

The record includes Clarence "Frogman" Henry's R&B classic "Ain't Got No Home," which Tuba recasts as "I'm just a lonely tuba player, and I ain't got no horn."

"That song told his story," said Craig Klein. " 'I'm a lonely tuba player.' There's an underlying darkness to it."

IN JANUARY 2004, TUBA and other musicians took a trip to South Africa. They played for the King of the Zulus. Tuba swam in the ocean. Then they flew home. He felt ill. Ronda Rose thought it had something to do with the long flight home. He didn't move much on planes and, given his size, flights were always uncomfortable. He went to the hospital after he returned home, thinking he had the flu. Doctors advised surgery to put in a pacemaker. He said no. So they prescribed some medication, but Walgreens was closed when he got home that night. The next day, Ronda and Walt didn't see him pass their store. Nor was he at the Square.

When they heard nothing after calling for him outside his apartment that night, Walt broke down the door. He found Tuba Fats dead on the floor. He was fifty-three. Nearby was an old, dented sousaphone.

"He told me when he went to Africa that his journey was done," said his sister, Joyce.

The coroner's office needed five hours to move him. They didn't have a body bag big enough, Ronda remembered, and they had to search their office for one that was. They wheeled him out, his feet sticking out of the bag.

Tuba once told an interviewer how he imagined dying—not unlike John Henry. "I wanna be onstage in front of a big audience," he said. "I wanna play that last note. I wanna set my horn down and just keel on over."

It didn't happen exactly that way. Like John Henry, though, Tuba Fats died when his heart gave out. The coroner's office called it an enlarged heart. An enlarged heart is a symptom of coronary disease, high blood pressure, and other afflictions that can be caused in turn by diabetes, poor diet, obesity, and drug use. But those who knew Anthony Lacen prefer to take this diagnosis as metaphorical. He had, they say, a heart too big for this world.

Walt Rose raised money among the French Quarter merchants. Tuba had an insurance policy, with a burial plot in

St. Louis Cemetery No. 1, not far from Jackson Square. His body was too big for the plot. They found a larger one out by the airport. More money was raised later for a headstone.

New Orleans had never seen a funeral for a tuba player like the one held for Tuba Fats. There wasn't room for everyone at Gallier Hall, the majestic old city hall on St. Charles Avenue. A brass band made up of the best musicians in New Orleans played "I'll Fly Away." Chosen Few trombonist Robert Harris sang "When It's Sleepy Time Down South." Gregg Stafford gave the eulogy. Tuba, he said, did everything he wanted to do in the short span of his life.

Mourners sang and cried and spilled out into the street.

That cold January morning, a couple thousand people snaked down Bourbon Street, through the French Quarter, past Jackson Square, and up into the Treme. His silver coffin sat on a cart pulled by two black horses, followed by a man holding a cherry-red horn Tuba had been given, which his sisters have kept. Clumps of musicians played at different spots through the procession, which moved so slowly that at times it felt more like a street festival than the up-tempo jazz funerals that the city was now used to. There was no one to organize the musicians and propel them, no one to move people out of the way. Fourteen tubas, and who knows how many trumpets and trombones. "I had never seen that many tuba players in one spot," said Julius McKee. "All these tuba players, some of them I didn't even know. They were huge guys. All of us playing the dirge together."

Tragedy struck as the procession came to an end at Joe's Cozy Corner bar in the Treme neighborhood.

The owner, "Papa Joe" Glasper, a retired construction worker, was a fixture there. He cleaned the streets around the Cozy Corner, and had one of the best jukeboxes in town. Second-line marchers and musicians often ended up at the Cozy Corner. Street vendors commonly followed these parades. They were the bane of Papa Joe's business, undercutting his beer prices without having to meet his overhead. He'd shooed vendors away a few times that afternoon.

One of them was Richard Gullette, selling beer just outside the Cozy Corner. He finally confronted Papa Joe. "Get back in the bar where you belong, old man!"

At this, Joe went inside his bar and came back out with a pistol in his waistband. Gullette lunged for him, apparently fearing for his life. Glasper, fearing the same for himself, pulled the gun and shot him dead. A jury found Glasper guilty of manslaughter, and he died in prison a year later, at sixty-four.

A juror later wrote to the *New Yorker* magazine, which had reported on the incident: It "was a case of both men letting their fear control their actions."

It is also the kind of incident Tuba Fats had had a gift for preventing.

WITHOUT TUBA FATS, Jackson Square "didn't have the same energy," Ronda Rose told me. "There was a huge void. He was not just a big man physically, but he was a big man to a whole lot of people."

"When he died," said Seva Venet, "something ended."

The Dirty Dozen Brass Band put out a gospel album, *Funeral for a Friend*, with his cherry-red tuba on the cover. Its first track is a jazz funeral version of "Just a Closer Walk with Thee."

A block from the Cozy Corner, and across the street from John Richardson's house in the Treme, is a grassy vacant lot at the corner of St. Phillip and Robertson. Richardson put in picnic benches and a sign asking those who use the space to observe rules of decorum, which most people do. Folks from the neighborhood clean it, and Richardson pays the real estate taxes. A metal artisan carved a sign from sheet metal claiming the space in Tuba's honor. Twenty years after the big man's death, "Tuba Fats Square" is where many parades end.

The year after he died, Hurricane Katrina came through and knocked down a lot. Emerging from the wreckage, the city turned its failing public schools into independent charter schools. But few charter schools are large enough to support band directors and marching bands. In New Orleans, of all places, music education has weakened. It's unclear how the town will continue to beget the kinds of musicians who gave it life for so long.

Anthony Lacen transformed the instrument most associated with the city of his birth, giving new possibilities to New Orleans and the music crucial to it, helping forge a new genre rooted in history yet looking forward and not frozen in time. As Chalino Sanchez had done in Los Angeles, he helped make the tuba a horn for kids to be cool with. Tuba's twenty-four-year-old grandnephew, Blake McCarter, is a tuba player in a brass band of men in their twenties. He claims to know at least thirty young tuba players around town.

All of this grew from a tuba player who seemed content just to spend his life doing his thing, shaping something original from the city's musical currents that ran through him. Tuba certainly traveled the world. But in the brass band renaissance that grew from New Orleans, he never had the recording contracts or the major shows other bands enjoyed. Dirty Dozen made some twenty albums, and played dates from Ames to Amsterdam. Rebirth Brass Band won its Grammy in 2012.

Tuba mostly stayed on Jackson Square. "He enjoyed being at home in his domain," said Leroy Jones.

Like any self-respecting tuba player, though, Tuba Fats was forever rebelling in his own sweet, peaceful way against the limitations that others imagined for him and his horn.

One final scene from his life that Gregg Stafford remembers:

Playing a club on Bourbon Street one night, Stafford stepped outside to find Tuba on the sidewalk towering above passing tourists and playing melodies on his sousaphone. This was after Tuba's first marriage had broken up, and he was living in a fleabag hotel and probably fairly desperate. Stafford, a New Orleans trumpeter also rooted in parades, had never heard a tuba playing melodies all alone. To Stafford, that's just not what a tuba was for.

"I said, 'Tuba Fats, how you gon' play on the street all by yourself? He said, 'I just play melodies, that's all I'm doing.' Well, that seemed awkward to me, out of the box, you know. But there he was on Bourbon Street at night. He said, 'Ain't nothin' wrong with me playing by myself. Who said I can't play on the street by myself? Who said I can't play melodies?'"

Playing melodies on the tuba—for himself, perhaps, as much as for the tourists.

FINALE

Chapter 35

The Tuba Player Who Had to Quit

"It gave me all this confidence, gave me an identity and purpose—the tuba did."

Stable tuba employment is so rare that those who find it hold on for dear life.

It is also the case that, given the beating the tuba exacts on the human lips and lungs, those who find such employment generally last about thirty years in it.

So, with the clockwork regularity you expect from cicadas, the best tuba jobs tend to appear en masse, then disappear about as quickly.

Players who found work after World War II were retiring just as the Tuba Woodstock generation discovered itself. Many who attended the seminal 1973 event moved into those jobs and hunkered down.

In the early 2000s, they began to retire. Stable, prestigious jobs came open in unprecedented numbers all across America, with symphonies in Columbus, Rochester, San Francisco, Boston, Milwaukee, New York, Cleveland, Philadelphia, and many other major cities.

Tuba twenty- and thirtysomethings, eking out livings playing weddings and teaching part time, raced to fill them, aware that the jobs might not come open again in their tuba lifetime. A nationwide game of tuba musical chairs ensued. Then the music stopped.

The Great Tuba Job Market of 2002–6 is today spoken of with reverence, nostalgia, even sadness. (Look for the next tuba job boom in about 2034.)

This is despite years of good news for the horn.

As the tuba pushed out of its ghetto of elephants, clowns, and whole notes, players got new repertoire. Ever more perfect tubas made the instrument easier to play. Tuba Woodstock opened minds to a collective tuba consciousness. As high school bands grew, more tubas were needed. And a new squad of tuba superheroes arrived to show youths what they might aspire to.

All this created a boom in tuba players across America. University tuba performance programs multiplied, using scholarships to attract students for whom the horn had been a musical, even personal, revelation. The late Roger Bobo, one of the tuba's great virtuosos and its first soloist, contended that no other orchestral instrument had seen such growth in players, repertoire, and instrument quality in so short a time. "There's never been anything parallel to that in music history," Bobo said when I interviewed him in 2014.

Problem is, stable tuba jobs have not kept pace. They remain painfully scarce, except roughly every thirty years. Rest of the time, the horn can provide a living for only the tiniest fraction of the young people who its promise inspires.

I was thinking about all that as I spoke with a fellow named Bobby Ortiz. I called Ortiz because his college instructor John Van Houten told me he had a compelling story about how people who fixate on a tuba career are forced to give it up, and what they take with them.

Ortiz grew up in Orange County, California. In high school band, he played flute and piccolo. But his junior year, he switched to tuba and found it more fun. A bit more manly, he felt. The flute, however, bequeathed him the lung capacity that made the tuba easier to play. Soon the horn became his life.

Bobby Ortiz went to California State University, Long Beach, to study tuba performance. He was part of the school's orchestra and took lessons from Van Houten. During those years, one night, he saw Øystein Baadsvik perform.

Baadsvik is Norwegian. He is also the only person in the world who makes a living entirely from solo tuba playing. Baadsvik has done this, in my opinion, by combining world-class skills with rambunctious musical taste and a zest for tearing at the scaffolding of cornball culture that surrounds the horn. His albums contain hip photography and no tuba puns. He tours constantly, often to those now multitudinous U.S. college tuba programs. (Baadsvik is also, as I write, the president of the International Tuba Euphonium Association.)

That night, Baadsvik played "Fnugg"—a short groove of didgeridoo-like funkiness that to my ears is made to be blasted from truck stereos at stoplights. On the piece, he uses a technique he invented and calls "lip beat," which adds a percussive sound to the tuba. *Fnugg* is Norwegian for "fluff," or "snowflake," and over the years it has become kind of a hit among tuba players. "This guy is playing [the horn] like a violin," Ortiz told me. "I said, 'That's it, that's the kind of tuba I want to play.'"

"That changed Bobby's life," Van Houten told me. "For the first time, he heard that the tuba wasn't just a one-dimensional instrument. He could use it to be a soloist. He had a path."

Ortiz would have to patch together various gigs—orchestras, community bands, teaching. But the horn required that kind of self-reliant, punk rock, DIY attitude. The faint of heart didn't take up the tuba. You had to learn creative marketing as well as music. But if he did, Ortiz figured, part of his career might then be as a Baadsvikian solo player.

He saved money to buy a tuba Baadsvik helped design. He brought Baadsvik to Cal State Long Beach for a performance and master class. He dissected "Carnival of Venice," that tubist cavalry charge from *Bill Bell and His Tuba*, until he knew it by heart.

Unwittingly, though, Bobby Ortiz had entered a system that allowed him to pursue his dream while making it almost certain he would not attain it.

THIS CONUNDRUM HAD to do with those university tuba programs. Universities began hiring tuba professors in the 1970s. Instrument instruction helped promote the prestige of the music department, perhaps the whole school. But in time, a self-sustaining system took hold. College programs, offering scholarships, never stopped forming, and high school marching bands kept feeding them students. They produced graduates who further saturated an already deadened job market, creating a "tuba education industrial complex," as one former tuba player termed it.

This is true of many instruments. But university tuba programs seem particularly untethered to any real-world market demand. I tried counting them all and gave up: the universities of Arizona, Arizona State, Michigan, Denver, Georgia, Northern Illinois, Southern Illinois, Illinois, Missouri, Iowa, New Mexico, Northern Alabama, Louisiana State, Mississippi, Texas, Oklahoma. Tom Treece counted more thoroughly and found nine hundred tuba performance majors at U.S. universities. Whatever the number, they turn out many times more tuba graduates every year than the country's total number of full-time, salaried performance tuba jobs, which themselves come open only about once a generation.

The tuba job market put me in mind of my college economics studies and Karl Marx's description of late-nineteenth-century industrial capitalism: vast, expanding numbers of equally skilled workers desperate for dwindling jobs.

This describes what faces many musicians, actors, artists, and singers. (I wrote part of this book in Nashville, a magnet for lone songwriters facing tough odds.) But few feel it more acutely and alone than one who plays the tuba. Nationally, there are more jobs as state governor than major symphony tuba chairs. Two hundred highly skilled players audition for every job. Nor are the couple of hundred U.S. military bands enough to absorb the tuba grads leaving universities every spring.

The tuba holds out such promise to those who take it up—teenage boys, in the main. "Most tuba players are people who are counted out, or they were this odd-fitting kid that found something that spoke for them," said John Van Houten. Van Houten said he was bullied badly in middle school until he took up the tuba. "It gave me all this confidence, gave me an identity and purpose—the tuba did. Tuba was the only thing I could do well."

Yet behind a horn of such optimism and possibility is a grim economic reality. Well into my tuba trek, I realized that across America is a hidden diaspora of former tuba players who have turned to careers that have nothing to do with the horn.

"I'm now a dump truck driver," wrote one respondent to a post I put up on a Reddit tuba group.

Another: "I'm a mental health therapist now."

"I moved to the woods. Haven't touched a tuba in a year and I'm much happier and healthier."

"I've since found a lane for myself in tech and I have a family now too," wrote a fourth. "I've only put down the horn for now, though."

Bobby Ortiz was among the best players his college produced. The horn moved him and he loved working hard at it. But as he studied, something ominous replaced the excitement that came with the horn. His tuba peers were planning other careers before they even graduated. Van Houten, one of the top Hollywood soundtrack session musicians, told him another tuba player was always there ready to take his job. Ortiz heard superior players at other Southern California universities.

A few years into this pursuit, Bobby Ortiz realized he wasn't so sure that passion was enough to endure a grind that approached soul-destroying.

"I felt I could have hammered it out," he said. "But do I want to be that starving musician? I said, 'I don't think so.'"

All this happened just as Ortiz was actually doing the kind of tuba playing he had hoped to do. One night, he walked onstage, his horn strapped to his body, fronting a brass ensemble, and played Baadsvik's "Fnugg" to a packed house that his sounds mesmerized. But that was his last big show. He sold his Baadsvik custom tuba a few months later. He was moving toward an interest in science, marine biology at first, then providing medical care for fish and animals. This different world thrilled him as the tuba had. It just offered a more balanced life. He applied at and was admitted to a veterinary school in Ireland.

With that, he seemed to leave his youth on the way to adulthood. Bobby Ortiz had to pursue the horn; had he not, he would have regretted it the rest of his life. Only the tuba couldn't come with him now.

Yet as he left it, the tuba was like a folk saint that still watched over him, repaying the love he had for it. The way he sees it, the horn taught him focus and the persistence to practice something over and over with precision until perfect—like cutting open the stomach of a tiny mammal—with pride in one's work the only reward. He cultivated a willingness to never stop learning, to roll with new situations; how to nurture love for what he does through daily effort, despite failure and strange looks from others.

The tuba taught him all this. It just couldn't fund a healthy, happy life. Instead, the horn prepared him for a life without it. A beautiful and selfless gift, he felt.

Today Dr. Bobby Ortiz is one of six exotic pet veterinarians in all of Ireland. A day before we spoke, Ortiz had removed the kidney of a Syrian hamster. He's repaired the wings of owls and done liver resections on rabbits.

Exotic pet vets, it turns out, are the tuba players of the veterinary world. They are few and far between, and when they get together, they have conversations about things that interest only them, that only they understand.

Bobby Ortiz never could bring himself to finally, cleanly, say that he was done with his beloved horn. He just gradually moved away from it, trying not to hear the doors closing behind him.

He married an Irish woman and they have a daughter. Bobby Ortiz is happy with his life and his family and is proud of his new profession. He has the priceless contentment of a well-meshed life.

Yet every so often, he goes online looking for used tubas, the way you scroll Instagram to see what your old flame is up to. At times, he remembers those shows, watching Øystein Baadsvik, and his own final Baadsvikian moment.

The last decade has taken him far from a musical career, happily so, and he regrets nothing about leaving the tuba. But "in my mind," says Bobby Ortiz, "I think of myself as always going back."

Chapter 36

Arnold Jacobs III

Brian

"There are times when you just say nothing. You just revel in it."

In a wood-frame house on a small lake in suburbs north of Chicago, Brian Frederiksen takes me through his downstairs den, which amounts to a museum to the great Arnold Jacobs.

His shelves are display cases for gadgets that Jacobs repurposed from medical supply houses and air-conditioning shops to measure his students' lung capacity: the Spirometer and the Inspiron. Now sixty-nine years old, Frederiksen has Arnold Jacobs' mouthpieces and supposedly the last tuba Jacobs ever played well after he had retired and sold his fabled Yorks to the Chicago Symphony. *Gray's Anatomy* and the laminated maps of the human head and torso that Jacobs called the Thin Man stand watch over the den, as they did for so long in Jacobs' studio in downtown Chicago.

For the better part of twenty-five years, Frederiksen was Jacobs' willing and unpaid driver, tour organizer, travel agent, videographer, and biographer.

Jacobs strode atop the tuba world then, a herculean figure to tuba players who toiled alone in orchestras and marching bands. They were proud to know that this teacher to whom so many musicians flocked was, like them, a tubist first, and one of the century's greatest. Jacobs urged students to hear the song in the music they were trying to play. Those who took his master classes and private lessons today count themselves lucky, and tell their own students of that time.

Brian Frederiksen installed grab bars in Jacobs' shower and soothed the great man when poor health and retirement winnowed his visitors and left Jacobs feeling forgotten. "This happens to the top symphony musicians," Frederiksen says. "I told him, 'The world won't forget about you.'"

To that end, Frederiksen videotaped 250 hours of Jacobs' master classes, which students today mine for insight. His students were "my boys," Jacobs often said. In those classes, they hung on his droplets of wisdom as if from some Buddhist monk, in awe of this man and his talent, and how he relished discussing how they might nurture their own.

Brian Frederiksen made all that happen.

He had taken up the tuba in elementary school. He was a big, nerdy outcast of a kid, as so many are when they find the tuba. The horn showed him something precious within himself. In high school, he heard Arnold Jacobs for the first time on the Chicago Symphony recording of Béla Bartók's *Concerto for Orchestra*.

"I've never been the same player since," he tells me. From then on, "I had the Arnold Jacobs sound in my head. Then it's starting to develop through my horn. Later, I would learn that you play two instruments at once: the horn in your head and the horn in your hand."

He attended Tuba Woodstock in 1973 as a freshman tuba student in college, then left the school after the next year. He enrolled in a conservatory in the Fine Arts Building on Michigan Avenue in Chicago, where Arnold Jacobs had his studio. But instead of taking lessons at the conservatory, Brian took lessons from Jacobs. After each lesson, he would have to sit and absorb what he had just heard. "I had that feeling every class with Arnold," he told me.

Such a brilliant light was intoxicating. So Frederiksen just hung around. He was the only tuba student in the Fine Arts Building most days, certainly the most consistent. "I started as Arnold's coffee runner, then as his assistant, then went out on the road with him," Frederiksen says. He helped Jacobs remodel his studio.

Upon finishing a Northwestern University master's degree in tuba performance, Brian enrolled in a community college data-processing course. The money he made from then on, most of it, came from computing and from stereo installation, back when elaborate sound systems were in vogue.

He auditioned for a symphony job or two—along with a couple hundred hopeful tubists. He scratched out an occasional freelance gig at a wedding or church. A musician, the saying goes, is someone who puts a $5,000 instrument in a $500 car to get to a $50 gig. That was Brian Frederiksen.

He knew so many tubists who studied hard, played as if their lives depended on it. Then one day they sold the instrument and you never heard from them again. He was this close to cutting all ties to the horn, too. Instead, a unique path presented itself: as Arnold Jacobs' acolyte. Maybe he made it happen by just showing up. Either way, he gradually became *the* guy close to the legend. He spent years doing whatever Arnold Jacobs asked of him with the devotion of a religious disciple for the sole recompense of being near the tuba's brightest star.

Jacobs retired in 1988 and spent the last ten years of his life holding master classes around the country. He didn't need the money so much, but he was a natural teacher and he fed on the students' energy and adoration. Brian Frederiksen managed the logistics, went on these trips, videotaped the classes, and watched as a light and lively spirit overtook Jacobs each time.

Almost a quarter century after Jacobs passed, Brian Frederiksen grows animated talking about those days. Those master-class trips, especially—just him, and Jacobs and Jacobs' wife, Gizella. The week they spent with the U.S. Marine Band in D.C. That week at Florida State, and another at the University of Oregon. Every night, he watched *Star Trek* with the Jacobses. "Arnold watched it when the show was on—then on reruns until the day he died. Every day."

Jacobs and Harvey Phillips, Mr. Tuba, were the tuba titans of the day. Brian was on a first-name basis with them, doing whatever they asked, for love and no pay. Their wives became his "tuba moms."

Once, he and Jacobs visited Phillips at TubaRanch in Bloomington, Indiana. Phillips had Brian install a new operating system on his computer, as Phillips had no understanding of it. This was laborious work at the time. The gathering was upstairs, but Frederiksen dutifully went down to Phillips' computer and got to it.

"I'm downstairs at Harvey's desk, with these floppy discs—remember them? It was boring but it was for Harvey Phillips, you know. Still, I'm getting bored to death. All of a sudden, who tromps through the door but Harvey Phillips and Arnold Jacobs to keep me company. Harvey has his recordings. I'm sitting at Harvey's desk. He starts putting recordings on.

"Every tuba player has hero worship for these two guys, whether they know it or not. But I'm sitting in there *with* them. I'm doing the computer *for* Harvey. They're starting to shoot the shit and they're talking about the old days. I'm just soaking it in. There are times when you just say nothing. You just revel in it."

In retirement, Jacobs yearned to have a book written about him and his teaching. Years passed and nobody came forward. Frederiksen watched this, anguished at the idea that Jacobs would feel that no one cared.

"Finally, I said, 'Fine, I'll do it.'"

Frederiksen embarked on a four-year journey to write the biography of Arnold Jacobs and his pedagogy and the Chicago Yorks and all the rest. He had never written a book, and once it was published, he never wrote another. He published *Arnold Jacobs: Song and Wind* himself under WindSong Press, an enterprise he started solely for that purpose. The book, with Jacobs on the cover playing one of the mighty Yorks, has sold twelve thousand copies.

"I could have made more money working the drive-up window at Taco Bell," he tells me during a visit. "Who would want to write a book about the tuba?"

But one of the best days of his life came in 1996, eight years after Jacobs retired and two years before he died. The book arrived. The Chicago Symphony store put it on display. After the concert that day, customers crowded in to buy the book. Jacobs arrived and was surrounded by people asking him to sign it. Brian stood off to the side, beaming at the sight of Jake reinvigorated as he accepted the adoration of concertgoers.

Arnold Jacobs died in 1998, at home, in his sleep. He was eighty-three. His son Dallas called Brian, who was doing computer work in a downtown Chicago office. Brian took the news to the orchestra's hall on Michigan Avenue. The orchestra president went down to interrupt the rehearsal and announce it. From there, Brian went to the Fine Arts Building, where he told Tommy, the elevator operator. "That's how word spread."

Two months later, they held a memorial for Jacobs. Harvey Phillips, Bud Herseth, and Gene Pokorny spoke, and brass players from the orchestra played. Through his students, his family wrote, "the contribution of the Arnold Jacobs tradition and method of teaching will exist for generations to come."

But for Brian Frederiksen, a lot seemed to halt right then.

Jacobs left an old tuba to his faithful, longtime, unpaid assistant, who now lives on Social Security, an occasional computer job, and the memories of his days with the master.

Arnold Jacobs had something profound and new to give the world through his teaching. Brian Frederiksen was sure of that. He was allowed to be there by his side, make plane reservations, watch *Star Trek* on television, and film those master classes. Who else can say that? It connected Brian to the tuba he loved. Otherwise, he might have just left the horn and no one would have heard from him again. Presence was all the pay Brian needed.

Much of what Frederiksen has done since is in service to Jacobs' memory. Digitizing those master class videos, for one. He maintains a website dedicated to Arnold Jacobs, with links to dozens of articles and interviews and a history of the York tubas. He has even compiled a bibliography of all the books on physiology and psychology that Jacobs owned. He sold Inspiron breathing apparatuses online to tuba students, until the manufacturer discontinued the item. He also stocked the Breath Builder, a plastic tube with a ping-pong ball used to expand breathing, and the Voldyne, which measures and expands air inhalation. Frederiksen sold them at brass instrument conferences for several years, presenting videos of Jacobs discussing his teaching philosophy, a series he called *Arnold Jacobs Almost Live*. Sales, though, were already falling when Covid came along to finish them off.

Jacobs' wife and son have passed away. A daughter-in-law is in Florida. Jacobs' teaching indeed lives on in his students, on a YouTube channel, in a couple of books, a smartphone app, and in that wood-frame house by that tiny lake in a suburb north of Chicago.

"Arnold went beyond the tuba, that's why he's remembered," Frederiksen says.

I agree with him. Jacobs' story was monumental, and I have spent considerable effort telling it. But just as interesting, I tell Brian, is his own story. The story of a guy who devoted himself to a man unknown to all but a tiny sliver of the country's population, then to that man's legacy, without payment or much else in tangible return.

Brian plays occasionally in an amateur community orchestra. For a while he was giving a local kid tuba lessons in exchange for weekly lawn mowing. During Covid, he and a trumpet player sat on his lake dock at three o'clock on Memorial Day afternoon and played "Taps"—part of *Taps Across America*.

Don't get old, Jacobs used to tell his students, you won't like it.

"Well, I did, and I don't," Brian says.

He lives in that house that his mother paid off before she died. He navigates it with difficulty. Before one of my visits, he tore a meniscus and the stairs down to his den grew treacherous. He can no longer walk around the lake. How long can I live in a house with stairs? he wonders aloud, and what am I going to do with all this tuba stuff?

He works out three times a week, to preserve his ability to walk. But soon, he tells me, he may be unable to make it down those stairs to the den. Then he may just have to abandon all that he has assembled—the gadgets, the Thin Man, the mail room for WindSongpress.com, the master-class videotapes.

Then he may have to finally close the door on all the Arnold Jacobs stuff, all that Brian's life has been about, and have no choice then but to leave it down there to gather dust.

Chapter 37

The Perfect Tuba

Zig's Last Horn

"He was trying to save the factory by making tubas."

By 2009, the good times for Zig Kanstul's company were ending. During the first years of the new century, the company had a hundred employees; the economy raged, and so did horn sales.

But the mortgage bubble recession of 2007 had drained a lot of that. Plus, Chinese makers were undercutting Kanstul's student horn business. "My father thought instruments were recession-proof," said Mark Kanstul, Zig's youngest son. "The Chinese disproved that." Competition from the two conglomerates—Conn/Selmer and Yamaha—also intensified. They spread money around to players to endorse their horns.

That's how his son Jack remembers it. Kanstul Instruments didn't have money to pay players, or to do much advertising at all. High school bands that had used Kanstul horns switched to Yamaha.

Plus, there was Zig's longtime mistress, and problems with her daughter, and conflicts with his sons, and workers who saw what they could get away with and did.

Had there been a younger worker Zig had prepared the way Foster Reynolds had prepared him, perhaps things would have been different. But Zig was wary that anyone he taught would end up competing with him. "We're not here to teach people," he'd say. And none of his sons wanted to learn the trade.

I visited his factory in 2014. He once had dozens of employees; now there were fifteen or so. This was years before I embarked on this project; I was just following a hunch. I interviewed Zig Kanstul with Jack. We were surrounded by golden and silver tubes and by horn bells lined up like the mouths of a choir, ornate metal intestines, calipers, mandrels, lathes, lines of trombones and euphoniums, and everywhere the smell of brass. One great thing about being a reporter: You get to see factories and how things are made. I was in awe of the Kanstul shop.

Zig Kanstul lived amid all this. He had the talent to make some of humankind's most elegant metal creations. His horns could express the deepest musical creativity the human brain could muster. Yet he seemed gray, suspicious, joyless. Jack did the talking; Zig spoke sparely. He seemed wary of opening himself too much, afraid to part with information. I wasn't sorry to leave the interview. "That was my dad," Jack said when I met him again years later.

My assessment, accurate on its face, later felt unfair. We all come to be who we are as the result of a lifetime of experience that others can't fully comprehend. I might have been like Zig were I in a life-or-death struggle with cheap Chinese imports.

To compete, Zig was turning to high-end versions of the instruments he once made for student bands. Into this dire situation had stepped Bob Carpenter and Tom Treece, with their York tuba metallurgical data. "Zig could spot somebody coming who'll waste his time," said Charles Hargett, his former sales manager. "He didn't see that with them. He thought, these guys are serious. They became friends, and Zig didn't make friends."

The resounding success of the Kanstul bell in the Orlando Philharmonic rehearsals had energized Carpenter and Treece. But Zig was already there. He wanted to get started immediately making tubas. Not just any tuba—the Chicago Yorks. What better way to restore lustre to the Kanstul name, and carve a new market niche, than to reproduce the perfect tubas, the All-American horns that boldly broadcast the confidence of a country in the postwar world. It was the final piece in his strategy to save the company.

That he *could* bring them back, that he could make a tuba in America again, the way York had done—this Zig Kanstul did not doubt, though he was now past eighty. His factory testified to his abilities. Who else had set up an independent plant like his? He had a David's pugnacious chip on his shoulder when it came to industry Goliaths. He knew their might. He perhaps saw himself as another Bill "Pops" Johnson. All this might explain why, when all he had to do was make trumpets and go out revered with a million in the bank, Zig Kanstul took on this new project.

"He was trying to save the factory by making tubas," his son Jack told me. "What my dad said was this: 'Sometimes you gotta do something nobody's done in a while.' "

His friends Dale and Diane Olson hadn't seen him for a time. Then, "at one point, he told me, 'I'm going to duplicate the York,'" said Dale Olson.

"It was a challenge," said Diane Olson, "the one thing he had not done."

So Zig Kanstul took the leap. He may have seen no other choice for his factory. He retooled to make high-end tubas. The cost of this alone, before even one tuba was made, was close to $200,000. "It was desperate," said Jack Kanstul. "My brother Mark tried to convince him not to do it."

Kanstul made its first York-inspired tuba in 2010. At least a dozen players across the country insisted on updates as the process began. A new tuba maker in America—a miraculous thing. No tuba player imagined it possible. They followed each development. One day that December, Bob Carpenter answered the phone, and Stan Freese was on the line. Freese is a boisterous Anaheim tuba player who had spent years at Disney and became its top talent booker. He could legitimately claim to have hired more tuba players than anyone on earth. He had played the tuba on the Great Wall of China, visiting the country with President Richard Nixon in 1972 as a soloist with the University of Minnesota. He was a tuba player at home in the world of media promotion, and he knew all the top musicians in Southern California.

He wanted to help promote what they were making, which, as Freese saw it, was "the world's greatest tuba." He wanted to know more York history to market the horns. He was organizing a Tuba Christmas celebration, with hundreds of tubists, and wanted a Kanstul tuba at the event. From then on, Freese took to dropping by the Kanstul factory on his way to Disneyland.

The team contacted tuba pros to hear their opinions of the horn. One was John Van Houten, a frequent Hollywood soundtrack tubist. "It was a magical time," Van Houten said. "They were really on to something. I was taking the horn to every job and coming back with notes on how it played."

Carpenter and Treece wrote their life histories into a press release. They were, they felt, recreating the knowledge, detail by detail, that had vanished with York workers.

Carpenter thought often of these workers. In the 1930s, their technology was primitive, yet they had figured out so much that was flawless. The taper of the bell, the braces, the metallurgy, the crafting of the lead pipe. That happened, he figured, because the real Yorks had grown from a lush environment of brass tinkering, thick like a rainforest, from which the tiniest new ideas and approaches sprang to life like new species from the needs of daily labor. So much of what York workers did, Carpenter imagined, was trial and error, inching forward despite occasional failure. Hunches and homemade remedies that worked became tried-and-true solutions. Such an innovative environment, once destroyed, could not be recreated.

Carpenter and Treece spoke a lot about that to me—about the know-how that left America when laboratories like the York shop closed.

I had seen this, too, in writing about opioids. As factory floors and tool-and-die shops died, their towns were drained of jobs. But those towns also lost the intangibles of community defense. They were deprived of the skills, and the approach to life, of people like Bill Johnson and his workers, who had been dedicated to the optimistic idea that progress came with hard work in minute steps.

I did not think it a coincidence that our national epidemic of opioid addiction hit these towns first and worst. This thought returned to me when I least expected it—in this tuba endeavor. A culture seemed to lose something huge when it no longer knew what it took to make stuff as intricate as, say, the perfect tuba.

To relearn some of those skills, Treece and Carpenter turned Carpenter's big old Holton tuba into a virtual research project. They permanently attached the bell Zig Kanstul had sent them. They soldered new braces on the horn in better places so the tubes didn't wobble with the air vibrating through them. They learned to trim the metal so the horn was more in tune with itself—a process I can say I still don't fully understand. They learned to "de-stress" a tuba by strategically loosening and tightening screws. The grateful Holton now played better than ever.

Meanwhile, Kanstul designed several new tubas based on the Yorks. Carpenter played Stravinsky's "Firebird Suite" on one of them. He sent an email to those following the project that he was amazed at "how loud, deep and present" the horn sounded. He and Treece took Kanstul tubas to the Midwest Clinic in Chicago and, he wrote, they "showed the tubas like crazy."

Just two years before, they were in Treece's living room blowing horns into a spectrum analyzer, charting high overtones to the wafting of low-fat Pop-Tarts. Now it seemed that they might be part of recreating the two legendary Chicago horns.

"What a great year!" Carpenter wrote in an email to the group on the last day of 2010.

But there was a problem.

The problem was that Zig Kanstul, who walked the earth understanding more than almost anyone else about brass instrument making, didn't understand how to sell a professional-grade concert tuba. Kanstul Musical Instruments was a new brand to pro tubists. What's more, few players had the backing to afford expensive horns, and many of them already had instruments. Those who were interested often didn't control the purchasing decision. Any orchestra needed to find a donor to pay for a new tuba. Zig had to lend horns to these players, sometimes for months, so they could hear them in concert halls. Trumpets sold quickly, tubas took their time. He didn't have shelf space to store them and couldn't wait for them to slowly find buyers. In his rush to recoup costs, some horns left the factory with problems he was unwilling to recognize.

Yet making tubas challenged Zig and renewed his energy. He gloried in it, spent hours puzzling out the tiniest tuba conundrums. He was doing what he was meant to do, and he likely felt blessed to be doing it so late in life. It kept him nimble and alive.

In all this, though, he was stretched between his artisanal desire and relentless cost constraints, the commerce of the question. By 2013, he told Dale Olson, "I used to have a million dollars in the bank. I don't anymore."

"He wanted to be remembered for those tubas," said John Van Houten. "But those things were dripping blood. He wasn't making any money."

Zig had fired his son Jack years before. Now he welcomed him back as sales manager. Zig had borrowed from what his sons called "hard money." These, I learned, were legal lenders that his sons describe as existing somewhere between banks and mafia loan sharks. Interest on the debt was $700 a day.

"He was borrowing money to keep the thing going," Jack told me. "Yamaha can afford not to make a penny for years on a project. Zig had bills to pay; he had money tied up in these tubas."

"He also misjudged the tuba market," said Steve Ferguson, the horn dealer in Pasadena. "Zig made some really good tubas, but he wasn't catering to the modern market. He was catering to the superfans, the older guys, who looked upon the Yorks as these holy grail horns. His tubas were beautifully made, but [they were] looking back instead of looking forward."

Maybe the decades-long search for the perfect tuba led to such dramatic improvements in the horns that what had been the holy grail in times of tuba deprivation was no longer as sought after. Tuba players were leaving behind their confinement that earlier generations had so keenly felt. Maybe their adulation of the Yorks was only a sign of how limited their options had once been but were no longer.

In the end, Kanstul Instruments produced a hundred or so York-inspired tubas, across a half dozen models of varying sizes and keys. Not a bad number for an independent firm. Doing so, however, indebted the company without saving it and foreclosed other ventures. Kanstul Instruments never did produce the biggest horn, the 6/4, the linebacker, the truest Chicago York replica. There just wasn't money or time.

In November 2016, his health long failing, Zig Kanstul went into the hospital and died there a few days later. He was eighty-seven. He had spent a lifetime abusing his body with cigarettes, poor diet, a lack of sun, family stress. And his workshop was now in debt. Workers had taken advantage of him; they slowed production, then argued they needed to work overtime. If he loved his tuba project, it seemed to some who knew him to also be the final weight on his shoulders.

"He had worked so hard and he was tired," said Dale Olson. "I think the tuba hastened his death. Everything he had done in brass instruments had worked. Except this."

A couple hundred people attended a memorial for Zig in the factory's shipping bay a few weeks later. A local school marching band played. The Citrus College Jazz Ensemble backed Arturo Sandoval and other trumpeters who serenaded the gathering on their Kanstul horns.

Mark Kanstul, his youngest son, who had worked in the factory for years, struggled to keep the company going. But the competition was too fierce. Kanstul Instruments was now a place where professionals came for horns. Yet it had costs—and had to support lives—that required far more sales than a boutique pro shop could generate. And, said Mark Kanstul, "I wasn't my dad. I didn't want to live there. I didn't have that drive. I wasn't the patriarch."

Kanstul Instruments closed for good in 2019, the last large independent owner-operated brass instrument factory in America. A Kansas City company bought all that tuba tooling.

Zig Kanstul wanted to make great tubas in America again. He had gone into business for himself when the entire industry he loved was consolidating into what he despised. This tuba project probably showed how desperate he thought things were getting. But maybe it's not too romantic to also think of it as Zig Kanstul's final act of rebellion. His David flipping off the brass Goliaths as he goes down swinging. The big guys barely noticed, of course. Yet it seems the country loses a lot when a pesky fellow like Zig Kanstul departs. Or maybe that's just me, too far immersed in this topic. But, I mean, what kind of gigantic combination of skills and chutzpah do you need to decide, in your eighties, to make tubas?

Dale Olson later published a book on the history of American brass instrument design from the 1800s all the way to Zig. *Zig Kanstul: The Last of the Great Masters*, he called it.

Mark Kanstul remembers a conversation with a euphonium player who wanted to know the Kanstul magic for making a horn that plays at the highest level. "I told him, 'There is no magic.' The magic is the knowledge that comes from having gone through it so many times. The magic went to the grave with Zig."

BOB CARPENTER AND Tom Treece watched all this from afar. They had been frequent visitors to Kanstul's factory. But the tuba project that began in Treece's living room had moved long ago to Zig's hands. They weren't brass craftsmen.

Mexican corridos of the kind democratized by Chalino Sanchez are often about lone, simple men in a doomed confrontation with power but who fight on anyway, knowing they have little chance. The more I learned about Zig, the more his story of fierce, prickly independence felt like a Mexican corrido. It seemed to me that his life could only result in this final act of attempting the perfect tuba. Maybe to do anything else was just impossible. It would be to deny what he was, and to turn his back on the talent that gave him purpose and made him happiest.

After all, on the first page of Dale Olson's book is this quote from Zig Kanstul: "I like making horns," it reads. "I really like making horns."

Chapter 38

Rio Grande Valley

Roma Ascends

In the Rio Grande Valley world of high school band, 2003 stands out as the year when everything changed.

That year, the two poorest enrollment areas in the state of Texas produced the Valley's two best high school bands: the Roma Mighty Gladiators in marching; the Lopez Lobos in performance.

At Roma, Al Cortinas had retired. Under Rudy Barrera, Roma beat all comers in marching competitions that fall. Thus, that November, the Mighty Gladiators boarded charter buses and headed to their second state championships in a row—held that year in the Alamodome arena in San Antonio.

They arrived the day before, staying at a La Quinta Inn near downtown. Most of the kids had never spent a night in a hotel. They walked the property in awe, ran into one another's rooms. One kid called 911 by mistake. Many weren't quite clear on how the showers worked. Josué Alanis, the euphonium player, took a shampoo bottle and a packet of soap as souvenirs. Orlando Herrera, who was now a sophomore euphonium player, was afraid to answer the telephone the next morning when Rudy Barrera scheduled a wake-up call.

The district had found money for them to eat well in San Antonio. That evening they went to the city's River Walk, packed with restaurants, but all the kids lined up at the Dairy Queen, the only eatery on the walk they knew from back home.

They woke early the next day to practice at a nearby high school, then boarded their buses again for the Alamodome. The dome stands high above the freeway on the southeast edge of San Antonio's downtown. The kids grew quiet as their buses sidled along the arena and rolled into its parking lot.

Josué Alanis, a junior by now and remembering the Valley victories that fall, had arrived thinking "Nobody can touch us." But there, outside the Alamodome, he and the others descended into a lot full of bands from Texas' largest metro areas.

"They were all tall White kids," Alanis said. "We walked off the bus with our heads down. It was intimidating. We were all kind of short Mexicans from down south on the border. Nobody knew us—this tiny little band. Their bands had two, three hundred students on the field. It was just incredible, the sheer number."

Josué often liked to mess around, get a laugh from his friends. There was none of that this morning. The Mighty Gladiators formed up outside the stadium. No smiles. Everyone looking straight ahead. "I remember the silence. In line, ready to go," he said. "The other bands were having a grand old time. Just another day for them. For us, it was all or nothing."

They stood in the tunnel leading to the stadium's field and ready to perform. The minutes dragged by. Each kid stood alone in the dark with an instrument, at attention, waiting for their moment to begin. It was November, and the dome had air-conditioning, but Josué Alanis sweated like never before. "That was the longest time, just standing there waiting for the next band to get off the field," he said. Legs quivered; fingers trembled. Thankfully, no one threw up.

Then their time came. Roma administrators had purchased new uniforms. Red fronts, black backs, black pants, and military marching hats, known as shakos, black and trimmed in silver, with a white feather atop it all.

They moved out onto the Alamodome field and into marching formation.

Orlando Herrera had never been to San Antonio. He was one of those who hadn't really known how the La Quinta Inn shower worked. Now he stood in formation in front of this stadium and was overwhelmed. "When you pass the threshold from the tunnel into the dome, it was the biggest thing we'd ever seen," he said. He could not believe that he was fifteen and on this field staring up at sixty-four thousand blue seats rising to the rafters.

"It just felt so surreal," said Juan Guerrero, then a senior marching with a huge Miraphone sousaphone. This was the moment that Juan felt the tuba section had been working toward since he practiced the instrument frantically on his family's porch in seventh grade. "We were making school history," he told me, and he was terrified of screwing up.

"It was breathtaking seeing all those people and how huge the place was," said Alberto Diaz, the trombonist. "But we just went and did our thing. Our bodies did what they were trained for."

Up to then, the Roma band had only played outdoors. Raymond Alanis, also a sophomore, stood under his sousaphone and realized as the band began to play that the Alamodome created a nasty echo. Neither he nor those around him was sure when to begin playing. The rap on that snare drum that signaled a start to their performance sounded like five or six drummers going off. "We felt like [the echo] never ended," he said. But they trusted their drum major and their counting and that those around them were doing the same, and together they marched across the field. Parents in the crowd gasped as the school's name flashed across the arena's Jumbotron in huge letters: ROMA HIGH SCHOOL.

Eight minutes later they ended. They marched off the field and assembled outside. They had to wait for the rest of the bands to finish to learn that they were one of ten to move on to finals. Thus the Mighty Gladiators had no time to celebrate. Out in the parking lot, they ate in their uniforms, their instruments by their sides, and prepared to perform again an hour or so later.

As the final ten bands set up to compete, Rudy Barrera took a seat in the bleachers. He watched his kids move out of the tunnel and onto the field for the second time that day, on their own and out into the world, far from all they knew. They played "Cantus Laetus," a piece influenced by a Gregorian hymn that heavily featured the brass section that by now was Roma's strongest unit. "You plant the seed of work ethic," he said, "and you hope at some point you can let go and let them take over. You have to in this profession. There are so many hours of devotion to the craft, but at some point, it's out of your control."

Two hours later, the ten final bands wound up their performances. Each took seats in the bleachers. A couple of thousand kids sitting in bunches, according to uniform: one blue, one green, one red, one black. Judges conferred for an eternity.

In Texas band finals, the results are read from bottom to top—the band that places last on up to the first-place band. Through it all, bands must sit still, displaying neither disappointment nor exhilaration.

Finally, the roll call began. Another band was the first school called. The Mighty Gladiators sighed in relief almost in unison. At least they were not tenth. The announcer continued. With each name that was not Roma's, Barrera's kids rose slightly from their seats, fists pumping, teeth clenched. "You keep expecting your name to come up because, you know, all these bands around you are incredible," said Orlando Herrera. "People started cheering when our name didn't come up. Our name didn't come up at sixth, then our name didn't come up at fifth. And then it did."

"Fourth place, Roma High School."

The Mighty Gladiators seemed suddenly to lapse into collective muscle spasms. "People were doing these involuntary movements—crying silently, wanting to jump up and down—all without saying anything," said Josué Alanis. "It was so weird, but it was the best feeling in the world. Nobody thought we were going to rank that high. It didn't seem possible."

The top marching bands that day were, in order, from Dallas, Houston, Austin, and the Mighty Gladiators from little Roma, Texas.

THE NEXT DAY, Rudy Barrera took the kids to a mall in San Antonio, and that afternoon they boarded buses for the four-hour ride home through the south Texas brushland. Josué Alanis doesn't remember the ride. He figures he fell asleep from exhaustion. But as the buses finally turned up Highway 83 that night and the empty road led the band into Roma's downtown, they were met by an escort of police cars blasting sirens and flashing lights that took them on a slow roll to Roma's beautiful plaza, which is bounded by cliffs overlooking the Rio Grande on one side and Our Lady of Refuge Catholic Church on the other.

There to meet them were mothers and fathers, siblings, grandparents, teachers, county commissioners. They waved signs and flowers and honked the horns of their work-worn pickups. Mothers stood outside their cars jumping and cheering, and dads stood behind the mothers with their jaws jutting and their eyes glistening.

The kids poured off the buses. Mayor Fernando Peña, owner of Border Hardware, Roma's lone hardware store, was in the crowd. So was school superintendent Jesus Guerra, a Roma High basketball legend in his day.

Roma was no longer a basketball town. It was a band town now. All that money spent on teachers, instruments, uniforms—all that felt justified. That night, there were the speeches, applause, hugs, and beaming parents that a moment like this naturally creates.

"We just felt so important," said Orlando Herrera.

When it was over, the kids boarded the buses and the motorcade of police cars, with sirens and lights blasting, escorted the band and cars full of families through downtown and along the highway to Roma High School, where they went to the band hall and, as they always had, laid their uniforms on chairs ready to be cleaned the next day—shirt and pants folded on the seat, coat around the back, shoes below.

ORLANDO HERRERA WAS a sophomore that day.

Over the next two years, the buzz surrounding the band intensified. Its demands on his time deepened. He eagerly committed to it. He began courting his girlfriend more steadily. She played clarinet in the band and had been on the Alamodome field that day as well. Then there were Friday football games, band competitions on Saturday.

"[Band] was all I was doing and everything I wanted to do. I eventually stopped going to Mexico," he said. Orlando made All-State on the euphonium his junior year. His senior year he was the first All-State euphonium chair in the state of Texas.

Orlando graduated from high school and turned eighteen in 2006. That year, cartel warfare flowed across the rest of Mexico—to Juarez, Acapulco, Tijuana, the western states of Michoacan and Guerrero. In the town of Miguel Alemán, gunfights erupted on weekends and shoppers would hit the ground as bullets flew. Drivers had their cars taken at gunpoint. Violence chewed up a generation of Mexican kids Orlando's age.

Orlando and several high school band friends instead joined another flow that year: of Roma band students heading off to college. The Roma system set up by Al Cortinas, supported by Eloy Vera and Walter Watson back in 1994, was now doing what they expected it could do.

Up to then, college had always been for kids of Roma's small, educated middle class, mostly the children of teachers. The band's success changed that. "Band became people pushing each other to do more, and by doing more, [kids] saw what was possible," said one former student I spoke with.

In the Rio Grande Valley, band directing was becoming a growth industry, providing middle-class jobs close to home, near family, with a degree and the stability of a respected profession.

The first Roma tuba player to do this was Lizardo Hinojosa. He had graduated in 2000 and was the first of Roma's low brass players to head to Texas A&M University–Kingsville, to study tuba and music education under Richard Morgan, who had recruited him after years of visiting the high school at Al Cortinas' request. In the fall of 2006, Lizardo returned to the Roma district as its tuba instructor and a middle school band director.

No one in Orlando's family had gone to college, and he knew nothing about what it entailed. But band, he thought later, had taught him to face challenge undaunted. Roma's band had come out of nowhere and caught the attention of college recruiters. Counselors were asking Orlando and his friends about their college plans.

Orlando Herrera was having a hard time imagining life without band. He wanted to marry his girlfriend, but she was wondering how he could support a family. Band was fine for high school, but how would it pay the bills? Well, now, band directing was a way he hadn't considered.

"Some of us realized, 'You know what, I really like doing this. Maybe I want to keep doing it in college, keep doing it forever.' And that was that. I just didn't want to let it go."

He accepted a scholarship to Kingsville and joined the stream of tuba and euphonium students arriving from Roma High School to study with a new professor named Yutaka Kono.

Kono was a native of Japan. He came to the United States as a high school exchange student and never left, studying the tuba in New Mexico, Minnesota, Kentucky, and the University of Texas, Austin. At Kingsville, he became professor for the half dozen Roma low-brass veterans of the 2003 Alamodome performance.

Kono had them organize concerts and visits from other musicians. He insisted they hold master classes—teaching their peers and critiquing their playing. When they arrived at their weekly lesson unprepared, he didn't need to do more than give the slightest look of disappointment—as if there was nothing sadder than wasted talent—for them to feel the burn. Even when they were prepared, he'd find ways of pushing them.

He urged Raymond Alanis to buy his own tuba rather than relying on the school's instruments. "He was also teaching us how to be professional musicians," Raymond said. "I started performing in local orchestras there because of him. He gave my name out to these orchestras. I was very honored that he trusted me in doing that."

Above all, Kono wanted them to think beyond technique. He wanted them to interpret each musical phrase, to think about the story each piece was telling. What did you think of this piece? His question had no right or wrong answer, and this left them unsettled. It took a while to find the words—sometimes they never did. "Those were the most difficult moments," said Josué Alanis, also attending Kingsville. "I can still remember feeling nervous when he'd ask this. But he wanted us to make music, to have it be more than notes and rhythms on a paper."

During his college years, Orlando would return to Roma to visit and there he would hear the stories of the Mexican boys he had once known across the river. A kid in his grandparents' neighborhood in Mexico was killed—rumor was he was tied to trucks and pulled apart. Another friend was fleeing enemies and on the run in Houston. Grim conversations about what happened to so-and-so grew common. A boy, several years younger, was a cartel lookout at fifteen when he was shot twice in the face by a rival group and died.

Listening to these stories, Orlando would recall that precious moment in 2003 when he walked through the tunnel and into the Alamodome. He had never been anywhere. But that day he stood beneath this massive structure, playing this strange tenor tuba, this euphonium, terrified he would mess something up, competing for his school from a town so far from anyplace Americans knew about Texas that no one could find it on a map.

It was too far-fetched for fiction.

There was something else that could not, of course, have occurred to him that day as he and his bandmates, in their black-and-reds, marched onto the arena's green turf floor for the very first time, and the immensity of the place made him shake.

But years later, and long after witnessing Mexico's descent into pornographic cartel violence, Orlando Herrera would realize that it was no exaggeration to think that maybe band and the euphonium had saved his life.

"I feel that way sometimes," he would say.

Chapter 39

Rio Grande Valley

Treviño at Lopez High

Almost as soon as George Treviño took over from Stacey Dunn as the band director down at Lopez High School in south Brownsville, he felt he was running out of time.

George Treviño is spectacled, short, serious, and driven, but he possesses an unexpectedly disarming smile.

He had come to view great world composers as veins of inspiration for his kids. Great composers wrote to fully express their grand musical visions, not minimize them for commercial reasons. Thus, their works were rich in musical ideas and brimmed with challenges that Treviño felt kids could meet if properly prepared. It was just a question of whether he had time to prepare them.

He searched for band transcriptions of works by the Russians Igor Stravinsky and Nikolai Rimsky-Korsakov, and the Italian Ottorino Respighi. Their works could lead his kids to awesome moments of power and unity with one another, with the music, and with the conductor. Band directing required staggering hours. Creating these moments, Treviño believed, was what made those hours worth it. "Those are moments you don't forget," he said. "I haven't experienced that anywhere else in my daily life."

His first such moment came in the summer of 1979, before he entered college. Treviño attended a one-week summer band camp at Baylor University in Waco, Texas.

A conductor named Stanley DeRusha led the band, preparing them for a Saturday concert. Treviño played alto saxophone. He had been through similar camps. But this one was different.

In daily three-hour rehearsals that week, DeRusha took the band through several pieces. One that Treviño never forgot was "Irish Tune in County Derry" by the Australian composer Percy Grainger. "Irish Tune" is a five-minute piece based on the melody to the Irish folk tune "Danny Boy."

DeRusha knew each instrument's part and used no sheet music. This amazed his young musicians. He could discuss the importance of each note, how one note in a specific chord needed to overpower the others, that this would lend the piece a tension to be resolved later on.

What impressed Treviño even more was something that he didn't immediately understand but that happened nonetheless. It was DeRusha's ability to bring out the beauty and importance in the piece's smallest moments. He could connect details of the piece to larger themes. In five days that summer, Treviño saw DeRusha nurture nuance in music. Under DeRusha's tutelage, seemingly minor moments became essential to creating larger crescendos. Even without those crescendos, however, these small moments had their own beauty and importance to Treviño.

After years of fairly rote band practices, Treviño, then eighteen, found the door opened to a higher realm of musicality that he had not suspected even existed. What's more, DeRusha felt it was enough to prepare his charges to experience the full power of moments like these in performance. That would teach them more than any lengthy technical explanation of what he was attempting.

Sure enough, during the Saturday performance of "Irish Tune," DeRusha was mesmerizing, drawing in the young musicians now that he had them primed. Those small yet essential moments built and the tension of the piece grew until finally, under DeRusha, the band resolved it with such force that Treviño was left pulverized and in tears.

The memory of that week never left George Treviño. He had diligently worked for years to achieve a level of technical skill, just in time to be ready for a master conductor to shape it into higher musical expression.

"I came back from it feeling, 'What was that all about?'—still trying to comprehend what I had experienced. It's something I've never forgotten. I'm still thinking about it today and I'm sixty-three."

Treviño decided then on a career in band directing. Before too long, his career took him to the newly opened Lopez High School in south Brownsville as an assistant to Stacey Dunn, and then as the school's head band director for twenty years.

He spent that career trying to lead his kids to the awe he had felt by the end of that summer camp at Baylor. In that pursuit, George Treviño came to believe in the power of small moments, tiny achievements, for only through them could larger ones be achieved.

At Lopez, Treviño was surrounded by the influence of H. E. Nutt. Nutt's ideas and Treviño's own mixed and filtered, synergizing into something new. For many years, Brownsville band kids had started their lives in band by learning to play one note perfectly. It was part of learning the fundamentals that would allow students to master pieces they once thought impossible. Treviño took this a step further.

To prepare them to play that note, Treviño sought something resembling meditation. He had kids first close their eyes and focus on the breath coming up through their throats, then relax their shoulders as the metronome clicked away. This allowed the tumult of the school day to fade and zeroed kids in on harmonizing parts of their bodies that they rarely thought about. All this before playing a note.

"Now they're thinking about their heartbeat. They're brought into this whole different zone," he said. "The idea is to become in tune with everything you're feeling and how you're having to adapt to play this note at a certain level. You're talking about the unity of everything you're doing—breathing, tongue position, relaxed shoulders, open throat, control and release of air. It's not just playing the note over and over."

Some assumed that students would be turned off. Yet Treviño found kids engaged when they approached one note this way. The collective pursuit inspired them, and the sound he got them to produce convinced them they had talent. "He made us feel like we knew what we were doing," said Nancy Casarez, a Lopez High clarinet player.

They sat on the edge of their seats, listening intently, striving to make that note. Start it right, sustain it evenly, and release it suddenly. Together.

"Everybody had to sound exactly the way he imagined it," said Ivan Valdez, a trumpeter in the Lopez band under Treviño. "What I didn't realize after so much rigidity and discipline is that when you put it all together—that's what gives rise to the magic, the creativity."

The Lopez band hall became, as years passed, not so much a hangout as a place of intense musical focus for the children of migrant farmworkers, cooks, and truckers at this forgotten southern tip of Texas. It was kids in rooms playing the same four measures twenty times. Asking Treviño how it sounded. Then doing it again.

Treviño and his assistants had to shoo students from band hall when they locked up late every evening. Youths wanted a sense of discipline in their lives, he felt. "When they get to experience it," he told me, "it gives them purpose and they become motivated with that purpose."

The rudimentary exercises he insisted on were essential training for that. The pieces Treviño assigned were rich enough to inspire students to the love and joy of what they were creating. Tasting what they could accomplish, Treviño believed, could fuel their desire to keep working at it. To get them there could be life-changing for his kids, as it had been to him.

This was what drove George Treviño. He was not there to be his students' friend. He was there to help them find something they might never find again if it didn't happen now. Every day, therefore, was as serious as life. It was a chance to get better than the day before, to move a step closer to the goal. This had little to do with getting 1s in band competitions. Rather, it was to help his kids develop a musicality that allowed them to feel what he had felt on that stage at Baylor University all those years ago.

It was just a question of whether each year, amid the hubbub of high school, George Treviño had the time to get them there.

Chapter 40

Rio Grande Valley

Symphony No. 6

In 2002, a rising high school sophomore and French horn player named Armando Hinojosa transferred to Lopez High School in Brownsville, Texas, because he wanted to be in its band.

Lopez High was not yet ten years old, but the Lobos had become one of the strongest bands around. Armando had heard it at football games. Two friends were members. Its discipline under George Treviño was legendary, its sound was startling.

This is what Armando Hinojosa felt he needed. No insult is intended, but simply to state a fact, Armando was not a great French horn player. He wanted to be, though. At his current school, he was cutting classes, not practicing his horn. This somehow came without consequences, and to Armando that seemed wrong.

At Lopez, George Treviño held the conducting baton in his fist and ran the band the same way. He had been an all-state sax player in high school, something he believed he achieved not because he had natural talent, but because he worked methodically. His daughters went through his Lopez band program, and so strict was he that they didn't talk to him for weeks at a time. Yet as schoolmates dropped out of school, his students held on to band and its discipline like a life raft. During marching season, it resembled boot camp: five push-ups for this, laps for that.

Armando Hinojosa was looking for exactly that. "Having discipline would make me a better player, a better student," he told me when we met years later in Brownsville. "I wanted to be in a really good band—like, with the best," though where he would fit in it was, to Armando, not altogether clear.

So he enrolled in Lopez High School, well south from the rest of Brownsville, amid the mesquite and the trailers and not far from the wall separating the United States from Mexico.

Armando landed in Lopez's junior varsity band as its lone French horn player. Truth is, he spent that school year hiding. He was naturally timid and knew his skills were lacking. His lips grew numb at the exercises Treviño put the band through. Armando kept at it, yet he grew afraid to even play at times for fear he would bring shame on himself and the brass section.

These misgivings magnified after he was promoted, the summer before his junior year, in 2003, to varsity band. Two French horns had graduated, and the section needed bodies. With that, Armando Hinojosa moved up and into the French horn's lowest, fifth, chair—proud of the promotion, yet terrified he'd ever be asked to play more than half notes.

THAT YEAR, THE Lopez Lobos band got their fifth chance to compete for statewide 4A Honor Band, after finishing second four times in a row.

The Honor Band competition is among the most important in the Texas band world. No marching is involved, just performance. Schools up for Honor Band consideration send in recordings of three pieces. Over each summer judges hold a public event at the convention of the Texas Bandmasters Association to hear and rank each band.

Being chosen as Honor Band is important. But the much bigger deal is that the selected Honor Band then performs at the Texas Music Educators Association conference held in San Antonio the following February.

Each time Lopez had been up for Honor Band consideration, George Treviño had attended the convention. However, waiting all day to hear from judges tied him in knots. His being there wouldn't change anything. The prospect of hearing his band ranked second a fifth time didn't appeal.

What's more, it struck Treviño that the disadvantages Lopez faced made it unlikely they would ever win against better-off high schools from north Texas. That no longer bothered him. One day at school, he had casually asked a custodian how the week was looking. "All I can do is worry about today," the man replied. That struck Treviño as wise, and his perspective changed. "This is what's important—the day-to-day stuff that has to get done. We're going to make ourselves better today than we were yesterday. Just keep forging ahead and committed. All I can do is worry about today. So I took my mind off the prize."

Instead of going to the Honor Band judging that year, he went to the coast with his family. It was a hot summer day, and George Treviño was not at all regretting his decision. That afternoon, he may have been on his second or third margarita when he noticed he had several messages on his phone:

"Hey congratulations!"

"Just heard. Great news!"

"Awesome job. We'll talk later."

Not one of them mentioned why they were calling.

"I think," Treviño told his wife, Lucy, "we just won Honor Band."

She was ecstatic. High schoolers from the poorest part of the state, forgotten even by Brownsville itself, had risen from the Rio Grande ranchland and mesquite to, finally, Honor Band of Texas.

Treviño, too, was elated. But he immediately felt an enormous weight settle on his shoulders that sapped the day of its relaxation.

As the fall of 2003 unfolded, the Lopez Lobos went to marching competitions and played Friday night football games. However, the minds of George Treviño and his students stayed focused on that Honor Band concert the following February.

So much about Texas seemed wrapped up in the concert. Lopez was small, and so far south. The kids were the children of restaurant workers, migrant laborers, custodians, and construction hands. Occasionally, they were greeted at competitions with "beaners" or "wetbacks" by tall White kids from schools in suburban Dallas or Houston. If this didn't happen often, it was common enough to sear memories.

Yet they had persisted and here they were. The kids buzzed with excitement and fear, amazed that it was they who were finally chosen after years of Lopez bands coming in second. So many people back home were hoping for them, not daring to expect too much.

"We were representing the Valley," Treviño said. "We had to show we were worthy."

The six pieces the band would perform had to be just right. It was then that Treviño remembered a piece he had played in high school. *Symphony No. 6* by Vincent Persichetti.

Persichetti taught at the Juilliard School in New York City, and he was considered, by the time he died in 1987, one of America's finest twentieth-century composers. Harvey Phillips had commissioned two pieces for tuba from Persichetti. Al Cortinas had chosen *Symphony No. 6* as he began pushing his Roma band to greater musical heights.

Symphony No. 6 was a huge work for a school band. It was long, almost sixteen minutes, in four movements. It had haunting melodies, a rhythmic dance movement, a contemporary section, then built to a sudden jolt of an ending. Yet at times the piece, Treviño said, "is so exposing," requiring small sections of the band to play alone, unhidden, and unafraid.

He thought of the piece as a painting. "You're admiring colors from a distance, then you get up to it and you really see the details and the technique." All that was in *Symphony No. 6*. Treviño placed it at the middle of the performance to drive the band to the end of the show. They had to get started right away. He didn't wait for school to start. He gave them the music that summer.

Over the next months, as he worked with his musicians late into the evening, George Treviño lost weight. His blood pressure rose. He would bolt awake at night imagining what might go wrong.

His students, meanwhile, arrived most mornings before band hall opened. Christine Jauregui was a senior flute and piccolo player and set up in a chair every day next to the band hall's Coca-Cola vending machine, missing lunch to practice, and discovering an appetite for work she didn't know she had. "It surprised me how passionate I was about it," she said. "This was the first thing I was really good at."

Her best friend, Estee Hernandez, played bass clarinet. "I'd get home at nine or ten, then wake up and do it all over again."

Toward the end of *Symphony No. 6* comes a moment for the French horn section to stand alone. Five notes, that's all it is. The notes reprise the theme of the symphony and prepare the audience for the ending. They had to be right.

As practices for the Honor Band concert began that summer of 2003, it was quickly clear that whether the band succeeded or not depended on the French horns playing these five notes boldly, purely, and filling the hall with their sound. It became just as clear that the weak link among the five French horns, and in most need of assistance, was the new kid, Armando Hinojosa.

Armando was slowly acclimating to this band for which he was probably not ready. He found it comforting that Eddie Salinas, the leader of the French horn section, went to his teachers not once but three times to ask about Armando's grades and ask for extra assignments Armando could do to pull them up because they needed him in the section. So, Armando practiced and studied harder.

After school, Armando had to drive the family car to pick up his mother at work, drop her at home, then drive back to Lopez for band practice. This made him late. Not understanding why, Treviño kicked him out. "I can't have you showing up late," Treviño said. Armando was in tears. He brought his mother, Blanca Hinojosa, to meet with Treviño. "I was like, 'Please don't kick me out. It's because I have to pick up my mom.'" Hearing the full story, Treviño let him back in, and Armando and his mother arranged a different system that allowed him to be on time.

That did little to cure Armando's fear of failure, yet he noticed that more advanced players messed up, too, and didn't let it weigh them down. "You'll get it," they told him. Still, it's safe to say he never felt fully at home that year as the band prepared for the greatest moment of its ten-year existence.

Adam Kramer was the Lopez brass instructor that year. Kramer is a trombone player from Connecticut. He had come to the area in 1996 as an assistant band director at a Brownsville middle school, then stayed and moved to Lopez High when Treviño took over. He and his wife, Mina, a piano professor with a degree from Indiana University, were just married and a long way from home.

In Brownsville, students "were the hardest-working kids I've ever been around," Adam Kramer told me. "I'd drive them home. Dirt floor, no running water. But they didn't believe in obstacles. They just work. It's not like that in most places."

As the concert approached, one of Kramer's jobs was to forge Armando Hinojosa into a real French horn player ready to perform those five crucial notes. "It's just start-sustain-release—you're going to do that," Kramer would tell him, "just like we do each day." Armando didn't have the best ear, couldn't always hear his mistakes. Then there were the intricacies of French horn fingering to get used to.

Over these months, there was no epiphany, no one moment where Armando got it and became the horn player he and everyone else wished he was. "It was just layers and layers of hard work," said Kramer. "It was glitch city for a long time."

Armando never budged beyond the section's fifth chair, but he did improve. He learned to hear his mistakes and play with more power. "For me to change from the timid-playing Armando, it took a lot," he said, "a lot of reflection. We were doing history. I had to step up."

The day before the concert, the kids boarded charter buses for the four-hour ride north to San Antonio. George Treviño, so focused on the performance, remembers the trip as quiet. "We were going for one thing only," Treviño said. "They knew what was at stake." Others remember it as more boisterous. For his part, Armando spent the hours wallowing in nerves and fear, then pulling himself out of it with energetic mental pep talks in which he told himself he would be great, that nothing else was permissible.

Brownsille schools purchased black tuxedos and gowns for Lopez band students for the first time. An hour or so before the concert, the kids donned their new concert attire, feeling sharp, yet unsmiling, pondering the enormous task ahead. They filed onstage and took their seats before a darkened hall. Then the stage lights went on. All eyes on the music or on me, Treviño told them.

The three levels of San Antonio's Lila Cockrell Theatre, with seating for twenty-three hundred, were filled to standing room only with music teachers. Many had come up from the Rio Grande Valley for this moment, including a contingent of music professors from University of Texas, Brownsville. Most of the crowd, though, was from the rest of Texas, curious about this band they'd never heard of.

The kids onstage saw none of that, however. The stage lights in their eyes meant they could see only three rows of people and after that a bank of stark white light. Thus blinded to anything but Treviño, they began to play and midway through their concert, they came to *Symphony No. 6*.

Throughout the piece, Treviño felt the band rising to the moment. His focus was now complete, and the students met that with the same intensity. It seemed together that they grew unaware of their surroundings, lost track of time or place. It was just them, Treviño, and the white curtain of light. "We were all connected," said Gerry Treviño, a trumpet player that day.

Persichetti wrote the symphony for professionals, not for high school kids. But to Adam Kramer watching from offstage, the students seemed to elevate. They were true musicians playing a piece of extraordinary nuance at a startling level. "George was the master of getting kids to play like that," Kramer said.

The band hurtled toward the ending and those five notes that the French horns had to carry alone. Before those notes the French horns have several measures of rest. During those measures, Armando Hinojosa had what he called "a flash"—an image of all the practice he'd gone through to be on that stage, even as fifth chair, and of all those repetitions of the five notes he was about to play. "I think it gave me that boost of confidence that we're going to kill it, man. Show the world who Lopez High School is!

"I didn't feel overwhelmed. I felt good, like I was supposed to be there. I had the same passion as everybody else. Then we hit those five notes and it just felt so good."

The notes pierced the hall.

"Those five notes," Adam Kramer told me, "represented all of that work that we did, from the directors down to the kiddos, all coming to an agreement on how we were going to do it. And they did it. To hear it performed like that—just those five notes—I can't even explain it, but I get chills right now thinking about it."

Persichetti ends his symphony moments later with the band playing what's known as the chromatic scale—a term for all the twelve notes of Western music—played all together for four seconds. It is jarring.

In the months before the show, Treviño had worked the band for weeks on the symphony's ending. It had to be crisp, sudden, *pow!* In class, the bell would ring for them to go on to their next period, and Treviño would keep them for two or three more run-throughs of that dissonant finale.

That night onstage, each student took one note, and this note blended with all the others so that the dissonance did not feature any instrument above another but instead formed one enormous, unified mountain of sound.

Each note started, sustained, then suddenly, joltingly, perfectly, released.

"I remember silence," said Adam Kramer, "then deafening applause."

Ninth grader Ivan Valdez placed his trumpet on his knee and looked out onto the curtain of light from which now pulsed surreal undulations of acclaim.

"Mr. Treviño turns around and presents us, the audience is clapping, and then he walks off," Valdez told me. "That's usually what he does, but this time the audience would not stop clapping. It felt like an eternity. Mr. Treviño had to come back, and the audience clapped even louder."

"I was in disbelief," Treviño remembered. "That's what broke me out of the, I guess, the trance I was in. I had never experienced that, at other people's concerts or my own. Not just the applause, but where it was happening. We still had half the program to go."

Adam Kramer's wife, Mina, was in the audience. All around her, she said, people wanted the moment to continue, "having just heard that performance and not wanting to let it go, but to reflect on it. They were not ready to go on to the next piece."

Ivan Valdez could not see one face in the theater, but he realized then the place must be packed. "We were looking around, like, is this normal? I remember being confused and didn't know what to do."

Armando Hinojosa sat dazed and numb. His mother, Blanca, sat near the rafters in tears, watching this ovation of teachers from across Texas for her boy and his band. Her son had played those five notes better than he ever had. Along with his bandmates, Armando stood, bowed, then sat, as the audience they could not see cheered and didn't stop.

"It was," he said, "the best feeling."

THAT NIGHT, ADAM Kramer was in a hotel elevator when two directors from Rio Grande Valley schools saw his Lopez High ID badge.

"That moved us to tears," one of them said. "You represented all of the Valley."

Band directors would approach Kramer at conferences like that for the next couple years.

"They would walk up to me and say, 'You all spoke for the entire Valley that night,' and they would say that to us over and over."

A few days after the concert, senior Eddie Salinas, the French horn section leader, stopped George Treviño in the halls at school.

"So, what do we do next?"

"Nothing," Treviño replied. "There's nothing else. That's it."

"I was like, 'What are you talking about?'" Salinas told me. There had to be more. He realized he missed the striving. Thirsted for it. He had learned to love the teamwork, taking his French horns and with them perfecting a musical phrase by playing it over and over until they got it right. Playing one note carefully. All this had come now to enthrall Eddie Salinas and he didn't realize it until it was over. All that drilling had prepared them all to receive the final beauty of their creation onstage that night. The hard work, the journey, once seemed so arduous. Then it turned out to be the whole point and Eddie Salinas had trouble imagining life without it.

SALINAS IS NOW a full-time freelance musician in Galveston, Texas: French horn in two symphonies, bassist in three rock bands, teaching private lessons, consulting on band programs, and running a summer music camp. He still meets musicians and teachers who were in the audience that night in San Antonio.

"I'm still blown away, even as a grown man," he said. "High school was fine, you know, but what we learned in those practice rooms was unparalleled. We were kids. How did they get us to do that? What did they put in the water that we were down for that? There was nothing to pursue aside from a good performance: the best thing you could possibly put out—one time.

"But that doesn't go away. You have that level of demand of yourself. I don't know how to do other than my absolute best and whatever that is, that's fine. I'm not trying to strive for perfection. None of us were under the illusion that was possible. But we came pretty damn close."

Twenty years after that evening, I spoke with Ivan Valdez. He had thought about it often since then, and believed the band's performance was made possible by "that meticulous, careful discipline—the fundamentals of working on a tone. Sometimes people don't understand how important these 'insignificant' things may be. This is everything."

The Lopez High dropout rate at the time was then close to 66 percent, Ivan remembered; kids left school to support their families, they got pregnant, their families moved, or they got involved in gangs or drugs. Yet all of his band peers graduated. Ivan went on to get a PhD and study diabetes as a biomedical researcher. When I spoke with him, he was in medical school studying to be a doctor.

"Mr. Treviño," he said, "was able to translate his passion for the music to a group of kids who were not particularly talented individually but together could generate this magic that had people in a standing ovation. I'm sure he had offers to go elsewhere. He never left, out of his commitment and his love for the kids. The way he conveyed that love is through that discipline."

They graduated with the tools to pursue other goals in life, the most important of which, Ivan thought, was how to not stop taking small daily steps toward a larger purpose.

"And it all starts," he said, "from just holding one note."

Chapter 41

Willie Retires

"I'm grateful for that note."

In the year 2002, the China National Symphony Orchestra was about to embark on its first international concert tour.

The Cultural Revolution had ended decades before. Tubas were no longer banned. Yet the country's level of tuba production was still far behind, as Kevin Powers and Fred Marrich were discovering. So, too, was the quality of China's tuba playing. That meant the National Symphony had no tubist to ensure that the orchestra's sound would not embarrass China before foreign audiences.

Which is why, one day, Willie Clark received a call from the symphony's conductor, Li Xiaolu, asking if he was free to fill in. After leaving Disney World, Clark had embarked on a master's degree in tuba that he was just finishing up. He was open to an adventure and flew to Beijing.

At the symphony, "nobody acted like they could speak English until after the first month," he told me, "then suddenly everybody spoke English." Then he was everyone's brother.

The tuba in China was feeling its exile. The tuba professor at the Beijing conservatory could no longer play, and could only describe to students how they were supposed to play. The school's tubas were peeling lacquer. Clark learned to count to one hundred in Mandarin to follow the measures of the music.

He stayed for a month of rehearsals, followed by a tour of Australia and Europe. Orchestra officials offered him a lifetime contract, but Clark had U.S. student loans to pay off. "If I didn't have those bills," he said, "I'd be speaking Mandarin today."

China was part of where the tuba took Willie Clark.

When we first met, he was fifty-five and leaving the U.S. Air Force Ceremonial Brass. The last time we met, he was fully retired yet staying busier than ever. He taught at Howard University and the University of Maryland, with various recording gigs and a brass ensemble through which he indulged his love of the chamber music he had discovered in John Weber's box of cassettes at Brooks Junior High. The horn had taken him from Harvey, Illinois, to the Tuba Fours in Disney World and the Orlando tuba scene, the fertile mind of Sam Rivers, and across the world from there.

Along the way, he collected what he called "Holy Grail" horns—horns designed to replicate the perfect tubas, the Chicago Yorks. He owned a York copy made by Nirschl, a German company, and one of the Zig Kanstul horns. Zig and his company were both gone. Tom Treece and Bob Carpenter were now focusing

Willie Clark in retirement. "Whenever I see a euphonium player, I think about Eugene."

their efforts on improving mouthpieces, which they saw as another neglected key to great tuba sound. But Willie loved the horn they had conspired to create.

He also owned a horn by Eastman, a Chinese instrument conglomerate. Chinese manufacturing expertise had leaped forward. Several Los Angeles companies were providing local banda players with sousaphones made in China. Eastman's silver-plated 836 could stake a claim as the latest replica of the Chicago Yorks, the great American tubas.

It's unclear what kind of brass Eastman used to make the horns. But it had apparently based the 836 on Yamaha's York copy—the YamaYork. So the Eastman 836 was yet another branch of the tuba's strange genetic tree that traces to those two horns made in 1933 by anonymous workers in a Grand Rapids factory that no longer exists.

Willie Clark not only owned an 836, he was also among Eastman's sponsored artists now.

He marveled that all this began with that one note that so captivated him—that open B-flat in sixth grade, playing the *Star Trek* theme in the band at Brooks Junior High School in Harvey, Illinois, conducted by John Weber.

"I'm grateful for that note," he said.

ON ONE MUGGY summer Saturday, as my tuba trek winds down, a brass band sets up under a white tent at a county park in the college town of Valparaiso in northern Indiana. Nearby stands a model-train track run by the Iliana Garden Railway Society, which has hired the band on the occasion of the society's annual Thomas the Tank Engine Day.

That is where I last see John Weber.

He is almost seventy-nine, diabetic, arthritic, has prostate cancer. He walks with a pronounced hunch. He had seizures awhile back. "Other than that, I'm fine," he says, smiling in his impish way.

John Weber once played tuba in brass bands across Chicago. But he cannot stand and play the horn anymore, so the gigs have tapered off. All but this one. The South Shore Brass Band in northern Indiana plays four or five times a summer, and Valparaiso is its last for this season.

This is a rare moment for John Weber to get outside. In Chicago, he fears he would be a target of the city's well-publicized street crime. This teacher and tuba player—who took his students to Disney World, to Indiana Dunes and McDonald's, up Michigan Avenue and along Lake Michigan, to see Miles Davis and Maynard Ferguson, and to hear master tubists change his kids' lives by playing "Flight of the Bumblebee"—now is confined in old age, alone, to a one-bedroom ground-floor unit of the triplex his parents bought when he was two.

His downstairs flat has been filling in around him with stuff accumulated through life that he has neither desire nor energy to move. An old reel-to-reel tape deck, stacks of sheet music, programs of concerts from decades past, antique cornets, Swiss alp horns, and two or three tubas. In a corner is the poster signed by his students at the celebration that Roosevelt Griffin put together in 2017. An upstairs unit contains three helicons. Helicons are marching tubas from the early 1900s.

I got to know John Weber through Willie Clark and visited him four times at his home in Chicago. Weber kids were everywhere by then. New York, Poland, Switzerland, Las Vegas, Washington, D.C., and parts of Chicago they had never seen before he took them there. Roosevelt Griffin heads jazz studies at Northern Illinois University. Many others are not musicians at all, but the values learned in a Weber band led them to professions of one kind or another. A month earlier, Weber and Willie Clark took a selfie together when Weber had an airport layover in Washington, D.C., for a few hours.

The only student John Weber knows nothing of is Eugene Campbell. I looked hard for Eugene. He was believed to still be in Germany. A German journalist searched online. U.S. Army public relations personnel did some checking, as did a veteran from an Army marching band in Germany Eugene once played for. Nothing.

Whatever became of Eugene Campbell is a question most Harvey kids from his generation, now in their fifties, used to ask themselves more often than they do now. Yet I imagine Eugene left his mark on every Weber kid near him in age. Or maybe that's just the storyteller in me. Intrigued by the idea of someone who rose from tough surroundings and used the euphonium, of all things, to overcome all that Harvey was crumbling into, then simply vanished, leaving a generation of youngsters, now adults, to wonder what happened to that magnificent talent they once wished they were.

"Whenever I see a euphonium player, I think about Eugene," Willie told me. "Still to this day, he's the best euphonium player I've seen in a lot of ways. They'd probably have mouthpieces named after him by now."

John Weber thinks often of his great student. He should have sent him that euphonium, he says, and he tears up remembering. His voice falters.

"I've been thinking about this for years."

THE SOUTH SHORE Brass Band starts up at that county park in Valparaiso, Indiana. A scattered audience in folding chairs sits in splotches of shade. Model trains with Thomas the Tank Engine's face attached do ovals on the large track.

Under the tent, the band in black goes through the national anthem and "God Bless America," then on to "Under the

Boardwalk." It will not be a long show. An hour, no more. But it's what John Weber can get and what he can do. So, after sixty years playing the tuba, he is happy to leave the house and grateful for this remaining gig.

The conductor calls for Leonard Cohen's "Hallelujah."

Sitting under the tent at the back of the band on this sweltering day, Weber arranges on his lap his grand Yamaha B-flat tuba that has been his faithful companion since he bought the horn forty years before.

Then he puts his lips to the horn once again and begins to play.

Chapter 42

Rio Grande Valley

Tuba Christmas

"I still love to see the kids' eyes light up when they sound really good."

Early on the first Sunday in December 2023, the last of the morning fog steams up around the Whataburger in Roma, Texas, as a brass sun breaks through an aluminum sheet of cloud covering the Rio Grande Valley.

The river from which the valley takes its name stands quiet. The highway that traces the river's meanderings starts to fill with dented pickups and shiny SUVs.

The first Sunday in December means, in the Valley's tuba world, that it's time for Tuba Christmas.

Eighteen Roma tuba students climb into a school bus and drive southeast for an hour to the town of McAllen and its Performing Arts Center.

At the wheel is Lizardo Hinojosa, the first tuba player to come out of Al Cortinas' band system and into music education. Hinojosa has been the Roma District's tuba teacher for almost twenty years now. He gives rides home to his students at night. "I'm tying ties at every concert," he says.

Band directing is a middle-class job in the Rio Grande Valley. Yet the responsibilities in the Valley make the job arduous, particularly in fall marching-band season. Hinojosa directs a middle school band, then teaches tuba to kids from sixth grade on up, moving from school to school through the day. Then there's Friday night football games and fall band competitions most Saturdays. Hinojosa has worked nineteen days in a row—a lot to ask of a man with a newborn at home.

Among the students in the bus is senior Justin Elizondo, the son of a truck driver and a homemaker. Elizondo is a tuba All-Stater for the third year running. He has festooned a tuba with red and silver Christmas tinsel. He's wearing glasses in the shape of a Santa cap. In other words, he's a long way from the scared eighth grader he claims he was at his first Tuba Christmas, unable to keep up with others on the horn he was already sure he loved. Through the big horn, he found his friends. Learned to focus. Learned what he was good at. By the following fall, he would be enrolled at Texas A&M, Kingsville, studying the tuba and music education on scholarship.

"Band changed my life," Justin says. "If I didn't pursue it, I would regret it."

The Tuba Christmas of 2023 marks the fiftieth anniversary of Harvey Phillips' first bash for the bass horn and Bill Bell. Some three hundred towns—from Anchorage to Austin, and Boca Raton to Boise—hold one.

Justin Elizondo at Tuba Christmas. "Band changed my life."

Nationally, Tuba Christmas is largely—I'll say almost entirely—a White-person thing, and generally an older-White-person thing. Many are players who once dreamed of a tuba career and can't bear to part with their horns, which they keep in closets most of the year. Tuba Christmas depends on this common nationwide tuba memory and those horns kept in closets.

Yet none of that applies in the Valley. Few families can afford the luxury of an expensive tuba tucked away. Many kids, in fact, chose the horn because they could *not* afford a band instrument. When they leave school, they usually leave the tuba, too. While they're in school, though, the horns are theirs. So in the Rio Grande Valley, almost all Tuba Christmas participants are Latino kids eighteen and under, like Justin Elizondo, brought to the event in school buses by band directors like Lizardo Hinojosa.

It's a reflection of band's importance to Valley towns nowadays that the region has a permanent population of literally hundreds of tuba and euphonium players between thirteen and eighteen years old. Before Covid, one of the largest Tuba Christmases outside New York City was held in McAllen when close to six hundred horns, I'm told, assembled in the town's Performing Arts Center.

In 2023, the Valley's Tuba Christmas attracts a somewhat tamer 350 horns.

Still, the sight of 350 tubas and euphoniums spilling from yellow school buses backed up like a New York traffic jam is one I never thought I'd behold. Kids pull in from San Benito and Harlingen, from Pharr and Mission, from Weslaco, Brownsville, Sharyland, Donna, Edinburgh, Mercedes, and La Joya, from Rio Grande City, and, farthest away, from Roma. Their horns come decked in holly wreaths, red and green tinsel, and blinking Christmas lights. The kids wear Christmas elf caps, Santa sweatshirts. They carry music stands.

I watch them saunter into the hall. They are kids who don't fit anywhere else, kids who are learning to create, kids who don't yet know all they can do, kids who can't run a fifty-yard dash very fast, kids who are certain they are going to college, kids who have made a sousaphone cool, kids without much social media influence, kids who are becoming leaders, kids who have learned to like hard work, kids who have unrequited crushes, kids who found themselves in this big beast of a horn and now cannot put it down.

They rehearse for an hour. After a break, they gather to play Christmas carols onstage—350 bass horns playing "O Come, All Ye Faithful." To one side, a seventh grader breaks into quiet tears because he can't keep up. Twenty-seven sousaphones stand at the back, draped in tinsel and snow, and Christmas lights blinking from their bells. The band's sound warbles and weaves up through the hall. Until, with "O come and behold Him," it gathers even the wrong notes and builds into a crescendo that is unashamedly, unabashedly, proudly low.

I stand there and this seems to me a wonderfully bizarre ending to this tuba safari of mine.

The man partly responsible for their numbers is at home in Rio Grande City nursing an inflamed sciatic nerve. Al Cortinas is technically retired, but he is still teaching band. This is his fiftieth year in the Valley. When he was elected to the Texas Band Directors Hall of Fame, a woman wrote to the newspaper that she never understood why Mr. Cortinas made her sit up straight and practice slowly—until she got older.

Indeed, in little Roma, Texas, his system evolved to discover the talent in youths who couldn't afford music lessons. Nurturing this once ignored asset allowed a school band from a speck of a border town to compete with the wealthiest in Texas and take its kids into a larger world.

That's a story worthy of its own symphony.

Al Cortinas keeps teaching beginning tuba—part time to middle schoolers in Rio Grande City.

One Monday, a kid bounds in to announce he won an All-Region tuba chair over the weekend. "I still love to see the kids' eyes light up when they sound really good," Cortinas says. "Animo"—borrowed from Roberto Botello so long ago in Crystal City—remains a motivating force in his life. Spirit and pride together.

He still has his collection of neckties. He remains "Mr. Cortinas" to many. Former students regularly approach him—a motel clerk, a lawyer; at a gas station, after mass. They remind him of his connection to their lives. One says Cortinas used to drive him home from band. Another says she now has a doctorate in education. Al Cortinas remembers their faces, far less often their names.

Before I leave the Valley, Cortinas and I meet at the Denny's in Rio Grande City. All of Roma's 2023 band seniors will head to college. It wasn't that way when he took over. By his count, eighty-one of his former students are now band directors, many of them in the Valley. Now *their* students, a third generation, are training at public universities in Kingsville, Edinburgh, and Austin.

Those who were his low-brass students just before he retired from Roma are now his bosses: Orlando Herrera, Josué Alanis, Alberto and Roberto Diaz, Raymond Alanis. All of them returned to the Valley as band directors in the Rio Grande City school district. Roma High on their résumé carries weight in the band world. Orlando remembers a job interview in another district at which they asked him for Roma's secrets to success. "I told them, 'There are no secrets. You just work hard.'"

Rudy Barrera is happily retired in Rio Grande City. Yet he, too, can't entirely let go. He judges competitions and teaches cornet part time to Roma middle schoolers. He cleans band instruments as a sideline. "Last year, I cleaned thirty-eight concert tubas from the Roma school district," he told me. "Also fifteen sousaphones, twenty euphoniums, and fifty trombones."

George Treviño took Lopez to Honor Band two more times, winning against 6A (in 2017) and 5A (in 2020) high schools. No other band director in the history of Texas has done that. He retired in 2020. His wife, Lucy, retired the same year from directing band at a nearby middle school.

Every senior in Treviño's first Honor Band graduated, and half of them went on to become music teachers themselves. Eddie Salinas consults high school bands. Nancy Casarez is an elementary school music teacher. She studied music at the University of Texas. Her clarinet teacher was surprised to learn she never had lessons and asked how she achieved her advanced sound. "I said, 'My band director in high school. He showed me what I could do.'"

Christine Jauregui (flute) and Estee Hernandez (bass clarinet) remain best friends. Christine is now a speech pathologist in San Antonio. Estee has a PhD in education and works for Texas Christian University in Fort Worth.

"Mr. Treviño told us it was hard, but he also didn't tell us we couldn't do it," Estee said. "I never really thought about what kind of gift that was to us. A bunch of little Mexican kids, whose parents didn't graduate from high school, who didn't have any money, didn't have any lessons. It's pretty radical what Mr. Treviño did."

Armando Hinojosa went to college hoping to get a degree in music education. But by his own acknowledgment, he wasn't serious, didn't understand how college was different from high school, messed around, dropped out, and wishes today he had not. He works for an O'Reilly Auto Parts store in Brownsville, and he still listens to classical music for the French horn parts.

IN 2023, TWENTY years after the Roma High marching band first went to the state finals in San Antonio's Alamodome, they did it again.

On-field props had by then become the thing in Texas marching bands. One band featured a volcano belching smoke. Another had nine chessboard pawns, each 12 feet tall and painted orange. I watched all this wondering what volcanoes and orange pawns had to do with marching and playing music.

A week later, I saw that Facebook map I mentioned, with a star for each 2023 5A school band finalist that year. Roma at the very bottom of that map validated the story that brought me to the Valley. The rest of the stars faithfully reflected the state's wealth—suburbs of Dallas, Austin, and Houston.

After years of writing about opioid addiction, part of this project was my search for counterbalances. For bulwarks against the marketing that indoctrinates us in the idea that happiness is something we can buy—from Taco Bell "Luxe Craving Boxes" to gambling apps.

High school band provides a quiet counterbalance. Unlike football, band is really about winning later. Most band members graduate from high school. How well a band does is best measured by how well its musicians are doing a decade or two later.

Yet watching the 2023 finals, it seemed Texas high school band risked becoming *footballized*. Band on steroids. Requiring almost year-round focus to the exclusion of everything else, supported by huge fees from parents, million-dollar budgets, and extravagant props.

If competing requires that a band be one of society's winners already, then we may lose what makes marching band such a precious sustenance to communities across America. "The haves and the have-nots—that is the antithesis of the true elements of the band world," said David Gregory, a longtime Georgia band director and judge. "If we're not careful, our own success will be our demise."

Amid all this, I called Bob Morrison, head of Quadrant Research, which studies arts education in America. American public school music education far outstrips that of any other country in both quantity and quality, Morrison said. "The very top of the pyramid are the large bands, with large budgets," he told me. "But those are the exception, not the rule. Most bands in the U.S. are Roma High School. Small communities, good programs that march and play well. That's the vast majority of programs. Roma were finalists without doing what the larger programs were doing with props. Just putting on great music."

In fact, Roma's was the smallest of the dozen band finalists in 2023. Its props were simple fabric panels of swirling blues, reflecting its excerpt from George Gershwin's *Rhapsody in Blue*.

Parents I spoke with said the key to Roma band is that parents let the teachers teach, work, criticize, and push their children to an extent apparently intolerable elsewhere. One mother told me, "Some parents ask me 'Doesn't it hurt to see the teachers marching your kids in the cold and the rain?' and I say, 'As long as there's no lightning, I'm fine with it.' That's why they're in the place they are."

Playing *Rhapsody in Blue* under the Alamodome.

Roma came in tenth that day, and the town serenaded the band with horns and sirens when the kids got home that night.

Justin Elizondo had a tuba solo in the middle of the Alamodome performance. It lasted only about twenty seconds. He had practiced it since May.

On the field that day, Justin remembered, he looked up at the Alamodome crowd and his right hand shook as he began his solo. But you know what? He was the tuba player from Roma High School. From a town of eleven thousand people so far to the south that Texans can't find it on a map.

So he mastered his nerves and he played it as he knew he could.

ONE NIGHT A few months later, Lizardo Hinojosa was at home. He was holding his infant daughter on the sofa as his wife cooked dinner. He turned on a YouTube performance of Ralph Vaughan Williams' *Concerto for Tuba*, which in 1954 was the lone major piece written for the instrument.

Lizardo had played it as part of his senior recital at Kingsville in 2006. He had practiced the piece endlessly for most of a year, phrase by phrase. The sheets of music wilted by the time he was done. He loved the concerto's soothing second movement.

As the music poured over him that evening, his little girl on his lap, Lizardo Hinojosa remembered that recital. Soon he was swept away by other images from his life. He remembered Al Cortinas, friends from high school, Rudy Barrera. He remembered practicing and competing with Jose Garza in high school. Friends who had passed on. Students he had taught. Band competitions. Meeting his wife in college. His kids and the house in which they lived.

This went on for several minutes as the concerto played. Connecting it all was one thing.

"I owe everything I have," he said, "because I said yes to the tuba one day in fifth grade."

ENCORE

None of the copies of the legendary Chicago York tubas have perfectly replicated the sound of the originals. Nor is it likely that one will ever do so.

Yet the search for the perfect tuba was hardly in vain. Today's tubas are easier to play, sound better, and invite virtuosity more readily than earlier horns. It's easier for kids to find themselves in tubas today.

Technically, of course, there is no such thing as *the* perfect tuba.

There may yet be a perfect tuba for each of us, however. Something that fills us with purpose and to which we eagerly devote our energies and creativity. A counterbalance to the addictive crud we encounter in this world. We may not find it exactly as we imagine it, or in every respect. We may detour to places we didn't know exist. But having that thing to strive for is the point. The journey seems a healthy, productive way to spend a life.

Arnold Jacobs was doing something like that, for himself and others, through his ideas of wind and song. Anthony "Tuba Fats" Lacen and Willie Clark were searching for that through their horns. A marching band became the perfect tuba for Al Cortinas, Rudy Barrera, Stacey Dunn, George Treviño, and John Weber—a vehicle through which youth talent and imagination could be channeled.

What is the tuba, anyway, if not a 12- to 18-foot tube for channeling imagination? It's a road of tortuous curves, straightaways, and U-turns where what begins as a primitive wet buzz can come out the bell one day, as J. R. Treviño says, as an embracing, majestic sound, echoing God.

Like a life. Like recovery from drug addiction.

It's just that, as Orlando Herrera says, there is no secret to it, no easy, magic answer. Just hard work.

We love those easy, magic answers, though. Corporate marketers and drug dealers know this. They spend great effort to convince us that those answers exist. Our national opioid addiction epidemic grew from the idea that the magic answer to all human pain lay in one kind of pill—prescription narcotic painkillers.

I'm often asked how one might prevent drug addiction, especially in young people. There are a lot of answers to that. But finding what fills us with purpose seems essential. That often requires hard work, postponed gratification, and sharpening our abilities. From that, we learn slowly to express our creativity, whether as carpenters, cops, landscapers, teenagers, nurses, professors, taco truck owners, bankers—or tuba players.

A few years ago, psychologists at several universities did experiments that they believed showed "Find your passion" to be deceptive advice. Believing that a passion is there just waiting to be found, they reasoned, may lead young people to give up on something when it gets hard to do.

An *Atlantic* magazine article described their work. One reader agreed:

> Passion develops from doing something well—from gaining expertise. This is usually confused with doing something well because one has a passion for it ... Most people I met who had a passion for what they did had no idea when they began—their joy developed by staying with something long enough to gain satisfaction from their expertise.

I guess that's why I drew such a breath of fresh air from the tuba and from marching band. They offer us lessons in how to confront our mass market culture of addiction. Stacey Dunn, Lopez High's first band director, told me one day, "What you studied all these years, you're seeing the answer to those problems" in the tuba and in marching band.

Maybe H. E. Nutt and Arnold Jacobs are the two greatest social philosophers of our time.

I still don't know how to arm young people against addiction. Especially today. So much around us wants to sell us fleeting pleasure and call it happiness. But after writing this book, when asked, I may say something like this:

Work to discover your own perfect tuba.

CODA

In the fall of 2024, the Roma, Lopez, and Rio Grande City high school bands all qualified for the Texas 5A Band Championships in San Antonio.

One November Monday, a couple of weeks before I turned in this manuscript, they were among the thirty-eight bands competing on the Alamodome floor.

Roma once again was among the twelve that advanced to the finals the next day. They came in twelfth. The top three bands were all from the Leander School District, a suburb north of Austin known as a center for high-technology firms and the people who own and work for them.

The following spring, Rudy Barrera and Stacey Dunn were inducted into the Rio Grande Valley Band Directors Hall of Fame.

On the morning of May 8, 2025, a few months before this book was to be published, John Weber, tuba player and longtime band director at Gwendolyn Brooks Junior High School in Harvey, Illinois, passed away in hospice care. He was seventy-nine years old.

John Weber
1945–2025

ACKNOWLEDGMENTS

As with all my books, *The Perfect Tuba* is based mostly on interviews I've done.

However, several books were essential to my storytelling:

- *Arnold Jacobs: Song and Wind* (WindSong Press, 1996) by Brian Frederiksen
- *Mr. Tuba* (Indiana University Press, 2012) by Harvey Phillips
- *Zig Kanstul: Last of the Great Masters* (KMI Publications, 2017) by R. Dale Olson
- *Season With Solti: A Year in the Life of the Chicago Symphony Orchestra* (Macmillan, 1974) by William Barry Furlong
- *Keeping the Beat on the Street: The New Orleans Brass Band Renaissance* (Louisiana State University Press, 2006) by Mick Burns
- *Roll With It: Brass Bands in the Streets of New Orleans,* (Duke University Press, 2013) by Matt Sakakeeny
- *Music, Mayhem and the Mouse: My "Tubazar" Life* (Skyway Press, 2023) by Stanford Freese
- *Barney, Bradley, and Max: Sixteen Portraits in Jazz* (Oxford University Press, 1989) by Whitney Balliett, which included his profile of Harvey Phillips, "Goodbye Oompah," written for the *New Yorker* in 1975

Several *International Tuba Euphonium Association Journal* articles were also important. Among them:

- The spring 2009 issue had eight pages remembering Fred Marrich.
- Joseph Agnew's article on the Chicago Yorks, in the journal's summer 2004 issue, was huge. I thank him also for spending a Zoom call with me.
- Paul Haugan's profile of Arnold Jacobs in the winter 1977 issue.

Peter Schwendener's 1984 profile of Jacobs in the *Chicago Reader* was also of enormous help.

In completing this book, I was quite limited in time and budget. So I am grateful to many people who made it easy, who quickly responded to emails, and who eagerly participated in interviews—all helping to move this project along.

Willie Clark and John Weber were mighty helpful and willing to meet up whenever I was in their respective towns. Roosevelt Griffin, Chris Davis, Frank Parker, Christopher N. Davis, and Landon Fuller all graciously spent time talking about their years in Weber bands, and their careers since then.

Bob Carpenter and Tom Treece were always eager to talk and answer the many weird questions I had about their attempts to recreate the sound of the Chicago Yorks. Thanks to Will Walker, Mike Roylance, and Claude Kashnig, all of whom met with me to talk about the Orlando tuba scene and playing with Sam Rivers.

Winston Morris, now retired as tuba instructor from Tennessee Tech University, was unfailingly encouraging, willing to meet or talk by phone and discuss his life and the tuba, even during years when I had still no plans to write anything. Thanks also to Tim Lawhern, Scott Mycowiak, Joseph Northcut, and Nancy Holland for their recollections about the tuba ensemble that played Carnegie Hall in 1976.

Jim Self and Paul Krzywicki both kindly invited me to their respective homes to talk about this project and their tuba lives.

Thanks also to the late Roger Bobo, Wayne Tanabe, Ed Firth, Bob Tucci, Dan Perantoni, Eli Newberger, Bobby Ortiz, John Van Houten, Robert Ryker, Don Little, Beth Mitchell, Sergio Carolino, and John Hagstrom. Carol Nowicke very generously answered my questions and provided me with oral histories she had done with students of Bill Bell.

Jack and Mark Kanstul, Robb Stewart, Charles Hargett, Steve Ferguson, and Dale and Diane Olson all met with me to talk about the late, great Zig and his life in brass.

The Chicago Symphony Orchestra's communications director, Eileen Chambers, was nice enough to arrange a meeting with me and tubist Gene Pokorny, who generously allowed me to view the legendary York tubas and attempt to make a sound on one of them.

Brian Frederiksen welcomed me to his home several times, willing to talk about his life and Arnold Jacobs. Brothers Paul and Peter Schwendener were, also, so thoughtful in interviews about Jacobs.

Thanks to Stacey Dolan, Rob DeLand at VanderCook, as well as Willie Owens and Rolando Zapata. Ruth Rhodes was so helpful in providing information about H. E. Nutt, then did a wonderful job seeking out problem punctuation and awkward phrasing in the manuscript of this book.

Kevin Powers generously took my many phone calls asking about China, tubas, and Fred Marrich.

In the Rio Grande Valley, so many people were willing to talk about the Roma and Lopez high school marching bands.

Above all, I thank Al Cortinas, whom I barraged with phone calls and questions. Rudy Barrera was equally generous with his time and patience. Eloy Vera was as well when I contacted him to hear more about the origins of the Roma band. George and Lucy Treviño met with me when I ventured to Brownsville. Stacey Dunn and Paul Flinchbaugh also generously answered questions about their lives as VanderCook band directors in Brownsville.

Thanks to Lopez former students who helped: Armando Hinojosa, Ivan Valdez, Eddie Salinas, Nancy Cásarez, Christine Jauregui, Estee Hernandez, Gerry Treviño. And to Adam and Nina Kramer.

Thanks to the former Roma band students, now teachers, who helped: Orlando Herrera, Josué Alanis, Raymond Alanis, Alberto Díaz. Lizardo Hinojosa was especially generous, taking my Sunday-night phone calls and recounting his memories of the first years of the Cortinas system at Roma High School.

I'd also like to thank Jim Egger, Richard Floyd, Bob Morrison, David Gregory, Scott Roeder, Danny Carrera, Claudina Anderson, Dorina Kingston, Dena Laurel, Danny Rentería, Eloy Garza, Frank Moreno, Juan Guerrero, and Justin Elizondo, and the parents of current Roma band members, for their help in this project.

I'm grateful to J. R. Treviño for his openness to talking about the tuba and his life over lunch in Harlingen twice, and many times by phone.

The chapters on Anthony "Tuba Fats" Lacen would not have been possible without the help of five of New Orleans' greatest musicians who help sustain the city's arts with their daily work: trombonist Craig Klein, trumpeters Leroy Jones, Gregg Stafford, and Mark Braud, and guitarist Seva Venet. Each of them spent time in person and over the phone answering my questions about their long-passed friend. I thank drummers Benny Jones and Jerry Anderson, as well as Kermit Ruffins, John Richardson, Kirk Joseph, and Roger Lewis of the Dirty Dozen Brass Band, Mari Watanabe, Hal Nester, Julius McKee, Quinn Sternberg, Jerry Brock, and David & Roselyn. Ronda Rose was so welcoming, inviting me to her home and answering questions about Linda Young and Tuba, whose love story I heard first from her. Thanks also to my friend, drummer Jeffrey Perkins, for a few phone contacts that got me in touch with the New Orleans tuba world.

Linda Young's sisters, Trula Vereen and Cora Young, and her nephew, Bryan Boysaw, were open to talking when I contacted them out of the blue, and welcomed my questions about Linda and her life.

I'd like to thank the Lacen family—Anthony's sisters and nieces—who answered my questions about Tuba when I just dropped by their Tenth Ward duplex one spring Saturday.

Thanks to Alfredo Herrejón, Juan Damian, Rigoberto Sanchez, and many others I've forgotten for their help on the chapter about banda tuba's popularity in Los Angeles.

Sam Enriquez, one of the best editors in American journalism, who hired me years ago at the *Los Angeles Times*, looked at part of this manuscript, as he generously has with past books.

Thanks to my editor at Bloomsbury Publishing, Anton Mueller, for his support of this admittedly strange project. And to my agent, Stephanie Evans, for even suggesting it might be a possibility.

Finally, to my best editor in many ways, my wife, Sheila, for her sharp eye, patience, love, and support in all that life and writing present.

To contact Sam and see more about his books, as well as *The Perfect Tuba* videos, interviews, photos, and more:

A NOTE ON THE AUTHOR

SAM QUINONES is a journalist, storyteller, former *Los Angeles Times* reporter, and author of four acclaimed books of narrative nonfiction, including National Book Critics Circle Award finalist *The Least of Us* and *New York Times* bestseller and National Book Critics Circle Award winner *Dreamland: The True Tale of America's Opiate Epidemic*. He lives with his family in Tennessee.